The Little Woman's Always Right

The Little Woman's Always Right

Jack Hulbert

W. H. Allen · London
A division of Howard & Wyndham Ltd
1975

To my favourite comedienne

The Little Woman's Always Right

1

It was St Valentine's Day, 1966. The party was a smash hit. You could tell that by the noise: everybody talking at once, great excitement. Close on a hundred people crammed into one small dining room, all standing up. No room to sit, it was like the foyer of a theatre on a first night just before the curtain goes up, everyone in high spirits. Still more people squeezed their way into the room, which should have been at least three times the size. A voice tries to be heard above the din:

'One moment, please.' Getting no result, the voice tries again, much louder. The noise subsides, the voice continues: 'This is a very happy occasion.'

'Hear Hear,' from all over the room.

'A golden wedding.'

Then the storm broke. A tremendous ovation from all our dear friends—overwhelming—emotional. A double forte chorus of 'Cis—Jack—congratulations', so loud that it must have been heard two streets away; but coming from an all-star cast, who could complain? Then cries of 'Cis—Jack—speech—come on, Cis darling—good old Jack—speech.'

Good old Jack protested and did a lot of 'Oh noes', but not too many, he was dying to have a go. As the shouting for speech continued, all the funny things I had thought of saying seemed entirely inadequate to such an hilarious moment. A grand party—a grand bunch of people, why should I spoil it? The clamant cry was 'Speech' so they had to have it.

'*My dear sweet friends, this is* The Hulbert–Courtneidge Saga: *a life-long struggle for supremacy.*'

1

This got a yell. I was away to a flying start. I continued, exhilarated:

'*First one goes ahead and then the other. Cicely Courtneidge born in Australia. Mother sweet and gentle. Father Robert Courtneidge, the redoubtable Scot. Daughter little change.*'

Big laugh from those who knew her well, which meant practically everybody.

'*1913, Brighton. Hulbert and Courtneidge meet for the first time. Complete disillusionment on both sides. They play the young lovers in* The Pearl Girl *at the Shaftesbury Theatre. Courtneidge the first to show a little interest, Hulbert bewildered. Courtneidge displays her genius for fixing things and fixes Hulbert, who finds himself under entirely new management. Courtneidge goes into the lead.*'

Gales of laughter and applause. I can't wait to go on.

'*1914,* The Cinema Star. *Hulbert goes into the lead. Sensational news—First World War. More sensational news—Hulbert and Courtneidge marry.* The Cinema Star *followed by* Light Blues. *Position about level. 1916, Financial Crisis. Courtneidge out of a job. Hulbert in one with a guaranteed long run at a marginal wage.*'

I thought this was a sure-fire laugh, but it missed.

'*The invincible Courtneidge to the rescue.*'

The laugh came here.

'*She makes a momentous decision and goes on the music halls. Result—great success as male impersonator. Starts a new career and goes into the lead. 1919, Hulbert comes out of the army just in time to go into* Bran Pie *at the Prince of Wales Theatre and snatch the lead from her.*'

The personal stuff, that is what they love. Such an affectionate audience made it almost impossible to go wrong. It was swinging along so well that I decided to make drastic cuts and finish while they were still laughing. I hurried on.

'*After a series of films and musicals they appear together in* Under Your Hat. *Position, neck and neck. They vie with each other for top billing.*'

I was safe on this one. An 'in' joke is always a certainty.

'*Courtneidge wins every time. Hulbert likes to be thought a nice man. Courtneidge runs the financial side and gives Hulbert an allowance. Hulbert asks for an increase to meet the ever-rising price of cigars. Request not granted. And that is* The Hulbert–Courtneidge Saga *to date.*'

The laughter was still at its height when I stopped. Pros, theatre people—the best audience in the world. Cis sailed in on the crest of the wave and made one of her characteristic spontaneous speeches, which she does with the greatest of ease when she is worked up and this party did just that. She spoke from the heart and got laughs as well without any preparation. Most annoying. And it was good stuff too.

Needless to say, she got a great reception when she finished. If anything I thought a little too much, but what does it matter? All good practice—give and take. Several friends said a lot of kind things, making little speeches about golden weddings and 'how do you do it?', etc., then gradually the party broke up. When the final guest departed, the place looked a shambles. Suddenly there was silence. It was startling —not a sound. Cis collapsed into a chair among the debris.

'Oh my feet.' Off came the shoes. 'Look at the place. Will we ever get straight again? I must have a drink. I've only had a couple of sips the whole evening.'

'Same here.' I filled two glasses.

'And I'm jolly hungry.' She looked round to see what was left.

'Cold cuts. Come on.'

We started in like two ravenous wolves.

'It's been a grand celebration.'

'Marvellous—sweet people—couldn't have been nicer.'

'Fifty years is a long time. Here's to a splendid lady,' I said, raising my glass.

'Thank you, darling, and here's to a "Fine Old English Gentleman",' she said, lifting hers.

'Not too old, I hope. But hasn't the time gone quickly?'

'Have you enjoyed it?'

'Yes. Have you?'

'You don't want to make a change?'

I took a step towards her. Two soft blue eyes sparkled. A radiant smile suffused her face, revealing that soft womanliness I always found irresistible.

'No, I don't think so. What about you?'

She got up from the chair. I took her in my arms. I was the happiest man in the world.

2

During the latter part of Queen Victoria's reign, so I am told, a handsome young doctor could be seen driving a phaeton through the streets of the ancient and venerable town of Ely, dressed in top hat and frock coat with a groom sitting at the back, arms folded. It was a very smart turn-out.

Advertising is anathema to the medical profession but this impressive outfit must have been a constant reminder to the local residents that the medical services of Dr H. H. Hulbert could be obtained on application. Mrs H. H. Hulbert looked very young and pretty sitting down to lunch in a charming old Georgian house discussing the events of the morning with her husband. He told her he had just bought a field and a donkey. Whether she thought this was meant to be her first anniversary present was apparently never explained, but when she raised her eyebrows Dr H. H. Hulbert replied, 'They were both going cheap'.

He was a man who had to be understood, rather eccentric. That was one of his capers, buying the oddest things. Being an excellent doctor, his practice flourished.

And then came the moment I chose to alter the whole course of his life. I plumped for Ely as the place of my kindly engender so that I could boast I had been christened in the great cathedral. Poor Father! Everything looking rosy and suddenly a bouncing boy arrives. The income of a country practice could hardly stand the strain of this added financial burden, so plans had to be formulated to migrate, as soon as reasonably possible, to a place where there were more people to the square mile liable to require medical service. London seemed the

4

obvious solution, so the three of us did a quick scarper to Cedar Gardens, Putney S.W.15.

It is quite extraordinary how one's earliest memories seem to conjure up the silliest things. I must have been around three or four then. The house we lived in had a garden running down to the river next to the railway bridge. In the centre of the nursery table there was a large china flower pot and my delight was to watch it reflect the passing train as it steamed rapidly, as I thought then, across the bridge. Even to this day the memory comes sharply into focus. I remember, too, my father and mother in the middle of the summer appearing on a stage in a large garden in what must have been a Gilbert and Sullivan Opera, which I suppose was a charity performance by the local amateurs. I did not know at the time why they were doing it or why they were wearing such funny clothes.

My mother had a beautiful voice and she was always in demand for charity shows. She could have been a professional concert singer, she was in that class, but, unhappily, ill health made it impossible.

My father, being a man of high ambition, soon decided the grass is greener on the other side of the river so we all trooped over and on the front door of number 732 Fulham Road was fixed a brass plate telling all who might be interested—and I was one—that it was the residence of Dr H. H. Hulbert, etc., etc. I could not read it myself but, when I was told, I was very proud that my father's name was important enough to be emblazoned on the front door. Gone was the phaeton with the groom sitting at the back, but the frock coat and top hat remained, with the sensible addition of an umbrella.

To the denizens of the salubrious suburb of Fulham he was a familiar figure. The frock coat was dark grey in winter and light grey in summer but always the umbrella—not rolled. He did his rounds on foot and by bus. His favourite seat on the horse-drawn vehicle was on top next to the driver, with whom he had animated conversations on politics and current events. The cost of living was very low in those days and so were doctor's fees, consequently Father gave lectures in his spare time on various subjects, including hygiene and breathing. I was beginning to get bigger and becoming more expensive to keep.

A doctor's job must be the most exacting and strenuous of all professions and, like a farmer, he is never finished. After an exhausting day poor Father would flop into bed and as soon as he hit the pillow a whistle would blow in his ear. Half asleep he took the whistle out and said, 'Hullo, yes.' And a voice on the other end of the speaking tube, at the front door, replied, 'It's the wife—Mrs Grimes, she's started.' And father would say, 'All right, I'll be round in twenty minutes. Keep her warm.' One thing I knew for certain, I never wanted to be a doctor when I grew up.

Today we deplore the tyranny of the modern telephone system. It would have been interesting to know what Father thought of that speaking tube, but he was a dedicated practitioner and never grumbled. As a member of the so-called privileged class, the only benefit he seemed to derive was working harder than any man of his own age. Educated at Bath College, now extinct, and Oxford, then having spent many years at St Thomas's Hospital as house surgeon, he toiled incessantly all his life.

I think I was five when I was first taken to the theatre. A vivid memory still, sitting next to my father in the stalls, wildly excited, longing for the curtain to go up, and when it did it was sheer magic. And even today I sit in the stalls longing for the curtain to go up. Admittedly, sometimes longing for it to come down, but the magic remains.

It was my first pantomime. A beautiful lady with beautiful legs and no skirt came on to the stage and my father explained that she was the Principal Boy, Dick Whittington, who was in love with Dolly, the Principal Girl.

'You mean they're sisters.'

'No, no, no.' There was a slight tinge of irritability. 'He's not a boy really, she's a girl.'

'Two girls in love with each other?' I was puzzled.

'Yes, no, NO'. He was very emphatic.

Father did not seem to be quite clear, neither was I. It was at the time of the Boer War and I assume we were not doing very well because the beautiful lady with beautiful legs and no skirt had suddenly joined up and was leaving for the front immediately. The shattering news was conveyed to us in a song of farewell she sang to

Dolly. This got me more confused than ever. How could she possibly go and fight the Boers in that outfit? Father's attempted explanation got us nowhere.

'She's not really—I mean—she's only pretending to—Oh, don't bother with it—just listen to the song.'

Which I did and was moved to tears, it was so emotional. I remember the words to this day.

> 'Goodbye, Dolly, I must leave you
> Though it breaks my heart to go,
> Something tells me I am needed
> At-the-front-to-fight-the-FOE.'

Oh, the way she sang it! That last line. What an actress! She put everything into it. She got so excited and so did I. She sang with such tremendous verve and gusto that a shower of spit came out of her mouth and was illuminated by the limelight on either side of the stage. It was the most dramatic thing I have ever seen. That did it. I was hooked, stage-struck, irrevocably, and still am.

Since experiencing that deep emotion I realise now I had witnessed a rare phenomenon. Few actors today can boast of having their destiny sealed by witnessing, in their extreme childhood, a combination of dramatic power and physical energy, with intense limelight making magic out of illuminated spit.

All this took place at the Grand Theatre, Fulham, situated at the foot of Putney Bridge on the Middlesex side, where it remained for many years a notable landmark. But like many of our ancient buildings it has succumbed to the predatory demands of commerce.

I told my father I wanted to go on the stage and here my story seems to be different to that of most youngsters. Instead of throwing a temperament and telling me not to be a silly child and stop talking nonsense, he was delighted and did everything in his power to help me right up to the time I made my first professional appearance.

As I grew older I found out he would have liked to have been an actor himself, so we had a lot in common. We visited the Grand Theatre frequently, but the next time the curtain went up there was no music, no beautiful lady with beautiful legs and no skirt. I asked my father why.

'This is a play, my boy—a drama. It's good for you to see everything.' I was all for that.

'Will that man in the funny clothes make us laugh in a minute?'

'I hope not,' Father answered hastily. 'It's Martin Harvey.'

'Oh, one of your patients?'

'No, no. He's a famous actor. Try and follow the story, my boy.'

I did my best and got very worked up when he, instead of the other chap, went to the guillotine. As I sat with my father seeing other dramatic plays, I began to realise I was entering a new world: a world of make-believe which filled me with a longing to grow up and become part of it. I began to dramatise life as I saw it in the theatre. I became conscious of the dim gaslight of the street lamps—the weird effect—the voice of the paper boy hurrying along the street and shouting, in the semi-darkness, the latest news item.

'Paper—Big British Victory—Five thousand Boers surrender— Paper.'

Then excitement—Father rushing out to buy one—the breathless search under the oil lamp in the hall—shouts of 'What does it say?' and Father's angry reply, 'Nothing at all.' I think Father had the same sense of drama, he never could resist the voice of that paper boy coming out of the semi-darkness, as he was always getting caught.

One of the most exciting events which frequently occurred was the appearance of the fire engine at night, drawn by two high-speed horses, going flat out through the pale subdued lighting of the Fulham road with the firemen shouting unceasingly 'Fire! Fire!' to clear the way ahead. My imagination was in flames. I was terrified, but thrilled by the dramatic impact.

Father's great love for the stage never abated and his unfulfilled ambition found expression in an entirely new aspect of his work. He became a very successful lecturer on voice production. I suppose it was the nearest he could get to being an actor and I am glad it remained at that. In spite of being a man of striking appearance and strong personality, I do not think he would have made it.

Voice production became the focal point of Father's career, and with his medical knowledge and experience he wrote several books on the subject. The success of his lectures enabled him eventually to set up in the West End as a Harley Street specialist, but that was a long way ahead. In the meantime, back to the brass plate on the door of 732 Fulham Road.

Father, having rowed for Magdalene when they were head of the river at Oxford, never missed seeing the boat race at Putney if he could possibly help it. Naturally, we were both terrific fans. We joined the crowds in Bishop's Park, all wearing dark blue and light blue favours. How I hated that beastly light blue. We watched the start. The crowds roared '*They're off.*' They shot past us, dead level, so I thought.

Father shouted, 'Cambridge is slightly in front.'

'Are you sure?' Greatly distressed I gripped his hand firmly. 'Perhaps Cambridge will catch a crab.'

My mother, who had been under the weather for many weeks, was now confined to her bed and on a cold December morning Father and I walked along the Fulham Road to the Post Office to send a telegram to my grandparents living in Bath. His graphic description of telegraphic communication and how a message could be sent anywhere in Britain in a matter of seconds was, to a kid of nine years, most intriguing. He further explained it was prudent to keep the message as short as possible as it was expensive. So Father boiled it down to three words—'It's a boy.'

As soon as my mother was well enough to move about again, the baby was christened Claude Noël Hulbert, the middle name being chosen as he was born on Christmas Day. Father now had two sons to support, which meant working harder than ever. He took it all in his stride, determined to be a good father and, as in most things he set his mind to, he had unqualified success.

Everyone who came to see Claudie in his first twelve months said, 'What a beautiful baby!' This I found difficult to accept. I had never seen a close-up of one before. Hardly beautiful, I thought. Red in the face, big head, and very little hair. But as we were both of the same stock I suppose I must have looked very much the same. He settled down very quickly and appeared to be quite satisfied with the set-up.

He dribbled a lot and cooed a lot, except when he had wind which annoyed him and he never hesitated in letting us know.

After a testing period of a couple of years I became 'Big Brother', his hero, a part I was very happy to play. So here we were, a couple of kids born into the privileged class with a wonderful father and mother. We had everything except money but that did not worry Claudie, he was far more interested in learning to walk. The small amount I got as pocket money was mostly spent on sitting in the gallery of the Granville Theatre at Walham Green, which was then a music hall, watching the dancing acts, and it was worth every penny of four-pence, the price of entry to the 'gods'.

I picked up quite a number of steps. I felt learning to dance might help me on my way to the stage, which still seemed as far away as ever. School was such a bore, why did I have to go on? I could read and write. I pleaded with my father, he just laughed, so I had to submit to the tyranny of education and had the distinction of developing into a very backward child although, at that time, I was not in the least concerned.

But what did concern me were the quarrels of my father and mother. I could not understand why two such lovely people could be so unkind to each other. Who could I talk to about it? Claudie? He was not ready yet; the only words he knew were 'tar tar', 'dad dad', 'pottie' and 'wee wee'. These rows flared up at the drop of a hat. I could not take sides because I loved them both.

Before Claudie's arrival my mother and I used to make frequent visits to my grandparents in Ealing, the Hinchliffs, my mother's family, all living together—a grandfather, a grandmother, three uncles and an aunt—and all of them specialists in quarrelling. In fact, seeing so much of it, I could easily have become a specialist myself, but I set my face against such lunacy, although I was only a kid at the time, and I have sedulously avoided rows ever since.

My grandpa was the one brilliant exception in that contentious family, a sweet old man with a long white beard; in fact he formed the perfect Father Christmas picture of all times, gentle and benevolent. A devout Protestant, loved by all who knew him, with never an unkind thought in his head, but mention the word 'Catholic' and he went into a Dr Jekyll and Mr Hyde routine: he blew his top. Coming from such a devout warm-hearted Christian, this caused the family to rock with laughter. I didn't. He was such a lovable old gentleman. Many a time did he take me on his shoulder for a ride round the room.

Christmas was always a great event in that house, and being the season of goodwill there was always a cease-fire over the holidays. The great moment, of course, was Father Christmas arriving with a sack full of presents—to me, the height of drama. I can hear him saying, to this day, 'And here's another present for little Jackie.' His voice was so like grandpa's. The same lovely white beard. He was so exactly the Christmas card Father Christmas, and yet . . . I hated myself for doubting—why worry? I loved the land of make-believe. Better not ask questions—leave well alone—just go on enjoying it, which I did and still do.

My three uncles were away at work in the daytime but Uncle George usually came home to dinner at seven o'clock. He was very kind and would always give me a tasty mouthful when I asked him, although sometimes he had difficulty in finding my mouth. I was very small as I stood there beside him guiding his hand, but I failed to understand why he poured out his beer and missed the glass. This I thought was very funny, but I was the only one who laughed. Mother was most displeased.

'Jackie, don't be rude. Just a slight mistake, your uncle is tired.'

He was a very kind uncle. He said to me one day, 'I am going to take you to the Hippodrome, to the big water show—elephants plunging into a lake.' And the night before we went he came home in extra high spirits.

'Here we are,' he said. 'I've got 'em. Two sickets for tomorrow night.' I thought this was a funny joke but nobody laughed nor did anyone laugh when he poured out his beer and missed the glass again.

The rows at Ealing were fierce, worse than at home. There were more people at it. As soon as one paused to draw breath another jumped in with renewed fury. Then they were all shouting at once. It was not pleasant, but the happy periods of peace made up for it.

It was on Ealing Common that a huge bonfire had been erected and the great day arrived when it was to be set alight. A day of jollifications, flags everywhere, bunting decorating the houses. I thought the illuminations in the evening were beautiful: the little glass lamps in different colours burning night lights, festooned over the shops, looking so pretty. It was a great night of celebration. I did not understand quite what we were celebrating—something about a Jubilee, a word I had never heard of. It didn't matter. As a special treat I was taken out at night to see the bonfire. It was ablaze, lighting up the whole common and the heat . . . it was impossible to go near. Wonderful—terrifying—here was drama indeed. I revelled in it.

Mother's health was not improving. The doctor attending her said she must get away from London's pea soup fogs and live near the coast.

Bexhill-on-Sea was chosen and I was sent to a small preparatory day school which gave me an opportunity to continue being an extremely backward child. Father came down weekends and holidays. We went out fishing whenever the sea was calm enough. Father disliked paying for the hire of a boat every time we went out, so he did a deal with the fisherman and became the owner of two fishing smacks, five large rowing boats and six skiffs. When he told mother she was not in the least surprised: 'Another bargain to add to the list I suppose.' Father enjoyed rowing out to sea on our fishing trips and I soon learnt to take over when he was tired. After those early years at Putney watching the crews practise, rowing was in my blood.

When the unfortunate subject of my future education was discussed and it seemed a public school was inevitable, my feelings were 'let's get at it and get it over and then . . . the stage'. Westminster was mentioned as a possibility. I acquiesced in the suggestion as it was a famous rowing school. Apart from that, however, there was more than a slight possibility the school authorities might not be interested in trying to educate a complete ignoramus. But apparently they were. I can only think they were running short of dough.

The first thing I did on arrival was to acquaint my house-master with my rowing ambitions. I was slapped down immediately.

'Your mind should be set on higher things. This is a seat of learning.' His beady eyes fixed me with a cold indifference. Our dislike was mutual. 'The school very wisely abandoned rowing two years ago—

it was taking up too much of the boys' time—which is just as well in your shameful state of illiteracy.'

This was a bitter blow and I didn't much care for the way he put it. Slightly backward, yes, but illiteracy . . .! I was really stung. I may not have learnt much, but at other things . . . I'll show 'em, I thought. Swimming—why not? I remembered the regatta at Bexhill where I had won several races. So I entered immediately for the school open championship, only to be beaten by a split second. Bitterly disappointed that rowing had been abandoned, I was now more determined than ever to stamp my name on this illustrious Elizabethan foundation.

I went into the gym, a very lofty building attached to the Abbey Cloisters. There was a full-sized ship's mast, fixed to the floor and the roof. On one of the top beams were painted the names of the heroes who had climbed to the top. I decided my name must go up there at once and immediately started on this mad enterprise.

I had no idea the base of a ship's mast was so massive, I could only just get my arms round. Laboriously I inched my way up. After gaining a few feet I was exhausted; it seemed impossible. I had to stop—my arms were aching, my legs were aching. A few boys started laughing.

'That's as far as anyone gets. Come on down, clever boy.'

'No, go on. You don't mind breaking your neck, do you?'

The words of the beady-eyed housemaster were still rankling in my mind. I gained another few feet and stopped again, exhausted. More boys came to watch. Now, I *had* to go on; I had an audience. Even in those days I had the actor's instinct. Now I would show off. I gained quite a bit more. As I got higher the mast got thinner. The audience grew. They began to cheer. I daren't look down. I was so high up, nearing the top, I could now grip the mast with my hands. The cheering increased—only a few inches more—I was there—.

The gym sergeant shouted, 'Put your hand on the top rafter.' The intense drama spurred me on. The rafter was just above my head. I had to hold on with one hand to leave the other free. Here was my first lesson in self-control, a lesson which I have never forgotten. A mighty shout came from the audience below. 'He's done it. Hulbert's climbed the pole.' The descent was just a matter of concentration.

It was a great day for me when my name was added to those of the valiant few on one of the top beams. Years afterwards, when I proudly took my wife to see how I had left my mark on the school, I found that the whole gym had been demolished and the names of those valiant few were relegated to the dust of oblivion. *Vanity, all is vanity*.

The climbing episode gave me a certain amount of prestige with the boys, and with that and the peculiar shape of my jaw I became well known as the chap with the pump-handle chin. I had no incentive to work. An appearance in the Latin play might have kindled an interest in the classics but only the King's scholars were included in the cast. Result: I continued to languish in obscurity in the bottom form but one. I found the biting sarcasm of my form master completely alien to my temperament and my 'shameful illiteracy' continued to flourish.

All I could think about was the stage and how soon I could leave school. I did not discuss this with my parents. They were so happy having a son at Westminster who had climbed the pole, that I had not the heart to disillusion them, and for their sake I had to pretend I was happy. I was just playing a part which, I must say, I rather enjoyed, but it soon began to pall and I decided to have another go at trying to leave and start on the stage as a child actor.

'I could do my lessons in the daytime,' I said to my mother.

'Jackie darling,' my mother said, with a note of pleading in her gentle voice, 'you can't leave now, you are doing so well and you are so happy there.' I could have kicked myself for overdoing it. 'Oh no, Jackie, it would be a terrible mistake to leave school now.'

3

'I don't want to hear another word. I am amazed at you asking such a question.'

This was coming from a house in Old Trafford. An outraged father was reprimanding his young daughter for daring to oppose his plans for her future career. He was an entirely self-made man and had done a very good job. His love for his daughter was implicit in his determination that she should enjoy that culture which he had never known. His severity increased as he continued.

'Judging by your school reports, you are not progressing as you should. An improvement must be made from now on and I tell you finally, you will not set foot on the stage until your education is complete.'

He was a remarkable character, coming from a very humble Scottish family who, by virtue of his natural gifts and self-education, was now a much respected citizen of Manchester. His young daughter, with a large amount of her mother's compassion and tenderness, took on an equal amount of her father's courage and determination, and even at a tender age she was a force to be reckoned with. The opposition became stronger.

'What about the pantomime? You let me go on the stage then.'

'That was only for a short season, darling,' her mother said very quietly.

'What about Midsummer Night's Dream? I did my lessons in the day-time. Why can't I go back on the stage?'

'Your education is so important, my darling.' There was a warm soft smile on her mother's pretty face.

Her father spoke with finality: 'Very shortly I am sending you to a finishing school in Lausanne.'

'Why?' asked the rebellious daughter.

'To make a lady of you,' thundered the furious father.

15

'I don't want to be a lady. I want to be an actress.'
Gently, her mother intervened. 'You're going to be both, my darling.'

During my school days Father took on a very lucrative appointment
as medical adviser to one of the Indian princes in Poona, which was
then still part of the British Empire. Claudie and I were packed off to
my grandparents at Bath. A direct contrast to the contentious Hinchliffs at Ealing, the Hulberts were a peace-loving lot—not a militant
among them. There were Grandfather and Granny, four maiden aunts
very prim and unworldly, and a cousin Judy, a few years older than
me. At meal times we sat at table: Grandfather, a high-principled
churchman, stern and severe, at one end and Granny, wearing her
little lace cap and looking the perfect picture of Victorian dignity,
at the other.

Granny was the superstar, adored by everyone for her sweet and
gentle nature, who in my opinion had unquestionably earned the right
to be billed above the title. An adorable little woman. Dear little
Granny, not an unkind thought in her head. Sharing everybody's
happiness, her angelic face crinkling with her merry laughter and a
tiny silver curl peeping shyly from beneath the little lace cap. Small
wonder she charmed everyone without even trying, and with all this
she had to cope with the inexorable austerity of my grandfather. She
must have seen certain qualities in him that I had never had the pleasure
of experiencing. They were both ardent Christians—the gay and the
serious. Which was right? Granny, I loved. Grandfather, I was afraid
of. He had my respect but not my love.

Entry Hill House, where they lived, was a palatial country house on
the outskirts of Bath in a beautiful setting of trees and shrubs with a
blaze of colour from the summer flowers.

My maiden aunts, in their cloistered security, remained unsullied
by the outside world. In fact my dear Aunt Eva, bless her, had never
been inside such an immoral place as a theatre and when I consider
some of the shows of today I think she'd got something there and I
must applaud her decision. In this rather unusual set-up meals were
served in the big dining room. Family prayers followed breakfast and
supper, conducted by the redoubtable head of the house—the servants

were summoned and we all sat round in a semi-circle. Sunday was a day of rest—no work of any kind, a most stringent rule. There was church morning and evening, and we all walked. It was about a mile.

Uncle Frank, Father's younger brother, was my sporting hero. He was a motor-bike expert; he rode for the Triumph Company in all the big reliability trials. His house in Coventry was stacked with trophies. Whenever he came to Bath for a few days it was my joy to be allowed to ride his bike round and round the tennis court.

Granny was a great companion and joined in a lot of our fun. My cousin Judy and I prevailed on the coachman to knock us up a trolley out of a wooden box and four old perambulator wheels and Judy and I used it to toboggan down a long sloping lawn to the tennis court. We were enjoying ourselves one morning and Judy said, 'Look who's coming.'

'Shall we?'

'Why not?'

The invitation was accepted with a certain amount of diffidence but with a lot of laughter. We helped her into the box with the greatest care and as we pulled the trolley along towards the stables we passed the coachman and the gardener who respectfully touched their hats. The polite salutation was acknowledged with a gracious smile and a regal gesture from the perfect picture of Victorian dignity. Granny was never put out of countenance.

'You're very naughty children. What will those servants think?'

'Granny, they loved to see you joining in with our fun.'

Peals of merry laughter; Granny enjoyed it as much as we did.

My father and I became very close friends and together we visited most of the theatres in London on a Saturday night. Father was not the man for waiting in a queue. If the pit was full in one theatre we hurried to the next and continued until we got in somewhere. I think he enjoyed it as much as I did. At a very early age I had been in every pit and gallery in the West End. It was the best possible training, seeing all the big stars of those days. My two heroes were Charles Hawtrey and Gerald Du Maurier. Just as there could never be another Pavlova or a Sir Henry Irving, these two, Hawtrey and Du Maurier, could never be reproduced.

Du Maurier's style was unique. He stood like a statue, motionless, a static figure, no movement or facial expression, except when necessary to convey an idea, then back to the static figure. It was complete economy of movement. His undeviating precision enthralled his audience and with the greatest of ease he held them spellbound merely lighting a cigarette, flicking out the match and putting it in the ashtray. So neat, so finished, so precise. He is credited with being the originator of 'the throwing-away-school'. Too many of our young performers today endeavour to do the same with the result they become completely inaudible. When Du Maurier did it you heard the lot.

Hawtrey was a different type entirely. He was not handsome and he was far from slim, but the fascination of his personality was completely irresistible: the slight drawl, the soft tone of his voice, the half smile as he spoke. Effortless in getting his laughs and completely controlled, as a light comedy actor he was paramount to all others. Of all the artistes of stage and screen, including the greats of Hollywood, I have never seen any to surpass or even equal the stylish and appealing charm of Hawtrey or the precision and expertise of the fascinating personality of Du Maurier. How unfortunate talkies and T.V. arrived a little too late to make perfect recordings of their two outstanding original styles for posterity.

Claudie had collected by now most of the odd five hundred words in common use, which enabled him to express his refusal to do what he did not want to do and great pleasure when he got his own way. He found the garden entirely to his satisfaction as a playground—no complaints. His big brother being mad about the stage, he had to be mad about it too. So Big Brother set about thinking up a pantomime for Christmas with a distinguished cast consisting of the four cloistered ladies, Claudie and myself. Here was my first attempt at stage production. One has got to make a start some time and this seemed to be the moment.

I got hold of a book of the current music hall songs and wrote some stunning dialogue between the numbers. Uncle Frank rigged up a proscenium and curtain at the end of the big drawing room, using his motor bike lamp as a 'front arc'. I started rehearsing Claudie in two short verses I had written for him, and here I encountered my first temperamental artist. He wasn't in the mood. He'd do it later. 'I want to go tobogganing,' he would say and start to go. 'No, no, not now, come back and I'll give you two bulls' eyes.' This was a daily occurrence, but I got him to learn the verses in the end but Judy had to make several quick dives to the village to get repeated bags of bribery.

On Christmas Day Claudie celebrated his sixth birthday by making his appearance on the stage with the startling announcement, 'I am the Demon King. This cave belongs to me.' Far from striking terror in the hearts of the audience it got one of the best laughs of the evening and the next best laugh was when Claudie dried up in the middle of a sentence and had to be prompted. This pleased Claudie as much as the audience, and he went on deliberately drying up. Although it was his first-ever appearance before an audience he seemed to possess the comedian's instinct for building up laughter. I had to drag him off the stage in the end. He was most annoyed and so was I.

All the drama had gone for nothing. *I* was the funny man and Claudie had entirely upset the balance, but as far as Granny was concerned I was the hit of the show. It was the song that sent her: *I never stopped running till I got home and the dog had my Sunday trousers.* She thought it was the funniest thing she had ever heard and talked about it long afterwards.

Claudie's triumphant debut fired me with ambition. Here was something to work on. He needed an author and a director; I decided to be both—good practice anyway. I concocted at once a six verse recitation about his daring exploits, one of which was hosing the chickens in the fowl house. Getting him to learn the words and remember all the movements required the patience of Job. He wanted to do this. He wanted to do that. He was tired of it. It wasn't funny.

I lost my temper on one occasion and slapped him smartly on the back of his hand saying, 'You're a very naughty little boy.' He burst into tears. It was the indignity and humiliation of being smacked by Big Brother, who was immediately stricken with remorse and wished he hadn't done it. Apologies were accepted magnanimously and peace was restored. The following two weeks called for the utmost patience, but gradually the words were learnt and the movements remembered.

Some thirty years later, there emerged from these early beginnings an act used by the B.B.C. for several months called 'The Hulbert Brothers'.

A musical evening was arranged for little brother's recital and invitations were accepted by most of the neighbouring houses. Aunt Amy played the mandolin, Aunt Eva the harp and Granny the piano. The entrance of the star was memorable; a musical flourish and a few dramatic chords from Granny and he walked on, primed with lemonade and chocolate cream to a big reception. He started with complete confidence. Laughter and applause all the way, great ovation at the end. A new type of comedian was born.

Father, having gathered quite a useful amount of rupees as payment for his medical knowledge, returned with mother from India. Needless to say, the Hulbert brothers were delighted to see them back home again and much rejoicing followed. Father resumed his work on voice production with renewed vigour and a little later set up in the Harley Street region as a specialist on the subject. I think Poona payed off not only in rupees but in physical energy. Father took on more and more appointments lecturing but with it all he still found time for our trips to the theatre on Saturday nights. His enthusiasm for the stage had increased and also his tendency to irritability, a venial sin in anyone working so hard. Some eminent men are collectors of antiques: period furniture, china, glass, etc. Not so father. He was none of that breed. He was eminently original. The cheap bargain he still found irresistible no matter what it was.

The bell rang one day. I opened the front door and a man with a horse and cart outside said, 'Where shall I put them?'

'What?' I was prepared for anything.

'Twelve glass-panelled doors.'

I told mother and once more the eyebrows were raised.

'He's at it again. He'll never be cured.'

One of his new appointments was lecturing at the Central School in the Albert Hall. This was an excellent dramatic academy run by a brilliant lady called Elsie Fogerty, who trained many artists for the

London stage. Father, who never missed a trick, found the school at that time had more ladies than men.

'My son could be available at certain times and would be only too pleased to read some of the men's parts. He's going on the stage when he leaves school.'

A few weeks later, the illustrious Miss Fogerty was taking the Shakespeare class in a large room at the top of the Albert Hall. She was addressing one of the lady students who was standing on a table.

'You will never learn to act until you have fully developed your imagination. Think who you are and where you are. Not in the Albert Hall. You're in Verona, not standing on a table, you're on a balcony. Imagine the soft night air, the trees tipped with silver from the moon. In the garden below, unknown to you, stands the man you love. You voice your thoughts: "Oh Romeo, Romeo, wherefore art thou Romeo." '

Miss Fogerty was not a young slim teenager, in fact she was rather buxom, but that line was spoken with perfect diction in a soft resonant voice and sounded the perfect Juliet.

'Now, my darling, say the lines.'

The young student had a go. Miss Fogerty winced slightly.

'More feeling. Think. Use your imagination. Standing in the orchard garden below is your beloved Romeo, the man you adore.'

But standing in the orchard garden below was a rather thin, gangling schoolboy with a pump-handle chin. Acting or no acting, if the imagination was stretched to breaking point there could never have been the remotest suggestion of that glamourous romantic character.

When we had struggled through to the end of the scene and Juliet said 'Parting is such sweet sorrow' she made it sound like parting is such sheer delight. I played the scene with many of the girls. How they must have suffered. It was all right in the Bottom the Weaver and Titania scene—the asses' head almost suggested itself.

With the principal of the school being a near perfect elocutionist —and by that I mean being the possessor of a well-trained, flexible speaking voice—the paramount importance of voice control was made obvious to all who had the intelligence to appreciate the fact. I was indeed grateful for those days. It made no difference what part I played or how completely unsuitable I may have been, it was all experience with scenes from *Hamlet, Julius Caesar, School for Scandal*, etc. Excellent practice.

The summer holidays were spent at Bexhill. Mother responded well to the bracing Sussex air and Father, who lacked nothing of the spirit of adventure, bought a motor car. He had a few cursory instructions from the salesman about the controls and how to use them. We were all waiting anxiously at the house for him to drive from the garage, wondering if he would make it, and he did. For this masterly achievement he got a hero's welcome. We were very excited and so was Father; it was the first time he had ever driven a car. It was one of those very early jobs—very high and upright which still suggested the horse and carriage without the horse.

'Where would you like to go? Hastings?' Father was in one of his jolly moods.

'Let's drive gently along the front,' mother suggested, wisely I thought.

'Right. All aboard. I'll start her up.'

That was father's big mistake. It should never have been said. The petrol engine is very sensitive and, like its predecessor the horse, knows immediately when it is in the hands of an inexperienced driver so does just what it likes. With a light heart father applied himself to the cranking handle and nothing happened. He tried several times; complete defiance from the engine. This started off a chain of events that could have gone straight into the immortal Harry Tate sketch.

Father paused to take breath then had another go. The engine spluttered slightly as if suppressing a laugh. Father's gay mood was gradually ebbing away. A grim determination took over. Mother and I waiting expectantly in the car, remained silent. One inopportune word would have sparked off a flaming row. Father tried flooding the carburettor. No good. He advanced the spark. No good. He retarded the spark. Continued defiance from the engine. Father, on the point of exhaustion, gave it another turn and the engine started, surprising us all. As soon as father got in and sat down it stopped. It happened again. Here was a new game. It was so funny, but Mother and I dare not laugh—the atmosphere was far too tense. Irritability was just waiting for its cue. The third time, Father rushed round and opened the throttle. The engine roared into action with a tremendous laugh, the clutch was dropped in and we shot forward half out of our seats. Then we settled down to a steady speed and reached the front unscathed.

It was a little embarrassing coming through the town on a busy shopping day because it was taking Father a long time to realise he was holding a steering wheel and not a pair of reins, and as some of the shoppers were trying to cross the road Father would shout 'Hupp' instead of blowing the horn.

Changing gear demanded skill and practice in those early days of motoring. The operating lever resembled a hand brake working over a ratchet and it was far from easy to hit the right notch. If the change was missed the engine raced and the car started running backwards downhill.

After a couple of days Father ventured further afield. All was well but whenever a hill was approached the light-hearted conversation in the car came to an abrupt end. Would father be able to change down, hit the right notch and at the same time look where he was going? Silently, we wished him the best of luck and for quite a while, with our fears abated, we could resume our light-hearted conversation very quickly. At the end of the sea front the road continued over Galley Head along the edge of the cliffs. As we approached, far from slowing up to turn round we gathered speed and rushed the hill, evidently with a determination to conquer this formidable height. Faster than we had ever gone before we approached the summit, then about half way we slowed down—a gear change would have to be made at once. Would father find that right notch?

He had a shot and missed. The engine stopped and we started to run backwards. Mother, being highly strung and with an artistic temperament, screamed: she was not suited to these kind of thrills. I shouted, 'Father, we're running backwards,' in case he hadn't noticed. Brakes were sluggish in those days and did not act quickly—not so Father. In a flash we did a complete U-turn and continued coasting down the hill the right way round. Having reached the bottom of the hill we stopped to give ourselves time to recover. Father's miraculous U-turn backwards was not appreciated by Mother who was on the verge of fainting; she thought Father should have more instructions before attempting any other hills, but I thought Father had surpassed himself.

4

Having spent three years at Westminster, becoming more and more backward, the question arose, what next? It was agreed that the ancient seat of learning, which had signally failed to give me an education compatible with the large sums of money my father had provided, would in future have to struggle on without me as best it could. I was overjoyed; the stage was within my grasp. Father was all set for it. Mother was not.

'He must go on.' She was most insistent. 'It must be Oxford or Cambridge.'

This was a shattering blow. I thought I'd made it. 'How could I possibly attempt the entrance exam?' I pleaded. I have my dear mother to thank for what followed; her faith in me was unshakeable. Nothing short of Prime Minister would have satisfied her ambition.

'Of course you could if you give your mind to it.' Mother had no doubts. Father's feelings began to change. It would have been easy for him to have vetoed the suggestion and avoided added expenditure but, like mother, he believed in me.

Suddenly I began to grow up. I was touched. I realised what it would mean, what it would cost him. Here was my great friend, a 'varsity man himself, agreeing with Mother, which he very seldom did. For the first time in my life I felt an appalling ignorance. I regretted bitterly those wasted school days and Father's money. Here was a chance to make amends. I had never thought seriously about education before but now it hit me right between the eyes. It was a challenge, a great opportunity, but how to do it? Hard slogging. It would have to be a crammers. Inquiries were made and father settled for Mr

24

The Demon King is wearing the sailor suit.

The Demon King, *in statu pupillarii*, dares Big Brother to defy the University statute of no white trousers with cap and gown.

I'm not quite sure *what* I'm doing here, but I was
certainly giving it the works.

University Drama Days

Sir Anthony Absolute talking to a lady . . . or is
she? Splendid make-up, but the hands give it away.

Sir Toby Belch? Not a bit like him, neither was the performance.

An amateur pierrot show—what better way of spending the long Vac?

On the way to the Senate House for graduation.
I'm just in, but only just.

It's an ill wind that blows no good. I got the lady.

Engagement, 1913. We've both changed a lot since then. It's probably just as well.

My arms should have been around Cicely, but Alfred Lester popped his
head up at the last minute. *The Pearl Girl*—1913.

Cicely as Chrysea in *The Arcadians*
—1911.

Borland's establishment in the Buckingham Palace Road. Mr Borland was a tall witty gentleman with no charm or warmth but quite pleasant and a good teacher. He always wore a well-seasoned frock coat, presumably to give him a more scholastic appearance, but it failed to work—he looked like an undertaker.

Insatiable optimism has always been a persistent feature of my make-up and it has helped me considerably in later years to deal successfully with a large amount of disappointments. The inception of this happy optimism can be traced to the dramatic moment when I was shown the syllabus of the University Entrance Examination. Without hesitation I announced I could do it in a year. After working with Borland for a couple of weeks he said, 'Three years and then it was doubtful.' Flouting his opinion, I worked harder than ever. It was exciting, a new experience, but the appreciation figure of my mental capacity remained at an all-time low.

Then by degrees the look of despair on Mr Borland's saturnine face began to fade. He started taking more time correcting my work and being more and more helpful. I became his model pupil, by no means the most brainy but the most zealous and persevering. It had now developed into a race against time. I asked him to let me stay on after hours and work on my own in the classroom where I had all my books and dictionaries around me. At first it was a definite no. I emphasised the advantages. I could be trusted to put out the lights and lock up. But again he said no: 'We don't want you overworking. We must be careful.' Here was something new. The first time I had ever been warned about studying too hard.

It made me laugh and I told him so. It made *him* laugh too, in fact I was always making him laugh. My fellow students were a splendid audience and these occasional interruptions of laughter made a welcome break and very good practice for me. When I cracked one of my best gags he used to put the palms of his hands together, lock them between his knees as he sat next to me and laugh his head off saying, '*Will* you get on with your work!'

I won the day about working overtime in the classroom and it paid dividends. It almost doubled the progress. Things were well on the move.

It must have been about the time I had just completed my first six months at Borland's. Cambridge was dimly visible on the horizon. Cambridge? Surely not? How could I explain such flagrant apostasy? But I had grown from childhood to adolescence. I was mad keen to get there. I felt I was more than half way and I still had another six months to go.

I realised that physical as well as mental fitness was essential so I used to walk to Borland's each morning and back home at nine in the evening. This kept me in very good shape. Saturday afternoon and Sunday I took off. I had a girlfriend, rather grand she was, good looking, tall and dignified. I used to take her out, not to dinner, I hadn't enough money, but to Earls Court Exhibition, and we would have coffee together sitting in the romantic surrounding of the artificial lake and illuminated grounds. We had warm summer nights in those days and I felt a hell of a guy with this splendid lady on my arm. She was my special one though there had been several others. Like the dramatic, the romantic had a great appeal. The sight of a pretty girl and I was in another world.

At last I got within a fortnight of the exam. I felt ready, I had done all that I set out to do. I had a fairly strong grip of each subject and even my friend in the seedy frock coat thought I stood a good chance. I was full of confidence but cautious. I made a list of the shaky bits. did a quick revision during the last ten days and felt easier in my mind. If I failed—well at least I knew as much, if not more, than the boys in the top form at Westminster and I had learnt in one year what had taken them five. Nothing in the world now to worry about, a good night's sleep before sitting for the exam—but things don't always work out that way. At the weekend, just before the exam at Cambridge, I said goodbye to Borland, who shook me warmly by the hand.

'Don't let anything worry you. Just relax, keep your mind clear and I think you'll pull it off.'

I thanked him for all he had done for me and left in great spirits.

I rang up the girlfriend, a perfect way to forget for a few happy moments the imminence of the exam. Her mother answered the phone and said, 'Come round, I know she'd love to see you.' I put on my best suit, the only one I had, not from Savile Row, off the peg at a sale, but it made me feel good. In the gayest of moods, light-hearted and light-headed, I was seized with a feeling of romance. In shining armour on my trusty steed, my pennant waving in the breeze, I galloped forward to meet the lady of my dreams.

Inside the house in St. John's Wood, as I awaited her arrival, I decided to fold her in my arms and embrace her without further ado. A knight errant works fast. I was shown into the drawing room and the door was closed. I watched it eagerly, ready to pounce the moment she entered and a voice immediately behind me said 'Hullo'. She had come in from the garden. This threw me a little, but recovering instantly I made the pounce and missed. I wasn't expecting her to sit on the settee. I crashed into the standard lamp but caught it just in time.

'Careful,' she said, affecting concern. 'Did you trip over the rug?'

'I must have done.' It was all I could think of in my embarrassment. The fiery spirit had been quenched—it didn't really belong in an Edwardian drawing room. I sat down beside her very gently.

'Well, how are you?' she enquired in a casual and indifferent voice.

'Fine. How are you?'

'Fine, thanks.'

I took her hand, which she withdrew immediately. I was getting nowhere. I tried again but the hands weren't available, they were adjusting an adorable wisp of hair. I sat a little closer. She rose majestically and approached the piano with all the dignity of the Queen opening Parliament. I got the message, but sadly lacking experience instead of taking the initiative and saying, 'So long, honey. Give me a ring when the mood changes,' I made the fatal mistake of giving her the exact feed line she wanted.

'What's the matter, darling?'

'Nothing. Go and sit down and I'll play to you.'

This was a definite brush-off. I seized both her hands.

'Please don't do that,' she said imperiously. 'I'm not in the mood.'

The romance was in pieces. I left in despair. I was shattered. Why, oh why did it have to happen now? I went to bed that night a broken man and slept like a top, which surprised me. The next morning I was determined not to bow to the storm, I would rise above it—fight it. A new kind of part to play. I began to relish it even. A new experience.

I took a tender farewell from my parents and set off for Cambridge. On arrival I made for Gonville and Caius College, where the Master and Fellows had graciously offered me a home for the next three years. It was just a little matter of passing the entrance exam and the others that would follow in due course. I was informed by the very efficient Minister of Information, the porter at the gate, that I had been allotted digs opposite the R.C. Church, just off St Andrew's Street. I took my belongings there and returned to Caius along Trumpington Street and King's Parade. I was in another world, one I had never imagined—the stately colleges—their antiquity. I was greatly impressed, but it was not until I returned years afterwards that I could appreciate to the full the ineffable charm and sheer beauty of this treasure of our heritage.

I sorted out the Minister of Information again. He told me a lot of interesting things about the College, especially the three gates: 'the Gate of Humility' on entering, feeling as you should unworthy of the great opportunity; 'the Gate of Virtue', as you proceed on the course of deep study, and finally the famous 'Gate of Honour', featured in all the picture postcard series and only used by undergraduates at the end of their third year on their way to a private entrance to the Senate House to receive their degrees. This gave my nervous system another sudden jolt and considerably increased my feeling of responsibility.

I dined in hall that night with the rest of the victims of tomorrow's ordeal and fervently hoped it would not be the one and only time. I turned in early to get a good night's sleep, to be right on the ball in the morning, but the church clock made a tremendous thing of letting all and sundry know every quarter of an hour exactly what it was there for. Going to bed before my usual time was a mistake to start with. I couldn't get off to sleep and I even had difficulty in worrying about my shattered romance, the noise that clock made was so compelling.

I got up the next morning feeling very tired, the last thing in the world I wanted. I entered the examination hall worried and depressed. I went to my place and read the questions quickly. There were three sections of St Matthew's Gospel in the original Greek that I recognised and started translating furiously. I glanced at the other questions; I could answer them all. It was just a matter of time. It was a most successful morning. The Latin translation presented no problems, including the unseen. It was the Maths papers I was uneasy about. I didn't have time to answer all the questions but I felt fairly safe on the ones I did. I tipped the porter at the gate to wire me the moment the results were posted outside the Senate House.

When I got home I told my parents, with my usual optimism, that I thought I had a fair chance and then braced myself for the cruel period of waiting. Surprisingly, my shattered romance was entirely forgotten. At last the telegram arrived. I looked at it stupidly. My stomach turned over. I felt my face turn red and hot. Beads of perspiration gathered on my forehead. Then frantically I tore it open. The message was short and clear. It read 'Passed third class'. I was in! I'd made it! Hilarious family rejoicing! Vindication of unwavering parental faith! Indolent ignoramus makes good! As we began to cool down I realised how much a father and mother are concerned by success or failure of their offspring. I was very happy for them. It was a load off my shoulders and I was happy for myself because I had found my own philosophy, found how much can be achieved by the simple method of sticking to it, of being an 'obstinate little boy' as my nanny used to call me.

On a bright sunny morning at the end of the summer of 1911, I entered Caius as a First Year man. The alternative name was 'Fresher'. I preferred the former. I was eighteen years old. 'Man', I felt was most appropriate and it gave me an entirely new outlook.

5

When the family that occupied the house in Old Trafford left Manchester they went to London and eventually established a home in the pleasant vicinity of St John's Wood. The father of the little girl was a remarkable man. One of those interesting types who start at the bottom and finish at the top. At an early age he set his heart on a stage career and with dogged determination reached the heights; not as an actor but as a producer of musical stage shows, and this is how he did it. He was a resolute Scot. From a strict but humble home in the poorer part of Edinburgh, he ran away and joined a touring company as a 'call boy'. He then earned a few more shillings by playing small parts. Self-education came from diligent reading and study in his spare time. He set great store by learning. He married a pretty English actress who became a great help to him in his creative work of producing.

While touring Australia their first child, a girl, was born in Sydney and as the name of the comic opera was Esmerelda, the poor innocent child got stuck with it. How cruel can loving parents be! On returning to England he took over the Prince's Theatre, Manchester, and the Theatre Royal. A big responsibility, but with his infallible touch they prospered, which was just as well as a son had now joined the Old Trafford ménage and, as in the case of my own father, up went the expenses.

His increased activity brought him notable successes, including some beautifully-staged pantomimes and two outstanding productions of As You Like It *and particularly* A Midsummer Night's Dream. *The press were unanimous: 'A sparkling production'—'The name of Robert Courtneidge will go down to posterity'—'A man of fine talent—the brilliance of his invention—his taste'. A glance at the programme would have been interesting. It contained the names of several well known artists of those days and right at the bottom it stated 'Peasblossom . . . Cicely Courtneidge'. Mercifully, Esmerelda had been dropped.*

The indomitable Robert, having proved himself to be a man of sterling qualities, now decided on fresh fields to conquer. Regretfully, the board of directors of the Prince's Theatre and the Theatre Royal were forced to accept his resignation. A course was set for London and the family took a tender farewell of the house in Old Trafford.

Fortune smiled on the adventurous call boy from Edinburgh. The West End was just waiting for a man of his creative talent and very quickly his aspirations were fulfilled. A couple of years and he was right at the top. George Edwards, a devotee of the sport of kings, whose colours could be seen on most of the race courses in England, was the ruling monarch of musical comedy. He was quick to sense the danger of opposition and hired Robert Courtneidge to produce the Duchess of Dantzig *which was an instant success. Once again the Scottish blood came to the fore and the offer of a partnership with the great George Edwards, which would have meant immediate security, was declined with thanks. Robert decided to go it alone. He took the risk and it paid off. He had two big musical successes,* The Blue Moon *and* The Dairymaids, *the latter with Carrie Moore and a new comedian with the intriguing name of Dan Rolyat, which is Taylor spelt backwards. It was on the strength of these two successes that he took over the Shaftesbury Theatre on a long lease. Not the present Shaftesbury Theatre but the one that cannot be seen any more because Hitler removed it one night in the Blitz.*

In its heyday it was one of the most popular theatres in the West End and it was here in 1908 that our Robert staged his first production, The Arcadians, *a delightful mixture of fantasy and the London season, one of the greatest shows of its time, in fact years ahead of its time, an innovation, something quite new in the musical comedy world packed with originality and invention. It had the delightful music of Lionel Monkton (the husband of Gertie Millar), the sweet voice of Florence Smithson, and the comedy of Dan Rolyat and the very funny Alfred Lester. Harry Welshman was the lover and the brilliant Nelson Keys was just starting. The final curtain fell on that famous first night to a hurricane of applause and another historical moment was created on the West End stage.*

When the great Titian was commissioned to paint The Assumption *to hang behind the altar of the Friare Church in Venice, what were his thoughts* as he left the ceremony of its installation? Or Michaelangelo as he left his masterpiece in St Peter's, Rome? Probably much the same as those of a happy and excited Robert as he left the Shaftesbury Theatre with the cheers still ringing in his ears. He must have felt himself great.

But that was about the last thing his stage-struck daughter would have felt, sitting in the train the next morning on her way to the finishing school in Lausanne to be made a lady. Less than nothing, just a little girl from Old Trafford. But being who she was, with characteristic resilience, she submitted to the process, which lasted about a couple of years. One could hardly blame her parents for not realising it was totally unnecessary. She was a lady by nature, just as her father was a natural gentleman.

At the home of the little girl from Old Trafford there was a scene of great rejoicing. She had just returned from the finishing school in Lausanne and was now eligible for an appearance in the Tatler with the debutantes of the season. Her parents were delighted. She was now all set for the stage and the sooner the better.

Her homecoming was exciting. She was about to start her professional stage career. May Kinder, playing Chrysea in The Arcadians, was leaving the cast to get married and at the age of seventeen Cicely Courtneidge attended several auditions and finally got the job, largely through the influence of 'Espy', Espinosa, who had trained her as a dancer and believed she had a future, but her father, fearing invidious criticism about father employing daughter, had turned her down. 'Espy' argued and won. He saw some indefinable quality in the verve and vitality which was to be part of the Cicely Courtneidge we know today. When you listen to old records of Al Jolson, Judy Garland, Jack Buchanan, to name a few, the voice is arresting, not for its beauty of sound, but for its warmth and fascinating characteristics which play such an important part in the making of a star.

Cicely Courtneidge was by no means sensational as Chrysea but that indefinable something in the voice seemed to presage a successful career. With a father an eminent producer, a mother an actress with three sisters in the business, one of whom was Ada Blanche, the delightful and talented artiste who had played principal boy at Drury Lane and a grandmother, Cicely Nott, an opera star at Covent Garden, the stage was in her blood. In any case, the show was a sell-out for months ahead. Cicely got an encore every night for her song and dance, which had not happened before. So everyone was happy

including the audience who applauded the company at the end of the show as
they lined up on the stage for the curtain call.

At the same time a similar incident was taking place at Cambridge in the theatre belonging to the A.D.C., the University Amateur Dramatic Club. In the line-up at the end of Sheridan's *The Rivals*, a slender but well-padded Sir Anthony Absolute with a pump-handle chin was bowing with the rest of the cast to the applause of a delighted audience of undergraduates, graduates with their lady friends, and dons with their families. The rather unusual-looking Sir Anthony was entirely unknown in the University but maybe the prominent chin had created a certain amount of curiosity and the A.D.C. were pleased to have a new member who would be useful to them in the future. It was a big chance and I had grabbed it with both hands. As far as the theatrical career in the University was concerned I was all set. I was extremely lucky and I realised very quickly the best way to learn the job was to do it in front of an audience.

The excellent Marlow Club, mostly members of King's College, including dons, was flourishing in those days and I played in some of their productions, including *The Knight of the Burning Pestle*. There were several amateur dramatic clubs outside the University and they were only too glad to recruit undergraduate talent. There were also all kinds of charity shows and every college had its 'smoking concert'. I accepted every invitation to perform. Wonderful practice for a song and dance appearance.

Cambridge is a world of its own, and an amateur actor can make a name for himself in that world just as a professional can in London, in the West End. Cambridge is about the best audience in the country and gives an amateur of undergraduate level confidence and the greatest encouragement. It is a unique place for training for the stage because it provides such excellent opportunities of appearing before an audience and so practising the job. The first thing I did when I arrived was to join the A.D.C. and I have much to be grateful for.

The next thing I did was to join the Caius boat club which I was mad keen to do after the bitter disappointment of Westminster. What a thrill finding yourself sitting in an eight for the first time! The

flashback to Putney—the Boat Race—Father's prowess at Oxford—
the excitement I felt as the boatman pushed us out slowly into midstream, the Cam sparkling in the sunshine. None of us had ever rowed
in an eight before. It was sheer exhilaration.

The cox shouted, 'Ready? Ready?' We were straining at the leash.
Again the voice of the cox—'Come forward, paddle.' What happened
beggars description. The boat rolled from side to side like an old
Cunarder crossing the Atlantic in a gale. First the oars went in so deep
in the water you could gardly get them out and then so high in the air
that you missed the water altogether. The coach, a senior member of
the club, mounted on a bike, was exhorting us through a megaphone
to get the blades into the water together. We were lucky if we could
get them in at all.

I went to bed that night very depressed. How different to what I had
expected! The next day was even worse. The third day no better.
Aching muscles, blistered hands and a red-hot bottom—why the hell
was I going through all this torture? I must be mad. The coach continued shouting instructions which, even if we knew how to do them,
we were incapable of carrying out. I was desperate, there seemed to be
no hope and it was at that moment that the 'Varsity boat went majestically down the river. A perfect picture of cohesion, complete togetherness, a firm grip of the water, shoulders swinging back together, controlled balance on the swing forward, all working as one man. It
looked so easy, which is the criterion of perfection as in every sport.
They must have been through hell when they first started, probably
most of them had begun at school.

My enthusiasm returned in a flash. My muscles no longer ached.
Let nature deal with the blistered hands and the broken skin of the
red-hot bottom. Of course it could be done—obstinacy came in useful.
Wasn't it Borland's all over again, starting from scratch? It seemed to
be a salutary lesson to us all. By the beginning of the Lent term the
freshers eight was entered for the 'getting on races'.

Then things really began to move and so did the boat. Goodness
knows why, but there must have been one brief moment during each
stroke when we were all doing the same thing, a split second of
cohesion. The winning crew was allotted a place at the bottom of the

lowest division of the Lent bumping races, in other words bottom of the river. Having won the 'getting on races' with comparative ease this extraordinary boat, rejecting the performance of the old Cunarder in a gale, had a marked tendency to move forward, rather fast, on the first day of the Lent Bumping Races. I was on the bow side in this extraordinary boat at No. 7 one cold winter afternoon waiting for the gun to set off the whole train of boats in the bottom division.

The start is somewhat tricky. As the boats must line up the prescribed distance apart, the cox of each boat holds on to a chain placed at regular intervals along the bank. The coach of each boat has his watch synchronised with the clock for the starting gun and tells the college boatmen to push the eight towards midstream at the start of the countdown. Being bottom of the division we had no boat chasing us. Our objective was to make our boat touch the stern of the boat ahead. The coach, looking at his watch, signalled the boatman to push us out.

The countdown started: 5—4—the tension was devastating—3—2. Match point on the centre court at Wimbledon or two runs to win with three minutes to go in a Test Match were child's play compared with this breathtaking drama on the Cam. Breathtaking indeed. I was gasping and we hadn't even started. The countdown ended. A slight pause. Bang!

Instantaneous reaction. Two short quick strokes, then swinging out to a full one, all the blades into the water together—our only bit of cohesion, repeating it as soon as possible, spending a minimum of time on the shambles in between, which meant a high rate of striking. In a matter of seconds we had gained half a length on the boat ahead and before we even had time to get our second wind we were overlapping and bumped them by the 'gut'.

The next night Clare IV had to start below us. Christ V is the boat we have to catch now and we did it in an even shorter distance. This made hot news in rowing circles and many of the experts came down to the start to see how we did it. Corpus III were our objective on this third night. The result was much the same as before. We literally shot into them just beyond the 'gut'. That made three in a row.

One more bump tomorrow night and we'd win our oars. Our coach discussed a plan of campaign.

'If Emmanuel III take you beyond "the gut" don't drop the rate of striking. You'll be getting your second wind, so make the most of it. Concentrate on those blades, into the water as one, that is vital. Don't worry about the rest. Emmanuel III are the best you've had to face so far, but stick to getting those blades into the water simultaneously and you'll have them licked.'

The dazzling prize of the oar was looming in the distance. The whole eight were madly keen and I was by no means the only one who was jittery. As we were pushed out by the boatman a few seconds before the countdown, a cross wind blew us slightly to the side.

'Touch her 2 and 4' the cox yelled, trying to get the boat straight.

The coach had started the countdown and the gun went while 2 and 4 were just finishing their stroke, which made them late, which disrupted our usual flying start and far from gaining on our rivals they reached 'the gut' well ahead of us. This was an entirely new experience. We had never been taken as far as this before. As we got our second wind they were two lengths ahead approaching 'Grassy'.

Our coach shouted, 'Get those blades in together. In–Out. In–Out.'

The crew responded.

'Give her ten. One—two—three,' he continued counting, slightly increasing the rate of striking.

The result was miraculous. His voice was drowned by the cheers of the crowd at 'Grassy'. We had shot forward. We were now only a quarter of a length away from our rivals, Emmanuel III, who were trying desperately hard to escape from us by bumping Peterhouse III who were just ahead of them. They were going up fast but so were we. Faster! We turned into 'the Long Reach'. A mighty cheer from the bank. Our bows had touched the stern of Emmanuel III. We caught them just in time.

From an old oak beam in the living room of our farm in Essendon that oar hangs immortalised and remains the pride of my rowing days. Sometimes when I look at it now I marvel at the importance I attached to rowing. I was obsessed. Caius had won the 'getting on races' so had won a place for another boat on the Cam. The flame of burning zeal still flickers; it never quite goes out.

I had ample opportunity of realising the extent of our success because in addition the college eight had done well in the First division.

A 'bump supper' was set up by the boat club and that was my first mad evening at Cambridge. We all dined together, all four college crews. We shouted and cheered, we sang, we yelled, no one interfered. We seemed to have had the freedom of the University. It was a wonderful get-together, all the different crews, great for making new friends, and all vying with each other to be the rowdiest. Then, as a slight diversion, we played rugger in Gonville Court with a pineapple.

One of the great surprises of the evening as far as I was concerned, was the number of senior members of the Boat Club who congratulated me on my efforts at number 7 in the boat. I had no idea I had been noticed even, but apparently I had become the focus of attention since we had won the 'getting on races'. I was told I was the mainstay of the boat, the most promising freshman, how lucky they were to have me. 'Well rowed, 7.' It was all too good to believe. After six weeks' strict training and then straight into a high-powered binge made it difficult to take it all in—except the wine, that presented no problem.

'Well rowed, 7,' was buzzing in my ears. I was way up in the clouds. I just couldn't get down. Not that I wanted to, I liked it up there. I was seeing everything through a beautiful soft haze—like a dream. Yes, that was it—*A Midsummer Night's Dream*, and I was Bottom the Weaver rowing 7, Peter Quince was in the power-house at six and Puck was coxing the boat again magnificently. The beautiful Titania threw her arms around me, saying with great feeling, 'Well rowed, 7.' I went to sleep that night on a bed of rose petals and lavender.

I was awakened the next day by Mrs Gibbs saying, 'I've brought your afternoon tea, I thought perhaps you'd like it before you get up to have dinner in Hall.' Sixteen hours' sleep had disposed of the Bacchanalian orgy and I was back to normal, realising with complete clarity that the good impression I had made on the Boat Club was reality, and not just a dream. So now I had made a start in the rowing world as well as the theatre. I was elated. My prospects couldn't have been brighter. But that was not quite the opinion of my tutor.

On Monday morning I received an urgent message requesting my presence at 11 a.m. in his study. I deemed it advisable to be very punctual, which accounts for my crossing Gonville Court as the clock was striking the hour. I hurried up the staircase to his room and knocked on his heavy oak door. Immediately a voice said, 'Come in.' I entered a typical college study—dark panelling, masses of books, rather austere, but comfortably furnished. My tutor looked very impressive sitting behind his desk, a splendid gentleman of high intellectual integrity. I did not receive the hearty congratulations I had hoped for. The atmosphere was on the cold side. Amongst the many papers crowding his desk I noticed a programme of *The Rivals*. He evidently knew what I was up to.

'Good morning, Hulbert. Sit down.'

'Thank you, sir.'

I could see he was a worried man. I was sorry to see this as he seemed so kind and considerate when we first met. In an endeavour to avoid our happy association becoming impaired, I decided on complete frankness. The eminent gentleman of letters came quickly to the point.

'Your multifarious activities in the University must make it difficult for you to work.'

'Yes, sir, very.'

'When do you work?'

'I don't.'

He took off his spectacles and wiped them with his handkerchief to give himself time to think of a suitable come-back, but I beat him to it.

'There just isn't time,' I said blandly.

'I suppose you realise you can't stay here in the University doing nothing?'

Such an inept statement could only be excused as coming from a man fighting on unfamiliar ground. I continued stating the facts with increased confidence.

'In the morning, I attend lectures and take notes. In the afternoon, I row and try to keep fit. In the evening, I am rehearsing a new show or playing in one or performing at a concert. As I am in training for the races a lot of the term, I obediently go to bed at 10 p.m. So when do I work. Frankly, sir, I am as worried as you are. What are we to do about it?'

The ball was now in his court. I waited for a hot return.

'I really must point out, Hulbert,' the glasses were now polished and back in position, 'this is a University not a drama school.'

'If I might be allowed to refute that statement, sir, I would say one of the best drama schools in the world.'

He rose at once to the bait.

'But you cannot get a degree in acting.'

'That's exactly it,' I replied. 'So what am I to do?'

No immediate answer came. He was slightly put out of countenance. I felt sorry for him. I came to the rescue.

'I must get a degree. That is understood. That's what I'm here for. I would like to transfer from Law to two "specials", History and Psychology. Attending lectures every morning from nine to one and working in the vacation. If you will leave it to me, sir, you need have no more worries.'

'Much as I appreciate your tempting offer of a life of equanimity, it would be imprudent to allow myself to be placed in the anomalous position of a tutor being run by his pupil.'

'I was trying to be constructive, sir.'

A slight suggestion of amusement flickered in the soft grey eyes behind the polished spectacles.

'Far be it from me to derogate from the merit of your suggestion, but I have a responsibility—'

'So have I, sir, to my father, who has made it possible for me to be here, and the moment I go down I must be in a position to earn my living as an actor and relieve him of a heavy burden. I must do everything possible to train myself and be ready to start professionally.'

'You certainly seem to know your own mind.'

'I do indeed, sir.'

As I heard myself talking, it sounded like somebody else. I had never talked like this before. It was the first time I had been addressed by a master as an intelligent being and it did something to me, it won my respect. Here was a man I could work for.

'I am asking you to believe my sincerity, sir.'

Again the eyes flickered.

'Of that I am convinced. It is a question of application and will power. Are you well enough equipped? I must have time to consider.'

I walked across Gonville Court figuring out the pros and cons. I made my chances fifty-fifty. If I failed I would have to think up another scheme.

Switching from Law to two 'specials', I knew *that* was a cinch. It was all a question of making him happy about my acting proclivities. But I liked him. He was easy to talk to. Clever chap. I was not in the least surprised when, in later years, he became the Master of the College.

I plumped for the History special as I thought it would be chiefly a question of memory, and the Psychology special as it had only just been started. There were only five of us in for it so we were pioneers and not likely to be ploughed. Dr Myers, who gave the lectures, was a great enthusiast and was most anxious to get the subject established. I knew I was on a plumb wicket. After a lapse of five days I received a note from my tutor.

> Dear Hulbert,
>
> I have arranged for you to take the two specials, History and Psychology. Please call tomorrow at 10 a.m. and I will give you the details. I enjoyed your performance in *The Rivals* and I am looking forward to seeing you in *The Knight of the Burning Pestle* near the end of term.

Splendid man. I could now go on acting, rowing, dancing and singing my way through college without a worry or care. At the end of the academic year in the 'May Week Races' I was rowing 7 in the Caius second eight trying desperately hard to justify the promise I had shown 'in the Lents'. Then came 'the Long Vac'.

Jubilant reunion with father and mother intensely proud of promising son. Hearty congratulations on the rowing, the acting and the compact with the tutor. The happy family, including little brother, moved for a few weeks to Bexhill, then a fashionable watering place. Lots of pretty girls, one in particular about eighteen with a long pigtail, looking beautiful. Passers-by whispering, 'That's Marie Lohr', the new actress. Promising son lost in admiration but never managed to meet her, not until years later when she had become famous. It was a hot summer, so much to do, good swimming, soft music in the evening, dancing attendance on pretty girls—what time was there left for working in the Long Vac? A time table had to be drawn up and strictly adhered to. And surprisingly it worked.

6

I returned to the 'Varsity in October a second year man, a great feeling. On arrival I threw my luggage into a cab outside the station—taxis had not yet appeared on the scene—and I was pulled along by a reluctant horse down St Andrew's Street, through Petty Cury and across the Market Square. Had the horse realised that a second year man was sitting in the carriage for all Cambridge to see, its performance might have been less perfunctory. On arrival at Caius, I deposited my belongings in the porter's lodge and called on my tutor, who shook me warmly by the hand and seemed genuinely pleased to see me. I had done some good work, I told him, enough to show I would never betray his trust. With a warm smile, he reaffirmed his confidence in me.

The next morning a wild rush on a bike to keep a nine o'clock history lecture and the routine started all over again. Then on to a lecture by Dr Myers, followed by a session in the experimental labs. A quick lunch, then down to the boat-house. I was promoted to coach one of the eights in the lower division and I found myself shouting instructions from the tow-path to the very boat I had helped to get on the river my first term. The growing-up process was increasing rapidly. I could hardly believe the change that had taken place since those wasted days at Westminster. But Cambridge was my world now with its endless possibilities. I found youth very enjoyable, and I have been trying to keep it right up to this present day.

There was a lady of means living in Cambridge called Maud Waraker who, being an enthusiastic amateur, took the new Theatre in St Andrew's Street for a week each year. *Jack Straw* by Somerset Maughan was the comedy she had chosen for this particular occasion and I was invited to play the title role, one of Charles Hawtrey's greatest successes. I had the temerity to accept without a blush, and this is where youth excells. It has no doubts or fears. It seizes an opportunity with both hands. To hell with caution. Experience comes later. Experience is like a notebook containing a list of mistakes, made in the past and stored away ready for quick reference to avoid a repetition of those mistakes. Youth suffers no interference. It forges ahead— nothing venture, nothing win. Never a thought that a bad performance might be prejudicial to future progress.

Fortune smiled on us. The show was successful and Maud Waraker took the theatre again the following term and invited me to play with her in *Little Mrs Cummins*. She was an amusing and likeable personality and playing the middle-aged comedy part she was very good, just as she had been in *Jack Straw*.

Among many of the shows I played in with other clubs was a triple bill, again at the New Theatre. It included a sketch I had written myself. You have to be young to take those sort of chances. My sketch amused the undergraduates but I don't think my revered tutor would have been very impressed. I hoped he hadn't seen it.

I don't know if it was the neat, trim figure or the golden hair that first caught my eye. It was hanging down her back in a long pigtail, a style decreed by the arbiters of fashion of those days. Was the front view as attractive as the back? It was well worth investigation. I raced ahead on my bike along Petty Cury to catch a glimpse. What I saw hit me for six. I nearly crashed. When I had recovered my balance sufficiently to have another look it was too late—she had disappeared round the corner. Would I ever see her again?

One afternoon, on my way to the boat-house, crossing Midsummer Common, she was walking towards me. I was going to risk giving her a smile. Why not? As I passed she stopped to greet a girlfriend so all I got was a close-up of the golden-haired pigtail again. These disappointments served to increase my interest. Our next encounter was walking through Petty Cury a few days later. We met face to face. I produced my most ingratiating smile, which was completely lost as she looked straight ahead and walked a little faster, right out of my life. And so ended a romance that never was. Very sad.

Twelfth Night was my next commitment, playing Sir Toby Belch. It could hardly be called type-casting—was anyone more unlike him? However, with ample padding as with Sir Anthony Absolute and with beard and whiskers to hide the pump-handle chin we got a little nearer to it. Life is full of surprises. A situation suddenly developed which in a play or novel would be criticised by the press as being highly improbable. When I was introduced to the girl who was to play Maria, Olivia's maid, at the first rehearsal I was so stunned and amazed I could only murmur, 'Oh—er—delighted—I—er—know you well by sight.'

'I know you do,' she replied, enjoying my embarrassment. She was even more attractive when she talked.

And as if this sudden encounter was not enough to send me up the wall, a lady arrived from London looking ideal for the rather majestic Olivia. The last time I had seen *her* she had been playing the piano and I had left the house a broken man. Where do we go from here? My thoughts were entirely nebulous. A very delicate situation—diplomacy was never my strong suit—and this job needed a Bismark. Play it by ear and hope she'd forgotten just as I had, I decided. I shook her warmly by the hand and as the incident in St John's Wood was never referred to we worked together as if nothing had happened. I must say I admired her for that. She turned out to be such a nice person. And so did Maria—she was a member of one of the local dramatic clubs and did well as an amateur actress. She did very well as an entertaining and amusing companion, too. We became great friends and had a lot of fun together. *Twelfth Night* was very popular with the university audience and I revelled in the part of Sir Toby Belch.

Herman Fink wrote a charming melody called *In the Shadows* and whenever I hear it played anywhere today, I am back in May Week at the end of my second year. While waiting on the stage of the A.D.C. theatre for the curtain to go up on Act II of *Pilkerton's Peerage*, the orchestra played this tune in the interval, and whenever I hear it now I relive the joy of those youthful days—a warm June evening, a full house, undergrads, parents, relations, girlfriends, the sound of merry laughter and applause, unforgettable moments. How often a song of yesterday becomes the signature tune of a fragrant memory!

The summer term was always the busiest for the college boat clubs, coaching their respective crews for the May Week races. The first division crews rowed in an eight-oared shell with sliding seats which was a merciful release from the red-hot bottom! I managed to get into the college eight which did well in the races.

The happy situation that existed with my tutor continued to flourish. It was all going splendidly, too splendidly; he had placed so much confidence in me that the original situation was completely reversed—the burden of responsibility was now on my shoulders. Was I doing enough work to justify this trust? It was impossible in term time to increase the output. After lectures and practical work in the morning the rest of the day was one long rush; rowing, rehearsing, acting, smoking concerts—I never stopped. There was no time for anything else. The Vac was my only chance. I would have to increase the timetable. The May races and *Pilkerton's Peerage* finished on the Saturday that marked the end of term. I did not stay up for any of the college balls—poor father had enough to pay out as it was.

My second year ended and I came down to start the Long Vac. Complete rest for the first two weeks and then work. A holiday at Bexhill provided many pleasant diversions but I managed to make a little progress. It was great being with the family again, but I was already looking forward to going back to the world I loved, especially since I was returning as a third year man. I went up for the Michaelmas term at the beginning of October.

The exalted status of seniority gave me even more confidence—too much. As I entered Caius through the Gate of Humility it gave me pause to think: watch it, Hulbert. Remember your father's excellent dictum: moderation in all things. As I walked through the Gate of Virtue I decided it would be best not to think. I looked at the Gate of Honour just across Gonville Court. One more year to go and then . . . could I beat the clock and scrape through? The gate was wide open.

There were no Bumping Races that term, only the light fours and the crock eights for the freshmen. I felt very uncomfortable rowing bow in the Caius four as I was responsible for the steering with a wire connecting my shoe to the rudder which I had to control by moving my foot right or left on the stretcher. It was a full-time job trying to keep one's form and synchronising with the other three blokes, but trying to keep a middle course on the narrow winding Cam as well made our outings a little too exciting. Too many near misses. Consequently, stroke was given this responsibility and he seemed to possess the unique gift of steering without seeing. A mad way of travelling. Four men all looking one way and going another.

Unfortunately, in our first race we drew the winners of the final. We held them halfway over the course and at 'glass houses' we were dead level. There they decided they were bored with us and very rudely rowed away to finish on their own, leaving us four lengths behind at the post. After all that training and practice! Undoubtedly, it was a quick way of learning to take hard knocks, a salutary lesson which I found in later years very handy in a theatrical career.

Then came one of the greatest moments of my life—an invitation to row in the 'Varsity boat. Here was a chance. A very slender one, but a chance. I reported at the 'Goldie' boat-house, carried out the boat with seven other chaps, all experienced oarsmen, and we started on our trip to Baits-bite Lock and back. The president of the C.U.B.C. rode his bicycle along the tow-path giving his instructions and comments *en route*. Rowing in that eight was sheer bliss. We glided through the water like travelling in a Rolls. With an easy swing, a firm grip of the water behind the stretchers, perfect synchronisation of blade work and leg drive, we moved at a cracking pace. It was all so easy. Never had I felt so comfortable or enjoyed an outing more.

As we passed the various college eights that had 'easied' and pulled into the bank to let us go through they saluted by rattling their oars in the riggers. Who was rowing did not matter, it was the 'Varsity boat they were applauding and as I was one of the crew, rowing bow, I thrilled with pride and excitement as if it was a reception at the end of a show. When we had an 'easy' the president emphasised the importance of getting a strong beginning to each stroke and holding out the finish to keep the stroke long. I was glad to hear him say this, these were the two things I had been concentrating on. We reached the lock in the quickest time I had ever done it. The boat travelled so well and so fast between the strokes. On the way back the president continued shouting instructions from the bank.

'Steady forward over the stretchers. Don't rush. That's more like it. Well rowed, stroke.'

He seemed pleased with our performance. I was delighted with mine. It was all so easy. As we shot round 'Grassy Corner' I was completely fascinated by the sight of my light blue blade as it dipped into the water with the others—not quite with the others—the president was quick to point this out.

'Bow, you're late.'

I realised this sudden lapse of concentration and got back into the rhythm immediately. The president had a nice warm friendly voice, such a contrast to most coaches and he certainly knew what he was talking about. The warm friendly voice continued, slightly raised, as the president was trying to keep up with us on his bike.

'Well rowed, 4—well rowed, 2—well rowed, 5. More work, bow.'

This surprised me. I was flat out anyway, going beautifully in my very best form. A little later on it happened again.

'Well rowed, 6—well rowed, 3. More work, bow.'

More work? I was giving everything I'd got. Just near the 'Pike and Eel' the soft warm voice was raised again making the same request. That did it, I knew then that style meant nothing. It seemed absurd to me that you were judged by the size of the puddle you sent down and no matter how hard I drove with the legs or threw the shoulders back, that wretched puddle never got any bigger. I should have thought the importance of style . . . but one had to bow to the inevitable and that was the end of a mad ambition, the nearest I ever got to a blue. What did it matter? Nothing could detract from that unforgettable experience, one glorious day in the 'Varsity boat.

At that time there was a friendly rivalry between the two big dramatic clubs, the A.D.C. and the Footlights. I was approached by the president of the latter to write and perform in their May Week show at the New Theatre. I said I would be honoured to accept, provided the A.D.C. had no objection. They were kind and understanding. It was a deal, and one more item had to be squeezed into a day already madly overloaded. And that was by no means the lot, the heavy clouds of final exams were darkening the sky. Who would attempt the impossible? Probably inexperienced, uninhibited youth, and that was me at twenty. It would have been sheer madness to have turned down the Footlights' offer, the big show at the theatre in May Week and a special matinée in London. After all, this was the whole object of the exercise. I went fearlessly ahead.

When I returned from the Easter vacation I entered my rooms in college, which I was entitled to as boat club secretary. I opened my bag and brought out the masterpiece which I had just finished. I sat down and made a few amendments. Better perhaps if I had amended the whole thing, but what did I know about writing shows in those days? Nothing. It was all an exciting adventure into the unknown. I just wanted to get at it.

Everything was happening at once—the show, the bumping races, the exams—all wildly exciting. I revelled in it, a fitting climax to my last term. We rehearsed the show in the evening. There were lectures in the morning and rowing in the afternoon. Not much time for last-minute study. If only the exams had come when things were less hectic. The pressure remained unabated until the last vital week and then the mad rush began in earnest. There were two of us at it, myself and my bike, secondhand when I bought it. Though it never had a clean or a drop of oil, the bike always got me there.

Early morning run with the crew and then training breakfast together. Frantic rush to the examination hall in *stata pupilari*. Late afternoon to the boat-house and into rowing togs. Early evening. First division race. Back to the boat-house, change from rowing kit. Flat out for the theatre, just in time to make up and dress for the show at 8. 30 p.m. Special permission from the captain and coach to retire to bed at 11.30 p.m. instead of the prescribed training time of 10.00 p.m. and then a good night's rest. A day in the life of a wild under-graduate. Quite a bit of coming and going, all made possible by the invention of the bicycle!

I sat in the examination hall in the morning reading the questions in the Psychology paper. It was a push-over. History came next. I started well. Dear prescient Mr Green, my director of studies, was so right with his tips, but there were one or two questions in a later paper that seemed to show my knowledge of the subject was not quite as comprehensive as it first seemed. Had I done well enough in answering the others to knock up the $33\frac{1}{3}\%$ to scrape through? What a tragedy if I just failed by a few marks! My fate was hanging in the balance.

The first night of the races was a thrill. I was rowing 3 in the college eight. We were high in the first division and made our bump just after 'First Post Corner'. The second and third night we were equally successful—we had the best college crew for years. One more bump on the last night and we'd win our oars.

The starting gun fired. We were away, my very life depended on victory. Irresponsible youth again. Success in sport transcends all other considerations. Amazing! Why should I be rowing with seven other oarsmen, showing a fanatical determination to bump the boat ahead, when I should have been concentrating entirely on the two vital things affecting my future: the exams and the Footlights show? But that's youth, thank heavens! First things first. The honour of the college. Up the Caius boat!

We were going well, travelling fast like the boat we were chasing, gaining all the time, but our rivals were almost overlapping the boat ahead of them. Could we catch them before they caught *their* victim? It was touch-and-go and they just managed to escape us by making their bump so we had to row over. It was a bitter disappointment, but we had pushed the Caius boat up three places, so there was cause for rejoicing and a happy way for me to bid farewell to my rowing days on the dear old Cam.

The first night of *Cheer, O Cambridge* was my last appearance at the 'Varsity as an undergraduate. Messages of good luck came pouring in and I got a delightful farewell message from the Vice Chancellor himself, who wrote me a note saying,

> 'I hereby give permission for your musical play *Cheer, O Cambridge* to be performed at the New Theatre, Cambridge, and I should like to add how sorry I am to know that you should think that the University could be entertained by such rubbish.'

A delightful finish to three glorious years. What a pity that a Vice Chancellor could have been so completely out of touch! The show was expressly designed to fit the festive mood of an undergraduate audience, plus relatives and friends, in May Week. With two brilliant performances by Douglas Carmichael and Munro Cuthbertson dressed in the most gorgeous and expensive gowns from a West End couturier we were half way home. Had Danny La Rue been on the scene in those days he would have had to look to his laurels. When these two undergraduates walked on to the stage the impact was staggering. They looked for all the world like two gorgeous mannequins displaying the latest creations at a fashion parade and the little feminine touches they put in got continuous laughter and applause, creating a most joyous atmosphere. Ladies were not allowed to perform in the university clubs in those days so men, dressed in the latest fashion, had to play women's parts. Several years later, Norman Hartnell carried on the tradition and emerged from the Footlight show to become one of the finest creators of women's clothes in the West End.

I went each morning in a state of dither to the Senate House to see if the examination results had been posted on the notice board, but nothing had come through so far. It was on the fourth day that the list of names suddenly appeared. I hurried forward, then I stopped. I daren't look. But it had to be faced. Frantically I searched for the 'H' column. I felt like I had done on the river, waiting for the starting gun. I found the column. I went over it several times to make sure. I walked away, dazed. I found it hard to think.

In my room I started packing to go down for the last time, leaving the world that I loved. I felt sad. Three never-to-be-forgotten years! Cambridge is written across my heart. I thought of the college I adored—and the ancient tradition of each tutor leading four young men in full academic dress through the Gate of Honour in Gonville Court to the Senate House, and I found it almost impossible to realise that one of those young men . . . the chap who had spent one glorious day rowing in the 'Varsity boat. I had a quiet laugh to myself when I thought of what the Vice Chancellor's feelings must have been as he was giving his blessings in the Senate House to the author of *Cheer, O Cambridge*. Whatever he thought, he can take comfort from the fact that his scathing message did me a power of good in my future career. It rendered me entirely impervious to adverse criticism in the national press.

As I came out of the Senate House a chap in the show told me a matinée had been fixed for *Cheer, O Cambridge* at the Queen's Theatre in London. I was delighted at the news. Another thing which helped to soften the blow of leaving my beautiful Caius was that the eight had been entered for the 'Ladies' at Henley and I was invited to resume my place at number 3. This was great news; some of the links were still intact.

7

My homecoming was a triumph—Father, Mother and Claudie, every-one was happy. I'm sure that, back at Cambridge, my tutor, the Vice-Chancellor, and even dear old Green were also rejoicing—that I had gone down for good!

Father did not lose a second. He had already notified the important West End Managers that a brilliant young actor would be appearing at a special matinée of the May Week show from Cambridge. This momentous news did the trick. Several of them turned up or sent their representatives with the result we got three different offers for my services. The one from Robert Courtneidge seemed the most reliable and the best bet. I was signed up on a three-year contract, starting at once, to appear in his new musical *The Pearl Girl*, which was about to go into rehearsal for the Shaftesbury Theatre. I could not believe my luck. At last, a stage career to start immediately. Then the awful truth suddenly dawned on me. I would have to give up Henley. It was impossible to do both, so the last link with Cambridge was severed.

I was very impressed when I met Robert Courtneidge. A man of substance, vital and resolute. He could have been one of the fellows of Caius. I took an instant liking to him. He told me about the play and my part. Harry Welshman and Iris Hoey were the romantic leads, Laurie de Frece and Alfred Lester were the comics and Ada Blanche, who had been the Drury Lane principal boy at the turn of the century, was playing one of the other comedy parts.

I was the light comedian in love with the soubrette. I asked him who that was and he said 'my daughter Cicely'. I found out that the delightful and talented Ada Blanche was her aunt. I had only vaguely

52

heard of Cicely Courtneidge and I wondered what she would be like. A soubrette? They were usually engaged for their looks. It seemed promising. It was arranged that I should go down to Brighton to meet her. She was at the Theatre Royal watching her father's production of *Oh, Oh, Delphine*. The company manager conducted me to one of the boxes in the interval. We climbed the stairs. It was exciting. I was about to meet a soubrette, a real professional actress. Dressed in my one and only best suit, just back from the cleaners, and wearing a gay tie, I was all set to make a good impression.

The manager opened the door of the box and we met for the first time. We shook hands. The polite smile that greeted my 'Delighted to meet you, Miss Courtneidge' vanished and a pair of blue eyes narrowed slightly as they focused on my face. Miss Courtneidge might have been a good actress but not quite good enough to conceal her disappointment. I'm sure I failed to conceal mine. She in no way fitted in with my mental picture of a soubrette. Where was the glamour and the fluffiness displayed so attractively on the picture postcards of those days?

This atmosphere of mutual disappointment permeated the scene. I couldn't seem to get a cue to start any of the funny stuff I was going to use. The jolly, light-hearted 'Varsity man failed to scintillate. An abortive attempt at conversation ended in a few desultory remarks. An usherette brought in afternoon tea with 'the management's compliments'. Miss Courtneidge had the two cups filled in a flash. She seemed to do everything at the double.

'You take milk and sugar?'

Before I had time to answer I'd got both.

Handing me a plate, she said, 'Have a cress sandwich.'

'Oh! Thank you!'

I took one and wished I hadn't. She looked at me and laughed.

'You remind me of the white rabbit I used to have when I was a kid at Old Trafford. It always had bits of lettuce hanging out of its mouth.'

She was highly amused. I wasn't. As I was trying to push the beastly stuff back and swallow it she asked, 'What made you choose the stage?'

She obviously thought I had been ill-advised. Taken by surprise I hesitated, 'Well . . . I . . .' and that was as far as I got. She was not the type to tolerate uncertainty.

'It's very hard work, you know.'

'That's just down my street. No trouble at all,' I said, shooting my cuffs and pulling forward my lapels to make it more impressive. Suddenly her gaze was fixed on the inside corner of my coat.

'Wait a minute—I thought so—it's the tab from the cleaners.'

She made a grab and it was off. I'd never seen anything so quick. I was furious I hadn't noticed it. All I could do was to thank her. How the hell had I missed it?

'I hope I did the right thing?' There was a mischievous twinkle in her eyes. 'Or did you leave it on to show it had just been cleaned?'

Normally, I would have laughed it off and enjoyed the opportunity, but I just couldn't get going. My introduction to a professional soubrette was a signal failure. It was definitely not my day. Better to make some excuse and clear off. As I opened the door of the box the light from outside fell on her as she sat down and crossed her legs. They were beautiful. Funny I hadn't noticed that before. Very unlike me.

The next meeting with Miss Courtneidge was a few days later when rehearsals started at the Shaftesbury Theatre. She was in practice clothes ready for dancing, looking even less like one of the glamorous picture postcard lovelies.

I had no idea professional rehearsals were so highly organised. Music, dancing, singing and dialogue all happening at once. Every part of the theatre occupied. The chorus singing with the M.D. in the stalls. Dialogue on the stage with the Governor. Dancing with Espinosa in the pit bar, and with Willie Ward in the gallery bar. I was enjoying an entirely new life.

In the dialogue department, after a few days, I was making rapid progress. The Governor, an ace producer, was very inventive, and exploited anything I had to offer in my two comedy scenes with Miss Courtneidge, building them up and laughing at what I put in myself. Then Willie Ward started on one of the duets. Being a rather elderly ballet master, he naturally went for ballet movement, the pretty stuff. Immediately the beautiful legs were displayed to great advantage, to say nothing of a delightful slim figure flitting about the stage as softly as thistledown. A new personality seemed to appear. My attempt to emulate these highly-trained moves reduced her to helpless laughter.

I said, 'What's so funny? I'm a chap that'll try anything, I'll go on till I get it.'

'No, no,' she protested, 'I would never be able to dance with you doing that stuff, I'd never stop laughing.'

So Willie Ward had to think again. With Espinosa arranging the other duet there was no difficulty. He went for the showy stuff, he was bang on. Such a nice chap too. I didn't know at the time he was to become a great friend to both of us.

I cannot think of any quicker way for two people to get to know each other than by rehearsing dance routines. Even after three years as a galley slave on the Cam, I was tired out by the end of the day and so was the indefatigable Cicely. We toiled together and sweated together. We had a common interest, a burning desire to create and perfect the end product, our two duets and our scenes together. Whenever the Governor was rehearsing and we were not wanted, Cicely and I would slip away somewhere and go through our scenes on our own.

On one occasion, the Governor was rehearsing the company in the Finale of Act I in the ballroom of the Helvetia Club in Gerrard Street, and as we were not in the finale we went off and found the ideal spot. It was a small stage at the end of the ballroom with the curtain down. We climbed up, went behind and started on our love scene, going through it several times to get the moves neat and tidy. The Governor had the rest of the company, principals and chorus, working at the other end of the ballroom floor. Then, suddenly, the caretaker who was cleaning our end of the room, without any warning, took up the curtain of our little stage and we were discovered locked in each other's arms. It got one of the biggest laughs we've ever had.

The Governor rose to the occasion and said to the company, 'It's a pity the rest of you don't show the same keenness and follow their example.'

That got a bigger laugh still.

As time went on, rehearsals became increasingly more exhausting. The Governor's temper began to rise and the artistes were beginning to show signs of nervous tension. The opening date was well on the way, the whole cast and the chorus were thankful for the weekend. I was not. I found it hard to tear myself away from the theatre. I was so happy there rehearsing. At least, I suppose that was the reason. As soon as we left on Saturday morning I was looking forward to Monday morning to start work again, or was it to say, 'Good morning, Cicely'? I was not quite sure. My thoughts were confused. She was so very—I don't know—she did so many things I liked. We had become great friends. She was such a help to me in the job.

During the last week we started having dress rehearsals every day. This was a revelation to me. The thousand and one things that went wrong, which I found highly amusing, the meticulous attention to detail, the hours spent on lighting, the dress alterations, shoes missing, stockings missing, men's shirts not delivered. Ties and socks coming tomorrow. Polo sticks on the way. I was amazed at the tremendous organisation required to put on a musical. The Governor giving vent to his wrath for inefficiency. Everyone on edge with nerves. My friend Cicely, who knew exactly what was happening, explained all these mysteries. She never missed a thing.

Then came the opening night. The tension had reached breaking-point. All wishing each other the best of luck. Telegrams, notes, flowers, most of Covent Garden seemed to be in the dressing rooms. The curtain goes up, applause and laughter all the way. Big laughs in my scenes with Cicely, huge applause for our duets. Wonderful reception on the final curtain. Everyone delighted, the Governor was full of praise.

'You've made a big success, my boy.'

Coming from him, that really meant something.

'Jack, you were wonderful,' Cicely agreed. 'Father's quite right.'

'I was thoroughly enjoying myself,' I replied. 'I felt so at home, it was just like Cambridge.'

I received a look of amazement.

'Cambridge! Do you realise what was at stake tonight? Success or failure. Our very life blood. This is London, the West End. Wake up, Little Boy Blue, you've made it.'

'Thanks to you,' I said, really meaning it.

Dorothy Ward in the arms of Harry Welchman, Cicely on the
left and myself in the middle. *The Cinema Star*—1914.

The start of Cis's music hall career
—as an officer in the Flying Corps,
one of the many male impersonations
that helped her to the top of the bill.

A cartoonist's view of myself and Phyllis Titmuss in *Une tasse de thé*—my first effort as a writer, with André Charlot.

Here we are as the Trick Brothers in *The Little Revue*—1923.

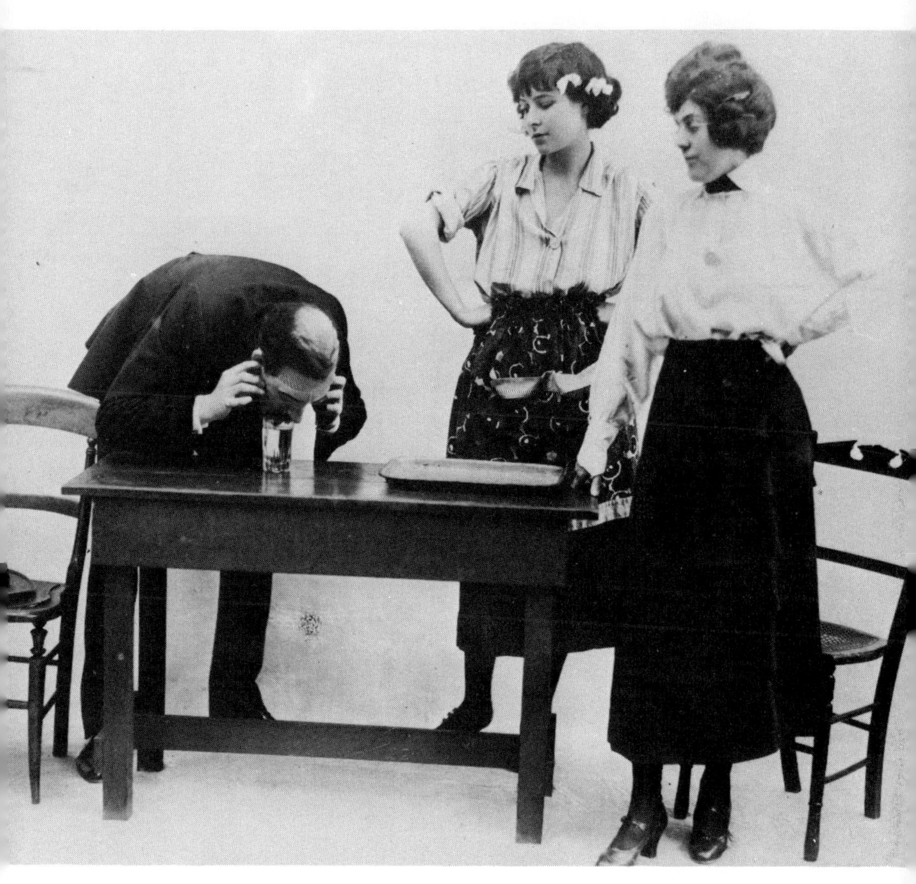

'...ut your fingers in your ears and drink out the other side of ...e glass,' says Cicely Courtneidge, Jack Hulbert does so while ...at Malone, Mrs Bobby Howes, looks on. The Hiccough sketch ...om *Pot Luck*.

The plumber in *The Little Revue*.

My favourite sketch—The Schoolmaster and The Boy.

It's Jack Hulbert again, behind three different moustaches.

The Ever Open Door.

Right to left: Cis, in a character role, May Bacon, and Yours Truly as a
brash American, in The Clock sketch.

A page from *The Sketch*,
December 19th, 1923. *Mander
and Mitchenson.*

'Mr Jack Hulbert "pops up" among the chorus.' *Clowns in Clover*—1927. *Mander and Mitchenson*.

Myself on the right with Paul Murray, my partner, and on the extreme left is our backer, Willie Gaunt. Next to him is Harry Welchman.

'Jolly good luck,' Todd Rich is saying and we're smiling back as if we hadn't a care in
the world, but that was just for the picture. A big night in broadcasting history—the
first time a London Opening Night had been televised. *Under Your Hat*—1939.

It took a long time to make-up
for this character of Colonel
Sheepshanks, but now I could
go on as I am. Stage version of
Under Your Hat—1939.

This is the scene where we meet Colonel Sheepshanks and his wife which gave us the idea to impersonate them.

Rehearsing a scene for the film version of *Under Your Hat* with Cecil Parker—1940.

'No, you got the audience eating out of your hand.'

'And what about you—terrific,' I insisted.

'Thank you, but you were wonderful to play with, you made it all so easy. Putting in things on a first night—improvising—you've got a nerve.'

Being a new boy, I hadn't realised the vital importance of the occasion. I took it all for granted; I thought it was always like this. I am glad I didn't know. Maybe that's how I did it. Uninhibited youth again. Cicely sounded a note of warning.

'Now we've got to wait for the notices in the morning. I wonder what the brutes will say. You'll be all right, they're bound to rave about you, but I'm the boss's daughter, don't forget, a target for sarcasm.'

But Cicely had nothing to worry about. We both got an excellent press and so did the show, much to the relief of the Governor. He was most enthusiastic about our prospects, he said we had a big hit and were in for a long run. Of all the people he certainly deserved it for a grand production. Father and Mother were overjoyed. Big brother was crowned with glory by little brother. What a blessing, the devotion of a family!

As the excitement died down and the weeks went by, I was still sorry when the show finished each night and I felt reluctant to leave the theatre, I was surprised I hadn't fallen for any of the lovely chorus girls. Normally, the sight of a pretty girl set me on fire. I tried to figure it out. What was the first thing I did on entering the theatre each evening? Knock on Cicely's dressing room door. No, that wasn't it. Just a jolly good friend with a dynamic personality and beautiful legs. Don't forget *that*! well, the whole figure was pretty good for that matter. But nothing to do with it. Not my type at all.

We had a slight tiff one night. Behaving like a kid and taking umbrage, all about nothing, I refrained from knocking on the dressing room door and took out one of the lovely chorus girls. The evening was a flop. Consumed with ardour, I wasn't even singed! It seemed an eternity waiting for the next evening, to knock on that dressing room door again, and when I did I must have conveyed a feeling of urgency. The 'Come in' I got was immediate.

Then followed the most ecstatic moment of my life. Not a word was spoken. It all just happened. The world stopped. The nightingale had not yet visited Berkeley Square but it had a try-out that night in Shaftesbury Avenue. When we broke apart, breathless and emotional, I asked her, in a shaking voice, 'When did you know I was mad about you?'

Her eyes danced with merriment. 'Right from the start.'

'Darling, you're wonderful.'

'And so are you.'

Brilliant conversation was not called for, I was too far gone. I couldn't even think straight. Cicely could, and without hesitation said, 'Now let's go and tell Father.'

Here was the quickest worker and the quickest thinker I had ever encountered. I was dazed. Marriage was the last thing in the world I had in mind. Romance, yes. But to settle down for the rest of my life was not on. Or was it? I didn't know, I was too dazed, too much in love. I didn't know where I was except being pulled by a hand across the stage and hurried in the direction of the Governor's private office. The moment we got there she opened the door and pushed me in. Her statement was clear and unequivocal:

'Jack wants to talk to you, Father.' And she went out, shutting the door.

Looking at me enquiringly, the great producer said, 'Yes, my boy, what do you want?'

I was completely foxed. That was it. What did I want? What was I doing here? What was I to say? I had to play for time.

'It concerns your daughter, sir.'

His expression changed. 'You're finding her difficult to work with?'

'No, sir no, far from it. She's the most wonderful . . .' Then inspiration came in a flash. I knew I could never spend the rest of my life without her.

And that's how it all began nearly sixty years ago. Pushing me into that room was the greatest thing she ever did for me. Her woman's instinct has earned my unfailing gratitude to this very day. I left the Governor's office deeply impressed by the charming way he gave his consent. His only stipulation was a long engagement. The Governor had an ace publicity man who got our picture in every leading news-paper in the country, including the periodicals, which of course helped *The Pearl Girl*.

So it did us all a bit of good. The show continued to run along merrily for months. Being an engaged couple, we were enjoying life to the full. Cicely, as a person, seemed to appeal to everyone. The family became great fans.

The Governor encouraged my desire to write by making me part author of the English versions of the Continental show *The Cinema Star*, which was to follow *The Pearl Girl* when that finished. I worked with Captain Harry Graham, a well-known librettist in those days. Being engaged to Cicely was another step towards taming the wild undergraduate, but it was the Governor who set about it in no small way. Not only did he smile on the Hulbert–Courtneidge alliance but he deemed it his duty to help it to prosper by trying to instil into his future son-in-law some of the finer points of stage technique.

Captain Harry Graham and I finished our work on the adaptation of the German book of *The Cinema Star* and from the first day of rehearsals to the opening night I came in for severe criticism from the Governor. I could hardly speak a line without being stopped. I knew instinctively he was right. Although I found it depressing and irksome, I knew I was gaining the most valuable experience of stage technique. After the success of *The Pearl Girl* it all seemed too easy. I knew it all. What I needed was slapping down, and at that the Governor was an expert. Not easy to take, I must admit, but to be taught by a man of his talent and ability was a great blessing and I am eternally grateful for the hell he put me through.

Apart from that they were happy days. *The Cinema Star* had an interesting cast. Cicely supplied the love interest, not with me this time but with Harry Welshman. I was one of the comedians, Cicely Deben-ham and the beautiful Fay Compton, who later became one of our finest actresses, brought great charm to the show. Laurie de Frece was the chief comedian and that great pantomine star, the magnificent look-ing Dorothy Ward, played the flamboyant lead with tremendous gusto. Since those days she has become one of our oldest and best friends. The first night was a stupendous success, even bigger than *The Pearl Girl*.

Happy days they were in London at that time, the halcyon days of peace. Life was leisurely, there was ample time to do things in this serene tranquillity. It seemed nothing could disturb that calm—calm which so often presages a storm—but, within days of our triumph at the Shaftesbury, the unfamiliar sight of young men in civilian clothes being drilled in Hyde Park by a Sergeant Major signified the storm had broken.

Anti-German feeling was running so high that *The Cinema Star* played to empty houses. As the Kaiser's armies swept through Belgium and France, the Governor was forced to take the show off, but as the war progressed the public clamoured for some diversion, so the long tour of *The Cinema Star* which the Governor booked immediately was just the job. The provinces were well supplied with theatres which were well patronised. We did great business. We toured the whole of the British Isles, taking well over a year to do it.

The Governor used to visit us periodically and I came in for the customary castigation. He would call a rehearsal and remind us of our responsibility to the paying public and keep going over the parts of the show that had deteriorated until we got back to the *status quo*. He was one of the few stage directors who had the experience and authority to do that, and his stern methods produced quick results. So many valuable lessons could be learnt from that Spartan training.

'My dear boy, you're not thinking what you're doing. You have lost your spontaneity. Make your lines sound like you're saying them for the first time. A musical comedy is played in a high key. You are not in that key. You are out of tune. Flat. You have lost your sparkle. You want to enter lightly, laughingly. You are dropping the speed. The pendulum must be kept swinging.'

He then gave an impression of a young man of today, which was quite embarrassing. Taken literally, it would be a disaster, but basically it was a hundred per cent right. To receive this superb training and at the same time be paid for it was a happy paradox, which I can appreciate even more today than when I was still only half-tamed.

Cicely and I were deliriously happy. The only wisp of grey cloud in an azure sky was the Governor's dour and stubborn resistance to an early marriage. He did not want us to marry until after the war. The first time the two young lovers made the suggestion it was rejected out of hand. We descended several places in the Governor's popularity chart and I deemed it advisable for the time being that any reference to this vexed question should be sedulously avoided. But my indignant fiancée was a Courtneidge too, determined to do battle, which I loudly applauded. Her eyes flashed defiance.

'That is by no means the end of the matter. He's got to be made to agree. We'll give him six months, not a day longer. The week after next when he comes up to Edinburgh, he'll be staying at the Caledonian. You can meet him in his private sitting room.'

'Me?'

'Who else? It's a man's job and this time no meekness. No shilly-shallying. You've got to stand up to him.' This was not the way I meant it to go at all.

'But my sweet darling Cis, your father has been so marvellous to me, he's given me his daughter, and is now giving me the best training in the world. I must show a little gratitude.'

The eyes were still flashing. 'We'll give him another six months, that's a fair compromise.'

In any circumstances this was a tricky subject to discuss with the redoubtable Robert Courtneidge, the most feared and formidable man in the theatre. His arbitrary rules governing his professional and domestic life created an impenetrable barrier. Against that he had a heart of gold and unlimited generosity. Much depended on getting him in the right mood. It was the luck of the draw. As I waited to cross Princes Street to get to the Caledonian Hotel, being held up by the trams and the traffic, I braced myself for a stormy interview. I had decided to take the plunge immediately. Entering his sitting room at the Caledonian I assumed a gay light-hearted air that belied the turmoil in my stomach.

'Good to see you again, sir.'

He was all smiles. 'I am glad you've come, my boy. We can have a nice quiet talk.' The mood was good.

'Splendid, then I'll begin—'

'No, you won't. I'll begin,' he said, warming to the occasion. 'I was very pleased with the writing you did on this present show, so I would like you to be part author with Mark Ambient of the next one which I am now preparing.'

I was completely taken by surprise.

The mood was too good. 'That's very kind of you, sir.' A benign smile from the Governor.

'Only too pleased, my boy. Now, what did you want to talk about?'

Being on the horns of a dilemma I felt extremely uncomfortable. To have answered that question at this juncture would have precipitated a crisis. It would have been a flagrant display of ingratitude. Wiser counsels prevailed. Better to retreat unscathed and make much play of the Governor's help and generosity. I asked him to excuse me as I wanted to dash back and give Cicely the good news.

On my way back I felt extremely lucky to have averted a stormy meeting with the Governor, but I now looked like having one with his daughter. Consternation! I think I would have preferred the former.

I found her in a state of frenzy waiting for the result. I was still in the street outside her digs. She couldn't wait another second and shouted through the window, 'Well, did you tell him?'

I seemed doomed to answer the most difficult questions.

'Wait till I come in.'

This gave me a second to think.

'Darling, your old man's a great guy,' I began.

'Yes, I know all that. What did he say? Come on, hurry, tell me.'

'Now listen, darling—'

'You haven't done it. You were a coward. I can see by your face you haven't done it. You don't have to say any more.'

'I haven't said anything yet.'

'Why didn't you stand up to him?'

'If you'd just let me explain—'

'Well, who's stopping you?'

I took advantage of a moment's pause and slipped in a potted version of what had transpired. Had I known her then as I know her today I would not have been in the least surprised that her attitude immediately softened. She is a most understanding woman once you can get the facts through to her by penetrating a verbal barrage. She would always laugh in the end.

8

The tour of *The Cinema Star* went on so long that gradually the whole cast had changed, and Cis and I were the only originals left. We saved a little money which would have enabled us to have enjoyed an early marriage but such an explosive subject had to be held temporarily in abeyance. During the latter part of the run I met Mark Ambient at Brighton where he lived, and we had several meetings about the new play, discussing the story line and the main scenes. *The Light Blues*, as the title suggests, was a musical comedy about Cambridge, so I was back on familiar ground. When the tour of *The Cinema Star* finally ended, I spent a lot of time at Brighton working regularly with Mark Ambient and we got the play finished in time to start rehearsing on the appointed date.

We opened in the provinces and had another hit. That delightful actor Edmund Gwen was dynamic as the father; dear Dorothy Ward had a big success as the actress who comes up for 'May Week' and Shaun Glenville, her husband, another of our great friends, was extremely funny with his soft unctious style as the harassed gyp. Cis and I had some good scenes and two duets, so we were happy.

There was a part to fill of a juvenile secretary to a Cabinet Minister. A boy in his teens was engaged. He was very young and very pimply, pompous and precocious, which was exactly the part, and he was very good, which rather annoyed me as I didn't like him. He used to talk about the plays he had in mind, the plays he was going to write. I found him a crashing bore. Just a silly kid in a minor role—and understudying me, which I found highly amusing because I knew he couldn't dance, or very little. His arrogance and conceit were such that he had the temerity to argue with the Governor on points of production and the Governor surprised us all by letting him talk. He saw qualities in this unusual character that I had missed entirely. I had no idea then I was talking to a genius. I am delighted to say that in later years we became very good friends and I laugh on looking back to *The Light Blues* when the name Noël Coward was entirely unknown. Right up to the time of his death his tenacious memory enabled him to sing all the numbers out of the show and he would have us in fits of laughter imitating Cis singing hers. I am very proud to think I acted with him at the beginning of a career which has shown him to be one of the greatest writers for the stage of all time.

The British way of life had now completely changed. Everything was geared to a mighty war effort. Munition factories and armament factories were working over-time. Thousands of wounded coming back from the front in train loads, thousands coming back on leave and thousands *not* coming back, their contribution and sacrifice so poignantly expressed at Wyndham's Theatre some years ago by that gifted woman Joan Littlewood in *Oh, What a Lovely War*. That contemptible little army that held up the mighty German thrust at Mons in 1914. Heroes every one of them, who made it possible for Britain to survive. Such a debt could never be fully discharged.

The war was obviously going on a long time, and it was the Governor's firm intention that we should not get married until it was over, but we dissented from him in the matter. Cis and I discussed the situation. We were playing Brighton—

'It's time we tried again—right away,' Cis said in a most determined voice.

'*We* meaning yours truly?'

'Of course.'

'Thank you!'

'Ring up the Albion Hotel and make a date. He likes walking on the Downs.'

So, once again, I acquiesced in the suggestion and we set off the next morning on one of these walks. It was all very pleasant. We chatted away, but all the time I was trying to steel myself for the ordeal I had to face. The saliva in my mouth was rapidly drying up as I searched for a suitable opening phrase. I found one. Not the best perhaps, but we were getting near the end of the walk. My mouth had now completely dried out. I tried to sound unconcerned.

'Cicely and I were having a little chat the other day about our engagement. It's over six months now, do you think—'

There was a distant roll of thunder and a vivid flash.

'Do I think what?' He stopped and looked me bang in the eye.

'We could get married now?'

Another flash, and a thunderbolt fell.

'Don't *talk* to me. Go away. Don't *walk* with me.'

'But, Governor,' I pleaded, 'I was only trying—'

'Don't *walk* with me,' he fumed. '*Go away.*'

'But, Governor . . .'

I was uncertain what to do. I just followed behind like a dog that had been called to heel.

'Don't *follow* me.'

He was still livid. So I stopped and started again a little farther back. I felt such a fool walking about ten yards behind him. Finally I gave it up and came home.

It took several days before the storm completely cleared. I met Cis ouside 'The Old Ship', and as we walked along the front I described the scene in detail. She was furious and started stepping out, and the more I told her the more indignant she became and the faster she travelled. I felt at any moment she would say, 'Don't *walk* with me.' I couldn't help laughing to myself, she was so like her father. His features, his walk, his mannerisms and gestures, his kindness, generosity and his indomitable fighting spirit—she had all these qualities but they were tempered by a sweet gentle feminity that evidently came from the distaff side.

Walking still faster she said, 'I am going to see him myself. I shall insist. Just after Christmas. All right for you?'

'Sure it suits me.' I was amazed at her unyielding tenacity.

'This time he's gone too far.' And she meant it. Her speed increased. We were now practically running.

As a matter of fact, Aunt Edie, the Governor's sister-in-law, and a most lovable character, and my mother, who now loved Cis dearly, worked so hard on him, on our behalf, that he had to give way; at last the wedding was fixed and the invitations were sent for February 14th, 1916, by my mother and Aunt Edie. But there were further complications. The tour, being so successful, was prolonged, but as the invitations had gone out and all arrangements made the date could not be altered so we had to forgo the honeymoon. We were playing a four-week season at Hull so we came back to London early Sunday morning for the wedding on Monday at St Paul's, Avenue Road, St John's Wood—Cis's Parish Church. My mother begged the Governor to give us the Monday night off and he agreed, provided the Hull Manager, a chap called Morton, gave his consent. The request was telegraphed first thing Monday morning to Hull.

The wedding was at 11.00 a.m. I can't remember much about it. I found it hard to realise it was actually happening. I vaguely recall the Governor looking very serious, a lot of people crying, Mother in tears and Father near to it. The only one who seemed to be enjoying it was Claudie, proud of his brother for making such an excellent choice.

Standing at the foot of the chancel steps when the vicar pronounced us man and wife, I was in a daze. I felt impelled to grab Cis's hand, take a call and say, thank you for being such a splendid audience. I was saved by the timely interruption of the vicar's homily on the sanctity of marriage. As the strains of the wedding march filled the church I couldn't believe I was walking down the aisle with Cis on my arm after all those months of waiting. Was it just wild imagination? It was not until we were sitting side by side in the car after leaving the church that reality returned and the ineffable joy of realisation.

I just couldn't utter a word and I think Cis for the one and only time in her life was rendered speechless. We just held hands. Words were superfluous. The most eloquent silence I have ever known and all remembered today as clearly and vividly as the day it happened that happy St Valentine's morning, 1916.

On the corner of Avenue Road a clergyman was waiting to cross over. As we passed he waved and gave us his blessing—an unexpected coincidence, but what a happy one!

The reception was at the Langham Hotel, later to become part of the B.B.C. When we had changed out of the wedding props to meet the guests, we were overwhelmed with affection and congratulations from everyone. Just before the bride cut the cake, the Best Man shouted for silence to read out the telegrams. He opened the first one and read it out to the assembly:

Certainly not—stop—come back at once—stop—Morton

The Best Man, hiding his embarrassment, hurried to open the next one. If this was vindictiveness on the part of Mr Morton of Hull because we dared to ask for a night off, it completely misfired. What did we care where we went? Cis and I were married, deliriously happy, and that was all that mattered.

We had a grand time on the train going back to Hull. Mr and Mrs Jack Hulbert and Miss Mo Finucane, one of the bridesmaids, were the guests of Miss Dorothy Ward and her husband, Mr Shaun Glenville, at lunch in the dining car. We got a tremendous reception that night in the show. The audience rose to the occasion and cheered! A Yorkshire audience can be so warm and friendly when emotionally moved.

After the show we had supper together in the Hotel. We were the only two there and, again, it didn't matter. We were together. As we were about to go upstairs to the bridal suite we were warned by the hall porter that there was going to be a raid. A Zeppelin was approaching Hull and we had better take cover. This sounded horrific—a Zeppelin with bombs, and coming at a very inopportune moment to say the least of it. Nothing much seemed to happen and after we had waited quite a time we turned in for the night, dog tired after the most exciting day of our lives.

Rosaline, Cis's sister, had been the other bridesmaid, but Charles Courtneidge, Cis's only brother, who was doing a splendid job as an officer in the Flying Corps, having transferred from the Cavalry, was unable to be present at the wedding. We had first met in *The Pearl Girl*, where he was playing a small part and understudying me. He was a splendid chap, I liked him immensely.

That charming actor Teddy Gwen had left the cast of *The Light Blues* to serve as an officer in the Horse Transport. Father decided the Army would give him a long-earned rest and joined as a medical officer. He was put in charge of remedial work at a military hospital in Crowborough. For the first time in his life he was able to slow down and enjoy a little leisure. It made him very happy.

The tour of *The Light Blues* was nearing the finish and the Governor decided to put it on in London. The time had now come for me to experience something entirely new—a flop. It had to come sooner or later and the sooner the better. A very important part of the training: learning to take it gracefully. The show opened at the Shaftesbury in 1916 but the public was not amused. An actor called Albert Chevalier took over in Teddy Gwen's part. He was famous as a singer of character songs, his best remembered is *We've been together now for forty years*. His songs, all of which he worked superbly, were mostly written by himself, and the one he wrote for the show was *I see life through rose-coloured glasses*, which seemed irrelevant with the Huns over-running most of Europe, and his performance generally, which was effective on the concert platform, seemed too slow and heavy for those stirring times and failed to please the public. Nor did *The Light Blues* do any better.

The Governor had nothing to take its place. So Mr and Mrs Jack Hulbert were faced with a very unpropitious start to a lifelong partnership. At the tender age of twenty-two and twenty-three they looked for the silver lining but the lowering clouds showed no sign of a break.

The other West End managements paid scant regard to the talent of Cicely Courtneidge who, according to their lights, had only appeared at the Shaftesbury because Robert Courtneidge was the lessee. This make me hopping mad. But I must admit I did not realise the potential that was there any more than they did.

We had just taken a flat in Great Portland Street, and were experiencing the excitement of having the first home of our own, choosing the furniture and fitting the flat out with all the essentials, buying this and buying that. Cis had impeccable taste, another facet I had not been aware of before. She made it look so cosy and warm. How to pay for it all became a very interesting point. Where would the money come from if we didn't start working again at once? But this sudden change in the family fortunes was timely. Up till now neither of us had had any practice in fighting off impending disaster. An unfamiliar situation had to be dealt with—looking for a job. Neither of us knew the first thing about it. I was hopeless. All I could do was to try and make myself useful in the house by becoming the handyman, which gave me a nice break from worrying, but the financial position remained unsolved.

I was in the dining room fitting a plug on the end of the flex connected to a standard lamp we had just bought. The flat being on the top floor, the noise of the traffic below was greatly reduced. I was enjoying the peace and quiet then suddenly came the gale warning: I heard the key turn in the front door. It opened and a hurricane burst into the dining room.

'Have you thought of anything yet? If so, what?' I looked round to answer but she'd gone.

'What are you going to do?' The voice now came from the kitchen.

'Ring up the agents again, I suppose,' I had to shout.

'That's no good.' The voice was muffled, coming from one of the cupboards in the bathroom.

'Well, I'll go and see them,' I shouted again.

'All right, I can hear.' This made me jump, she was standing immediately behind my chair. I don't know how she got there in the time.

'All right, I'll call on them tomorrow,' I volunteered.

'No, you won't—you'll ring up André Charlot and fix an appointment, that's what you'll do.'

'But, my darling, I don't know André Charlot.'

'And do it now. I'll give you his number.' She had the phone book in her hand.

'C . . . CH . . . CHA . . . Here we are. I'll get the number and you can speak.'

It all happened so quickly that I found myself talking to a man I didn't know from Adam who said he would be pleased to see me tomorrow. Cis interjected, 'Make it this afternoon.' To my surprise he agreed and suggested five-thirty. Cis certainly works fast. I was left trailing. The least I could do would be to pull something off. With these thoughts in mind I hurried along to the appointment. As I entered his office at the back of the auditorium of the Comedy Theatre,

I found myself talking to a large genial Frenchman with a slight accent and a lot of charm.

André Charlot, one of our biggest producers of the time, originated intimate revue in London where he reigned supreme for many years, and deservedly so. Apart from his impeccable taste in decor and colour, and his flair for originality, he had a genius for making stars. In addition to Phyllis Monkman, he found Beatrice Lillie, Gertie Lawrence and Jack Buchanan. They were just a few of the glittering personalities he introduced to the West-End.

In the interview I found him courteous and affable. The first thing he asked me was, could I do acrobatic dancing. I answered without hesitation. I think he guessed I was lying because he smiled as he said, 'I'll take you down on the stage to meet Phyllis Monkman.' He introduced us and said, 'It's up to you, Phyl. He looks right, you must say if he's what you want. Let me know. I'll be up in my office.' Phyllis Monkman was the current pin-up girl—a beautiful figure, a beautiful dancer and a most entertaining personality. I liked her the moment we met, she was warm and friendly. I decided on frankness and at once there was an easy camaraderie between us as a result.

'There's nothing to it really, I'll show you how simple it is. I'll stand on this table and dive into your arms. All you have to do is catch me. I'll show you how to hold me after the dive; your right arm will be under my chest and your left arm under my legs. I shall be lying in your arms parallel to the floor. Let's have a try.' She climbed on to the table. 'Are you ready?' she asked, poised for the jump.

'Yes,' I answered in a very unconvincing tone. She jumped, I caught her but not quite according to plan. I caught her legs with both arms instead of leaving the right arm for catching her round the chest, with the result that she was upside-down with her legs in the air and her hands on the floor. It was a most inopportune moment for Charlot to come out of his office at the back of the circle and shout, 'How are you doing?'

'Fine,' answered Miss Monkman from her upside-down position. 'See you in a minute.'

So here I was holding in my arms the pin-up girl of every officers' mess. I would have been the most envied man in London had I been seen at this moment, even if I was holding her upside down.

'Just let go of my legs and I can stand up. Let's try again.' Miss Monkman, as well as great charm, had great courage.

'Don't forget the right arm round the chest and stand perfectly still.'

She was on the table again ready to make another dive. I was tense with nerves. My very future depended on this jump. Irreparable disaster all round if I missed. Right arm round the chest—must remember that and stand still—Miss Monkman was in mid-air—she landed beautifully in my arms. I was astonished at the result.

'That looked all right.' Charlot had popped out of his office again.

'O.K. Guv',' said the intrepid Miss Monkman. 'Mr Hulbert's coming up to see you.'

It was almost a parental interest he took in his artistes and he treated them with the greatest kindness and consideration. When it came to money he was very economical, no one complained of being overpaid. I didn't argue about the salary he suggested. I was so delighted at getting the job.

9

The show was called *See Saw* and we opened to big business at the Comedy Theatre. Phyllis Monkman was the star with John Humphries, an excellent character comedian, who got his laughs without effort. I had two numbers with Phyl and a few odd bits in the sketches. Phyl and I soon struck up a great friendship. Apart from being a most fascinating and amusing lady she specialised in caring for people, helping them in their work, helping them in getting jobs, helping them out of trouble. As a close and sympathetic friend she was never found wanting. Cis and I to this day are proud and happy she is one of our chums.

Very quickly she taught me all that was necessary to know about the so-called acrobatic dancing, which really consisted of lifting her up, throwing her around and catching her when she sprang into my arms. The rest was the kind of stuff I was used to.

Having no Robert Courtneidge as my tutor I had to continue my stage training on my own. I spent a lot of time watching John Humphries every night from the wings, trying to see how he got his laughs with such an economy of effort. Apart from learning I had another reason for watching so carefully. I had seen John Humphries' understudy rehearsing once or twice and I knew that if ever he had to go on Charlot would go into his despairing act. Sure enough John Humphries got 'flu and the understudy took over. Charlot's despairing act was his best to date. With unashamed presumption I approached him.

'I know how you feel, Guv',' I said, trying to sound sympathetic. 'Let *me* go on. I *know* it. I could make up to look much older.'

The despairing act rose to its peak.

72

'I think Jack would do it very well'. Who else could have said that but Phyl, bless her heart. It tipped the scales, Charlot would always listen to his favourite artiste.

Thanks to his talent and expertise John Humphries had created a most amusing performance in the revue and as I tried to reproduce it as faithfully as I could I managed to get some of the laughs, which shot me up in Guv's estimation. I was now regarded as a promising comedian as well as a dancer. Phyl decided this called for a little celebration in her dressing room after the show.

As usual she was entertaining a posse of officers on leave who very kindly joined in and used their best endeavours to make it a go. Nice blokes. One I talked to a lot had a sore throat and runny eyes. I detected a cold and suggested ammoniated tincture of quinine which turned out to be no cure for chicken-pox, for that's what he'd got, and that's what I got a few days later. Very considerate of him to pass it on to me, but a month at home away from work was inadequate to compensate for the inherent disadvantages of this untimely ailment. Cis nursed me with great patience, and then Claudie, who was staying with us, picked up the infection, so she had to nurse him too. Then of course it had to happen, she got it herself so Claudie, who had now recovered, had to take over the nursing. The night I got back to the theatre the young officer, who was now both compunctious and uneasy, apologised for causing this untoward sequence of events, but what can you do except smile and play it down when all the time you want to deliver a trenchant censure on his carelessness. In short, tear him off a strip.

When *See Saw* finished Charlot engaged me for his next revue *Bubbly* which gave me a big chance. I had several good numbers and a very successful duet with Phyl. Arthur Playfair, another splendid character actor, starred with Phyl; Teddy Gerrard, a popular young actor of that time, added to the sparkle of the champagne. It turned out to be a big success for Charlot and it gave me, at a critical time, a chance to set my foot firmly at the bottom of the ladder in the West End.

Early one evening, after we had been running several weeks, the stage door-keeper was having a most unusual conversation with a soldier. Officers he was used to handling, but a private was a different proposition.

'Good evening,' the private said. The stage door-keeper looked surprised.

'Good evening, can I help you?'

'No, I don't think so,' the soldier replied, 'I just want my key.'

'What? Oh, sir, I thought I knew that voice. For the moment I was puzzled. So you've joined up?'

'Some time ago,' I told him. 'But I was only called up yesterday. I'm stationed at Grove Park and I've got to get back to camp after the show.'

'Well, good for you, sir.'

'It's not good for me, it's exhausting.'

My group was drafted into the R.A.S.C. and Grove Park was one of their depots on the outskirts of London. Dear Phyl was most disturbed but I assured her I would try and wangle a sleeping-out pass so that, for the time being anyway, I could continue playing. Guv' was very concerned, too, and he had to engage a chap to be ready to go on should my services become essential to the running of the R.A.S.C. In any case, I could not get away in the daytime so he would have to go on at matinée in any case. It was a cliff-hanger existence, but I was able to continue through the indulgence of a kind sergeant who loved the theatre and who, when he knew what I was up to at the Comedy, gave me a measure of adulation big enough for Sir Henry Irving himself.

For two weeks all went well. If only I could hang on for another two it would give me just enough time to consolidate my success and enable me, after the war, to pick up where I left off. It became a very busy life. One of the great drawbacks was lack of sleep and, out of sheer necessity, I used to curl up anywhere I could and have a snooze —on the floor, in a field, in a cupboard, anywhere—and I would wake up refreshed. A valuable experience which I have used right up to the present day. I always have forty winks in the dressing room before the show. It works wonders.

We were having an inspection parade one morning at the depot and the officer of the day did a neat double-take as he passed me in the

front rank. When we were dismissed at the end of the parade he came
over to me and asked the inevitable question: 'Didn't I see you last
night on the stage in *Bubbly* at the Comedy Theatre?'

I thought, Hullo, this is it. I could only say, 'Yes, sir.'

'Then how do you manage to . . . I mean . . .'

'Forty-eight hours' leave, sir—compassionate grounds.'

'Oh, I see.' The officer was still mystified. 'You're not continuing
in the show?'

'No, sir.'

'That's a pity—wonderful show—you were marvellous.'

'Thank you, sir.'

I sprang to attention, saluted smartly and was away before he had
time to ask any more questions. It was getting too dangerous. It didn't
take me very long to discover that the key man in the British Army
was the non-commissioned officer—the sergeant—and that became my
target in the army. I must go all out for a quick promotion.

An officer I met in Phyl's dressing room one night after the show,
when we were having drinks, was inaugurating the new technical
school at Osterley Park. It was at the time when the Horse Transport
was in the process of becoming entirely mechanised which meant
teaching men the intricacies of the petrol engine and the parts and
function of the transmission. Phyl immediately said, 'Private Hulbert
is the very man for you.' The officer agreed, delighted. 'Give me
all your particulars and I will apply for you at once.' And it would
have been in the bag had not some irate gentleman in the War Office
received reports of certain actors breaking out of camp and playing
in the theatre. I was instantly put on draft and sent to Sydenham.

While I was waiting to be drafted overseas, one very clear day in the
early afternoon on Sydenham Hill I saw the first daylight raid on
London. There in the distance was a formation of German planes
flying straight over the West End and the City, with the little puffs
of smoke of the anti-aircraft shells bursting just behind the enemy
planes—but always just behind. It was an amazing sight. As I gazed on
this clear view of London, wondering where the Comedy Theatre was,
it stirred a chord in my heart and I felt a little sad. Was this the shape
of things to come? Would this develop on a large scale? And it did,

but not until some twenty-odd years later when the trouble started all over again. How crazy the world has become!

My departure from *Bubbly* happened so quickly there was not even time to wish the chap who went on for me the best of luck. He was hardly known in those days, but he went on to become one of the most delightful and fascinating light comedians of our time. The name of Jack Buchanan became a household word in London and New York.

In the middle of all this excitement I was informed that I had been applied for and was being dispatched to the new Technical School at Osterley Park. This came as a great surprise and I wondered what had happened to the fulminating staff officer in the War Office who had thundered out the order, 'Put these actors on draft at once'. It must have got mislaid. I soon settled down at the camp and started to work out a plan for quick promotion.

In the meantime, what was Cis doing? Quite a lot. Something which called for courage and tenacity. To appreciate the full measure of these rigorous demands a picture of the entertainment world as it was during the years of the First World War, and just after, must be reviewed.

The live theatre was at its best, each large city in Great Britain had several excellent theatres and in addition there were various *Empires* and *Hippodromes* presenting twice-nightly variety shows all over the country. The *Halls*, a diminutive of music halls, pulled in the crowds with a popular star at the top of the bill and another at the bottom with half a dozen smaller acts in the middle like acrobats, conjurers, ventriloquists, performing animals, etc. These were the glorious years of live entertainment. There was no radio, no talking pictures, no television to impede the steady flow of money into the coffers of the creators of the live show. The established stars like Vesta Tilley, Marie Lloyd, Bramsby Williams, Clarice Mayne, and a host of others, remained firm favourites. The irresistible comedy of Harry Tate, W. C. Fields, Charles Austin, Wilkie Bard etc. kept them at the top of the bill for years. Not to mention Fred Karno's comedy team.

But from an artiste's point of view it was a tough assignment. A music hall audience could be the kindest and warmest in the country and, on occasions, the most impossible. Sometimes a Saturday night could be like a Cup Final—pandemonium, none of the hooligans could be chucked out, there were too many of them. Sometimes the turn preceding you gets the bird and the noise continues all through your opening number. You *may* succeed in quietening them, on the other hand you may *not*. Conversely, the turn before you goes enormously and the audience continue shouting and applauding all through your first song trying to get the turn back. Both situations are equally difficult to deal with and call for an unwavering display of guts. Much has to be endured, and many fierce battles fought, before reaching stardom at the top of the bill.

When *The Light Blues* finished and Cis failed completely to interest any of the West End managers, she staggered me by announcing she was going on the halls. I couldn't believe she realised what it entailed, but she flatly refused to be dissuaded. I was frankly terrified. My dear little wife, a singer of dainty little musical comedy numbers followed by a dainty little dance with twelve dainty little chorus boys. All so sweet and innocent even in those days it was old-fashioned.

> 'Some boys are glum boys,
> Some boys are gay,
> Some boys are keen upon work,
> And some are keen on play.'

Smashing stuff. I trembled to think what a wild Saturday night football crowd would do to that! But she was determined and as soon as I joined the army she gave an earnest of her intentions by having three songs written: a point number, a hospital nurse and an officer in the Flying Corps. All the innocent sugary stuff had been replaced by the down to earth happenings of the time. Being away in camp I could offer no assistance. She found herself a kind, friendly agent, Hartley Milburn, and in a short time he had booked a try-out date at the Hippodrome, Colchester.

Agonising moments were endured that day in the camp at Osterley Park as I waited to hear the result of her attempting to start on this perilous adventure. I managed to get through on the phone about eleven at night and I got the news. Big success—particularly the male impersonation of the Flying Corps Officer. I couldn't wait to see it.

I managed to wangle a weekend pass. I sat in the stalls of the

Hippodrome, Colchester, amazed. I couldn't believe I was watching the dainty little girl I had married a year ago. Suddenly, a complete change. A comedienne getting laughs. A fine sense of character. Gone for ever was the pretty musical comedy stuff. Here was the beginning of something I never knew existed.

In retrospect I realise now it was the turning point of her career. There was a hell of a long way to go to reach the top of the bill, but she was heading in the right direction. Success was assured. She was now in a position to refute the invidious things said about her as the theatre manager's daughter. The occasional rough house and the wild Saturday night failed to be a deterrent to the intrepid young Courtneidge, who proceeded doggedly to fight all opposition. It was hard going, a completely different life, tough, lonely but a stage training beyond price. You had to make good or you were out on your ear—and quick. Self-reliance became the cardinal rule. Always thinking about the job—improvement essential—working out new material—getting new songs.

At twenty-three star quality began to show itself. It was there right enough waiting to be developed. Cis was quick to appreciate the camaraderie that existed among these music hall artistes—the sympathy, kindness, good companionship, all fighting against heavy odds —the same camaraderie that existed during the war, with all working to the same end.

Jack Hayman, the manager of the Victoria Palace, saw her performance at Colchester and booked her immediately. Very taken with her work, he gave her second-star billing at the bottom of the bill. The London audience endorsed his opinion. Jack Hayman believed in her so strongly that she appeared at the Victoria Palace regularly throughout the whole of her music hall career, finishing up top of the bill. On the strength of her success at the Victoria Palace the contracts started to come in and she was booked to appear all over the country. The male impersonation seemed the chief attraction and so she soon became busy entertaining the masses twice nightly, as an officer in the Flying Corps, which I must say I enjoyed enormously and I feel I *am* entitled to say this as I had nothing whatever to do with it.

After I had taken a careful appraisal of the possibilities in Osterley Park I decided on a plan. There was a large lecture hall in the camp and all round the edge of the parade ground there were long sheds containing the various working parts of lorries—the engine, the transmission, the steering etc.—dismantled for demonstration purposes. The army demonstrators, who were mostly ex-garage hands, did their work efficiently but the so-called lecturers took a bit of a dive. I asked for permission to parade before the officer in charge. As I stood at attention in his headquarters, he obviously didn't know me from Adam, which is what I had hoped. He was the nervous fussy type and the interview was conducted on strict military lines. *The King's Rules and Regulations* must have been his favourite book.

He said, after I had applied for the lecturing job, 'What are your qualifications?'

This was the question I wanted.

'Been in the motor business since boyhood. Maintenance and repair work. Father kept a garage.'

'What makes you think you could lecture?'

'I was president of our local debating society. Had a large experience in public speaking.'

A more perceptive officer would have realised by now I was just the man they needed. He hesitated, so I put the words into his stupid head.

'Perhaps I could have a trial run.'

'Well, yes. I can't see anything against it,' he said, obviously scanning in his mind the pages of his favourite book. 'When do you want to start?'

My answer surprised him.

'In three weeks.'

'Why not tomorrow?'

'Must get my notes in order.'

Not having the foggiest idea how a petrol engine worked I got a pass and dashed up to town to buy some books on the subject. I daren't waste a second. Only three weeks to learn the lot because at the end of the lectures it was necessary to answer all the questions that were fired at you by the troops. In those vital three weeks it was swotting for an exam all over again.

I was a bit shaky on the first lecture, but it was good enough to land me the job and my first stripe as a Lance Jack. I tried to make the lectures crystal clear and keep the attention of the men by getting laughs, and this proved highly successful. I became well established as a lecturer and the humorous approach did the trick. The headquarters of the officer in charge adjoined the lecture hall and as the number of lectures began to increase the laugher increased proportionally.

I was sent for and hauled over the coals by this silly man who wanted to know what it all meant. I gave him a straight answer—the facts. I told him my main job was to keep the men *awake*. They had been up since dawn and by midday the moment they sat down in the warm lecture room it was hard to resist a cat-nap, but the noise of others laughing brought them back to full consciousness and a few more laughs kept them interested. I was thinking of some of the sermons I had suffered before the war and how I had to fight drowsiness and so often lost. He was unconvinced but had to acquiesce. I was awarded another stripe and became a full corporal. As the lectures continued it was rather like playing a part in a show and I was happy because I knew the chaps were learning something—I found this very rewarding.

Cis was now so firmly established on the halls that contracts were coming in for return dates. This meant new material, of course, calling for new ideas. Thanks to my success at Osterley Park I had no difficulty in getting a sleeping-out pass and weekend leave whenever I applied for it. This for the first time enabled me to help Cis with her act, in getting new songs and seeing her performance on certain weekends. Return dates meant new material.

In place of the Army Hospital Nurse song she came on wearing the uniform of a W.A.A.C.—Women's Army Auxiliary Corps and sang *The smell of the blooming onions knocked everything out of my head*. This is the kind of stuff a musical hall audience liked. It tore them up. The other numbers were changed gradually, but it was a long time before she changed the Flying Officer number. It had a little scene which she played with a girl and a Flying Corps Private which led into her final song. Claudie first appeared professionally in this sketch and went round with Cis for many months in some of the later ones. When the

Flying Corps hero was finally changed, Cis made her entrance as a naval officer. The scene got a lot of laughs and provided a good lead into her big finishing number as a naval lieutenant when she played a scene with the girl and Claudie, who was now an A.B. looking very smart. The male impersonation was still definitely the main feature of her act.

Most of the time she was playing the big cities in the Midlands and up North, but when she played the London suburban halls she was able to live at home and I could get back from the camp on a sleeping-out pass and help her with her new material. Contracts were coming in all the time and she was signed up for months ahead. It was hard work. With twice nightly performances it was sometimes a tough battle, but most of the time she faced a delightful audience. Endless travelling week after week. It was a question of how long she could stick it. The money came rolling in, good money too. So ended our financial crisis, which very kindly gave place to another of an entirely different calibre, but the particular crisis that suddenly darkened the scene we could have well done without.

Cis began to lose her voice and a Harley Street ear, nose and throat man insisted on immediate rest for six months or else. . . . If you pay a man for his experience and knowledge it would be madness to flout his instructions, especially when permanent injury is threatened. Rest, silence and fresh air were the simple and, at the same time, extremely difficult remedies to carry out. After endless enquiries and a lot of travelling, 'Yew Tree Cottage', on the edge of the Chiltern Hills, came to the rescue. It was a workman's cottage, ancient and charming in a beautiful country setting just outside West Wycombe.

We found various people who were happy to go and stay with her. There was Claudie for a start; her father was there once or twice, as was Rosaline her sister; P. G. H. Fender, the famous Surrey Cricketer who had become a close friend and was on leave at the time visited, and several others came periodically, so she was never alone. I had no difficulty in getting week-end passes and covered the distance from West Wycombe station to Yew Tree Cottage on a push-bike. We had many happy hours away from it all for a brief spell in the peace of this unspoilt countryside. It was a haven of rest far beyond the reach of the hideous sounds of war. The birds sang to the rising sun, the lowing of the cattle in the meadow proclaimed the importance of the hour. The clarion call of the cockerel from the cottage on the distant hill told the farmer the toil of another day was due to start and, in case he failed to hear, the cockerel called again.

The ear, nose and throat man should have been proud of his patient. His instructions were followed scrupulously. The vocal chords that had become angry and inflamed through overwork were suddenly surprised to find themselves no longer required to work beyond a slight vibration for a whisper. Such a thing had never happened before in the whole of their existence. I must say it amazed me. The threat of permanent laryngitis was rapidly receding. More examples of the little woman's dogged determination. The net result was overwhelming success. After three months she was allowed to return to the battle of the halls.

Reflecting on this today one is tempted to think set-backs of this kind should be regarded as a blessing. Nature sounds a note of warning, which it would be the height of folly to ignore. Adversity is a very unwelcome guest but a profitable teacher. From this long enforced rest at the beginning of her career, the little woman had learnt much. She was richer in knowledge through experience, learning how to conserve her vocal chords and get her effects without straining. One would like to warn beginners about the dangers of vocal strain but the attitude of many of them is 'things have changed a lot since your day'. That may be so but not with the vocal chords, they are still susceptible to strain and overwork.

Cis finally said goodbye to Yew Tree Cottage which had served her so well and returned to the flat in Portland Court, where she spent a few days getting ready to start work again where she had left off.

Back in London, there was one particular night that was very exciting. Claudie, Bill Fender and myself were there and we were treated to another Zeppelin raid. Just above us was a flat roof where I used to practise my dancing and Bill suggested we should go up there and watch it. In the night sky the flying monster was dimly visible. The sound of an aeroplane moving towards it through the darkness increased the excitement. Then the thunder of an explosion rent the air and a huge ball of fire lit up the sky as it fell to the earth at Cuffley just north of London. Night flying was an adventure in those days and the chap who went up and destroyed that Zeppelin won the V.C. to become Captain Warnford, V.C.

On another occasion, one night, we were all together again on the roof trying to spot the odd enemy plane that had ventured as far as London. In the dark an aircraft flew overhead. We started to rush from the roof. Bill shouted, 'Don't worry, it's one of ours. I can tell by the sound of the engine,' and just as we had become reassured there was a terrific bang from an exploding bomb. It had dropped about a mile away.

10

Cis's voice was back to normal and she was performing with renewed strength and fervid enthusiasm at the Hippodrome in Coventry. I came up on a weekend pass and was delighted to see the act going better than ever. The Flying Corps Officer was the main attraction just as before and Flying Officer Cis met several other officers from the aerodrome near by. When I entered her dressing room at the theatre she flung her arms round me and set off at a breakneck speed:

'How lovely to see you again. It's been so long, darling, hasn't it, nearly a week. Are you tired? Of course you are, darling. Have you missed me? I've missed you so much. How are you, darling? You look great. Are you happy to see me? Come and sit down and tell me lots more.'

More? I hadn't even said hullo yet!

'I've met such nice people here, mostly Flying chaps. Cliff Whitley, you'll love him. Dying to meet you as you're so interested in flying.'

I didn't know I was interested. I was under the impression I was terrified.

'It'll be so exciting for you going up for the first time. I know you'll love it. It'll be such a thrill for you!'

The next morning I reported at the aerodrome and was hurried into one of the huts and changed from a corporal to an officer by means of an army mac and flying head-gear. I have never been guilty of showing signs of bravery in my life, but when I climbed into that flimsy, dilapidated-looking aeroplane that morning I got near to it. Clifford Whitley was one of those cheery, easy-going, everything's-going-to-be-fine sort of chaps with an ingratiating manner which usually inspired trust and confidence. It failed dismally in my case.

It was astonishing to me that when we had finished bumping along the runway and became airborne, the plane was still holding together, but looking at it by and large I couldn't see any possibility of making a safe landing. Cliff chatted away but I couldn't hear much, the noise of the engine took over, for which I was very thankful. I was beyond polite conversation. This agony seemed to go on for ever and then suddenly I caught sight of the runway again rushing towards us at a tremendous pace. Then a bump and I thought, here we go, then another bump. I expected the plane to disintegrate. Another bump and the runway began to slow up until finally we stopped and, to my amazement, we were still in one piece—a fact almost impossible to believe. I stepped out of a nightmare on to the tarmac. Cliff gave me a beaming smile.

'Enjoy it?'

'Absolutely marvellous.' My voice didn't sound like mine at all. It was too high and shrill. Cliff shot a quick glance at me.

'Shaken you up a bit?'

'No, just excitement. So jolly glad to be back—I mean, to be back and know that I've done it.'

'Yes, grand feeling. I'm glad to know *I've* done it too. I've been certified unfit for flying.'

I was on the point of collapse before we landed but to show unconcern at this terrifying revelation required a superhuman effort. I was so stunned I did nothing, I never moved a muscle, which was evidently the right reaction.

Cliff seemed relieved as he said, 'I need a drink. How about you?'

I am not a great drinker, but there are times—oh boy! Cis as usual was bubbling over with excitement.

'Oh darling, what a thrill it must have been. I knew you'd love it. Did you feel sick? You look rather pale but then you're a good sailor so you must have been all right up there in the air.'

Nothing could stem the tide of her enthusiasm. Once again I hadn't even a chance of slipping in a 'Hullo, darling'. She concluded by saying, 'I'm so glad you enjoyed the flight. Wonderful experience. I'll fix it for you again when we go to Leeds.'

My insatiable desire to become a sergeant was well on the way to fulfilment. I set out to make myself indispensable to the R.A.S.C. The lectures had become the main feature of the training school and I was the only lecturer who kept the men awake, so the laughter technique had to be accepted by the officer in charge. He gave me no further trouble. The men enjoyed the lectures—I knew this because so many of them made a point of telling me. I had become famous in the camp not as an actor but as an authority on the mechanism of the army lorry. I had bluffed my way into a strong position and was sitting pretty, not quite in the sergeant's mess but very nearly.

In the same week that I got my third stripe, Cis, for the first time in her life, went top of the bill at Nottingham. So all was going well with *The Hulbert–Courtneidge Saga*. A musical hall star and a sergeant. The music hall star was going from strength to strength, learning all the time, gaining an experience which would redound to her credit in future years. And the sergeant? What had he learnt? How to keep a company of tired men awake in an overheated lecture hall.

Turning this over in my mind, relaxing after a splendid meal in the luxury of the sergeants' mess, I realised Courtneidge was racing ahead. Catching up, of course, was out of the question but preparations should be made for the future. A realistic assessment of weaknesses showed my voice to be in need of drastic treatment. I had done so much dancing practice, since I was fifteen, that I had practically danced it away.

How to deal with the situation? I read my father's book on *Voice Training*, an excellent treatise on the subject. He laid great stress on breathing, and described very clearly the necessary exercises. I remembered he had taught me these in the past but I regret to say I had given the subject scant attention. And now it was vital. I persevered with the exercises and learnt some speeches from Shakespeare which I recited while wandering around the edge of the camp or, more correctly, tried to recite and this showed immediately that the vocal weakness was appalling. There was no power, no flexibility, no clarity of articulation. I knew my singing voice was very dreary and weak but the speaking voice . . .! This was a shock.

I heard of a Doctor Alderson from one of the artistes on the bill with Cis. He apparently had trained several music hall performers with considerable success. I found him a great enthusiast and he told me he would have me singing in six months and that would strengthen my speaking voice, which I see now was all part of the same trouble. As I had a sleeping-out pass I went to him mostly in the evenings when I got back from camp. I worked hard at the exercises that he set and after a few months I could feel the improvement in breathing and vocal strength and a definite increase of flexibility and modulation in speech. I was working under great difficulties but the voice was definitely getting stronger and I knew I was on the right lines. I was building for the future. Look out, Courtneidge, here I come! I knew if I stuck to it I could overcome the great weakness and today, Heaven knows the voice is nothing great, but thanks to the inspiration Cis gave me in those far-off days I have been able to earn my living for over sixty years. Thank you, Cis, for setting the pace.

There was always a big flap in the camp when an inspection by some of the top brass from the War Office was about to take place and I was in the office discussing the last one with the officer in charge who was still apprehensive about the 'Learning with laughter' technique. Mind you, he was now pro Sergeant Hulbert, but he was a bit windy about the 'brass hats'.

'Have there been any complaints, sir?' I put the question to him bluntly.

'No, but I think this time it would be safer if you were not lecturing.'

'Surely, sir, we should show them we are progressive.'

The phone rang. It was a message from H.Q. The orderly officer was speaking, I could hear every word loud and clear coming from the phone.

'Message received 10.05 hours. Inspection of demonstration sheds 11.30 hours. Lecture Hall 12 noon. Sergeant Hulbert to be lecturing.'

I didn't have to listen to any more, this set the seal on the whole thing once and for all. I now had the authority I wanted. From now on I could do what I liked. I could have jumped for joy. With military precision, on the stroke of twelve noon, the door of the lecture hall swung open and the 'top brass' entered. There were about half a dozen of them, looking very important and formidable in their war

office makeup. I shouted 'Company, 'Shun' and the men jumped to
their feet. A very high-ranking officer in a very high-ranking voice
said, 'Carry on, Sergeant' which was extremely nice of him, and I gave
the troops the O.K.: 'Gentlemen, be seated.'

'Now, you lucky lads, if any of you find it too hot to keep awake
make yourselves comfortable by the radiator and your name and
number will be taken when you wake up. The army thinks of everything.'

Not a suggestion of a smile from the troops. They were overawed
by the presence of the War Office visitors, but there was a big laugh
from the 'top brass'. This broke the ice and from then on we were back
to form. The gents from the War Office stayed about twenty minutes
and laughed as much as the men. This put me in good heart. They
were progressive too. They had to be. They were an integral part of
the great war machine which was now pounding and grinding its way
to success. The will and determination were there as always in the past.
As a nation we were one.

I swaggered into the sergeants' mess and got a standing ovation.
One of them shouted, 'Jack, you're a bloody marvel, making those
brass-hatted monkies laugh. We're proud of you. This is going to
cost you money.'

Of course, a celebration. Drinks all round. Over the beer we discussed the value of laughter. A mixed lot, these blokes, mostly car
drivers and mechanics in civilian life with their own particular brand
of philosophy, which was down to earth and sound. Laughter was
high on their list of priorities. Splendid chaps all of them. One who
looked the toughest of the lot said, 'If you can make people laugh
you're quids in. It's the only thing that keeps us going, 'ow could we
exist in this 'ole 'ere if we didn't laugh?'

'That's right,' another wild uncouth looking character agreed looking at me. 'Jack's got the gift, 'e's got the knack and it's a bloody fine
thing to 'ave.' I was a little embarrassed but coming from these chaps
I was very pleased.

This was my first full realisation of the importance of laughter, not
only in the theatre but in real life and now today on the stage when
I hear the laughter of an appreciative audience my mind invariably

jumps back to that extraordinary conversation in the sergeant's mess during World War I and I am eternally grateful to my fellow sergeant who referred to the gift of raising laughs as 'a bloody good thing to 'av'. How right he was. How thankful I have been down the years, and still am, for the precious memory.

The work at the camp continued unabated. Hundreds of thousands of men passed through the school. The lectures were acclaimed by the authorities and continued without interference. The only difficulty I had to surmount was the Colonel, who sent for me and said, 'Sergeant Hulbert, in appreciation of the excellent work you are doing I would like to recommend you for a commission.'

This did not fit in with my ideas at all. I had grown to like the rough and ready friendship of the chaps I was working with, something I had never encountered before. It was too valuable to lose and so was my job. I had stumbled on something I could do and it was getting results.

'Thank you, sir. I am pleased you are satisfied with my work.' I started thinking hard for an excuse. 'Lecturing is a difficult job, sir—'

'And you do it very well.'

'I mean the men, sir, they're not easy to handle—'

'But that's where you excel. That's the whole point.'

The laugh-as-you-learn technique was now becoming a menace. I was up to my neck in it. Play for time was all I could think of.

'Sir, this is an honour . . . I feel unworthy . . . I don't know if I'd be capable of—'

'Think it over, Sergeant Hulbert, and I'll send for you in a few days.'

True to his word the order came through and once again I found myself facing a very determined C.O. Why didn't I say I hadn't the heart to give up the lectures and spoil the fun of the big boys in the War Office who could come down to the camp and enjoy a few laughs occasionally? The Colonel had worked his way up from the ranks himself and I assumed he would take a vicarious pleasure in seeing me do the same. A psychological situation—not easy to play. I would emphasise the basic fact that I felt committed to the lectures. A sergeant talking to his Colonel is bound to feel inhibited. Since our first meeting

I'd given it a lot of thought and decided the safest bet would be to write a short speech and learn it by heart. The Colonel was all smiles as I stood at attention before him for the second time. 'Good morning, Sergeant Hulbert.' I made a suitable reply, took a deep breath and started.

'May I begin by saying, sir, that in civilian life my job is appearing in front of audiences, trying to entertain, trying to keep their interest—I do the same here.'

'Perfect training for an officer,' the old boy said approvingly.

Again I'd hit the wrong tack so I hurried on.

'I must obey my conscience, sir, even if it means refusing an honour that is dear to the heart of most young men of my age. I feel it is my duty to repress with the utmost rigour even the slightest tendency to selfish ambition. England expects this day—' I left the quotation unfinished—I knew I was overdoing it. 'I mean, sir, the war machine is in full blast. Nothing must slow it down. If more trained men are needed immediately then those trained men must be supplied without delay.'

The colonel's expression was bordering on amazement.

'We, the instructors and lecturers of the Technical School, are proud of having the opportunity to do our humble share. We are conscious of the clamant cry, the extreme urgency for more trained men to maintain the efficiency of the war effort. In the circumstances I feel it is my duty to decline the honour you have so graciously offered to sponsor and I beg you to grant me the privilege of carrying on my work here so that I can continue with renewed earnestness and avidity.' I felt this was a bit prosy but the force and cogency of my plea did the trick. The Sergeant *v.* Colonel contest was ended.

All Cis's original bookings on the Halls had matured and she was now playing return dates. Her latest male impersonation was a fireman and she made her entrance sliding down the pole as then used in the fire stations for speed instead of stairs. I must have been mad to have thought of this with all its attendant risks. The small cage in which she sat to be hoisted right up in the flies out of sight of the audience enabled her to grab the top of the pole and slide down on to the stage. On the first night of this new scene she was up in the flies in position some twenty feet from the stage, hidden from the audience, but the small cage she was sitting in was not quite close enough to the pole. The orchestra started: her cue came. There was no time to hesitate and she had to spring and hope to grab the pole. By some miracle she made it and slid down to a big reception from the audience who knew nothing of the threatened tragedy. I nearly had a fit when she told me about it in her dressing room afterwards. We had to get the cage on another set of lines closer to the pole. In the second house there was no difficulty. It made a most effective entrance and it was impossible to dissuade Cis from continuing to use it. She argued it gave such a good start to the scene leading up to the fireman song.

It was just before the 1914 War and during it that the purely indigenous entertainment known as pantomime was at its best. The joy of the kids and the delight of the relatives finding an excuse to indulge in this lowbrow form of entertainment had become an essential part of the seasonal festivities. Musical hall stars were offered large sums of money to appear in these shows at Christmas time and Cis had a very lucrative engagement playing *Cinderella* with Little Titch as Buttons at the Theatre Royal, Manchester. It was her first starring part in a pantomime. She had a song in which she gave an impression of different types of soldiers singing the chorus and she made the American, who was one of them, a little careless where he stuck his gum when he had finished chewing; in this instance it was on the edge of the proscenium. I must admit this piece of vulgarity seemed rather incompatible with the sweet, ingenuous Cinderella. It caused a certain amount of adverse criticism, but the number went exceedingly well and the show had a long successful run at the end of which Cis returned to the halls.

I was sitting in the sergeant's mess one day having my dinner with the rest of the chaps and we were discussing the situation that was on everybody's lips. Rumours were legion. There was an atmosphere of excitement everywhere, but Sergeant Hattersley sounded a note of caution.

'There's a long way to go yet. I give it about another year.'

'Don't talk bloody silly.' My friend Sergeant Alf 'arrison was in contentious mood. 'If you want my opinion—' But nobody did. A heated argument started.

'Now shut up a minute. Take it easy. What's got into you all?'

'We're talking peace, ain't we?' Alf 'arrison turned to me.

'Now come on, Jack boy, give us your opinion.'

'I'm very optimistic,' I replied.

'Of course, there's a bloke wiv common sense. In my opinion them 'uns 'ave 'ad enough. We've got 'em on the run, ain't we? They're about to turn it in. 'Ow long do you give it, Jack boy?'

'About a month, I should think.'

As a matter of fact it was a good deal less. A week later at 11 a.m. a maroon went off with a terrific bang just above the camp. What followed beggars description. The noise of the explosion epitomised the sudden burst of agonising tension—the suffering—the torturing distress of war. In a flash all hell was let loose. Men cheering, shouting, women laughing, crying. The camp was deserted. London was the target. Anything moving in that direction was jumped on by the frenzied crowds. It seemed like a wild dream, beyond comprehension.

I had one thought only—Cis. Where was she? Birmingham. A district train got me to Euston, incredible scenes at the station again, a seething mass of humanity all shouting and singing. Fortunately I knew the departure platform for Birmingham. No chance to get a ticket—I hadn't even got a pass for that matter. No redcaps could possibly operate. It was a scene of utter confusion. Anyone in a uniform was mobbed. I was hugged and embraced non-stop with barely time to take breath. Nearly an hour it took to reach the platform and there, of course, a long wait for the next train. When it eventually arrived, the enormous crowd tried to push their way on. I took no chance and went straight for the luggage van.

Being a slow train, it was early evening when we reached New Street Station and here was a complete mad-house, even rowdier than Euston. The pubs must have done a roaring trade. Everyone was celebrating, singing and dancing, and I could see the only way to get through the station was to join in and gradually work towards the exit. I grabbed the girl next to me and danced her bit by bit in the right direction, grabbed another a little further on—I lost count of the number of females I danced and sang with. At last I was out of that station and like a streak of lightning ran all the way to the Hippodrome and arrived breathless, mad with excitement, mad to share it all with Cis.

She was on the stage in the middle of her act, which was a complete waste of time, there was just as much noise from the audience as in the streets, but that's the theatre. Come hell or high water you just go on. It must have been agony for her seeing me at the side. It was for me. At last the moment came, the curtain fell. She only took one call at the end. I grabbed her. It was just one of those great moments. After the second house, which was another painful waste of time, we dashed back to the Queen's Hotel for supper but they refused to serve us with a drink. On Armistice Night too! I couldn't believe it. I am even glad that hotel has since been demolished.

On the bill with Cis was a very popular American performer, Bill Anderson, who worked with a most amusing stooge, an adorable pony. Anderson said, 'Hetty King's upstairs, let's see if she can oblige.' She was delighted. She had all the equipment for making merry but no one to celebrate with. She lost no time in plying us with drinks and within a very short space of time we were in perfect condition for the midnight revels. We started singing in her sitting room. We decided anyone who was trying to sleep that night was crazy. The porter came up in answer to several phone calls of complaints but we very soon got him singing too.

We then went out of the hotel straight into the seething mass of yelling and shouting humanity outside to augment the volume of noise. A mighty cheer went up on our approach. We all linked arms, singing and dancing *Knees up Mother Brown* in New Street. How can foreigners accuse us of being lethargic, unemotional, all that stiff, upper-lip stuff? We may not be easily roused, but when we get going we're experts. Anyone worthy of being British and capable of standing up would have made merry with that jubilant crowd. Cis and I look back with the happiest thoughts to that hysterical night when she and I and Hetty King sang and danced *Knees up Mother Brown* with the masses in New Street, Birmingham.

I was still in a great state of excitement when I got back to the camp.

Soon I would be free to start work again. How soon? That would depend on . . . what? I went into the matter very carefully and the outlook wasn't very promising. It could be quite a lengthy business. In some cases special application could be made for key men or men in essential services. If only I could get a West End manager to apply for me. But were there any who were interested or even remembered my name? It was a sobering thought, but problems, however daunting, must be solved. The West End managers must be informed at once, I decided as I walked across the parade ground to answer a phone call one morning. As soon as I spoke, a voice the other end said, 'Mr Hulbert? I had to track you down here but it's rather urgent. I'm Sir Alfred Butt's secretary. He would like you to appear in an Anglo-French revue in Paris. Would you be interested?'

Interested. All I could do was to laugh.

'If you say yes,' the secretary continued, 'Sir Alfred will make an application for your release as soon as it can be arranged.'

My brain was doing strange things. It recalled the charming scene in Cis's pantomime at Manchester when the lovely fairy God-mother said, 'Cinderella, you *shall* go to the ball.' I don't know what Sir Alfred's secretary looked like, but as far as I was concerned she was beautiful. I phoned Cis at Leeds. She was just as astonished and de-lighted as I was.

Within a week I was on the demobbing list. Orders came through I was to leave Osterley Park on the following Tuesday and join a party being transported to the demobbing centre. I took a tender fare-well of the chaps in the mess, especially my pal Sergeant 'Arrison, who wished me 'the best of bloody luck', and after much hand-shaking and wishing them a quick return to civilian life I jumped on the lorry and we arrived at the depot somewhere in South London—Eltham, I think it was.

I went into the building with the others. My name was called. A few formalities. Papers to be scrutinised, forms to sign, and I was out, and when I say 'out' it was the quickest exit I ever made from any-where. I wasn't giving them the chance of calling me back if they found they'd made a mistake.

I ran down the street—I must have done a hundred yards in ten seconds dead—and I continued running until I was well out of reach. I jumped on a bus en route for the West End. On arriving at Great Portland Street I rushed into the flat and changed into civilian clothes for the first time for nearly three years, and as Cis was away I had a mighty job to find them. She was playing in Manchester. The train got me there in time for the second house. I banged on the dressing room door, burst in and presented myself.

One would have expected Cis to have been dumbfounded on suddenly seeing me in civvies but that was exactly what she wasn't. Immediately, she embarked on an excited monologue on the months of anguish and heartache she had endured in my absence. She never uses just a few words to express a thought. She goes for quantity, spoken at a breakneck speed; one of her most amusing and endearing charms. So here we were back to the status quo at last—the only difference being she was now a music hall star and I had a hell of a way to go to catch up; but I was all set to make a start. Vive La France.

Hartley Milburn fixed Cis for a month at the Alhambra, the Paris music hall, so that we could be together. It seemed a bit much to expect the majority of the Paris audience to speak English but the management were keen to have her and the money was good. I had never been to Paris before so it was great fun for me. A small flat near the Rond Point off the Champs Elysées was just right for the two of us.

The show Sir Alfred wanted me for was called *Hullo Paris* with a half French and half English cast. I had scenes with Gwenie Brogden and dances with Régine Florrie. I wrote a sketch for Gwenie Brogden and myself called *Une tasse de thé* about an Englishman trying to talk to a French lady using his schoolboy French. I thought it would be the best way of getting through to an Anglo-French audience. There was a very large section of Americans and British in Paris, hence the revue.

Dancing with that beautiful Parisienne artist, Régine Florrie, was exciting. She would dart back and forth, like the Dragon Fly she was portraying, then leap into my arms on the last chord of the music with perfect precision and timing—but not always. Some nights there would be a strange look in the eyes, an excessive brightness and the darting Dragon Fly would decide to dart in a new direction and I had

to do a bit of darting myself to avoid disaster. The audience, unaware
of this drastic change in the routine, applauded with great enthusiasm
as we left the stage. The first night had an added importance for not
only was it the première of a new show but the opening of a new
theatre, which had started life as The Palace and was subsequently
renamed The Mogador after the street which it adorned. The revue
was a hit. Playing in it was much more amusing than talking about
carburettor jets and piston rings.

Cis opened at the Alhambra, raising very little laughter at first but
gaining much appreciation at the end. The audiences admired the
vitality and technique of the young English comedienne. This was
much to her credit because the sickness she was suffering from being
synonymous with pregnancy, nothing could be less calculated to help
her in dealing with a Paris audience. Fortunately her figure showed
little change; she was still able to wear an Air Force Officer's uniform.
It could not have been much fun for her but it was a chance for us
being together, and she wanted that as much as I did.

But her engagement came to an end and she had to return to England for music-hall dates there. Drooping and disconsolate, I watched
the train pull out of the Gare du Nord. Paris in spring with all its *joie
de vivre* was no longer appealing to me. What was I doing in Paris
anyway with Cis on her way home to London?

A few weeks of this loneliness got me scheming again. I went to Sir
Alfred. He was in his office at the theatre, looking very cheerful,
obviously pleased with the way *Hullo Paris* was going. It seemed a
shame to disturb his complacency, especially after getting me de-
mobbed so quickly. I would put it as gently as I could.

'Good morning. Come in. Sit down.' He was beaming. 'What do
you want to see me about?'

'The show—I have never really thanked you properly for the big
chance you have given me.'

'Delighted, my dear chap, and you're one of the main props of
the revue.' His eyes were full of admiration. 'You've made a big hit,
but you know that of course, and now you want more money. My
accountant will be over next week, I'll arrange something—'

'No, no, please. It's not that—'

'Then what?' His eyes opened wide in surprise.

'Nothing really, I just wanted to thank you.'

'Quite unnecessary, but thanks all the same.' The benign smile reappeared. 'Once more my congratulations. Goodbye.'

The inescapable conclusion was depressing. I had muffed it. I left rapidly before I said anything that might be prejudicial to a future meeting. I decided to come right out with it the next time. That was equally disastrous; he just got tough and suggested I should read the terms of my contract again. At our third I tried to work it on compassionate grounds—baby on the way—should be with the wife—but to no effect.

While I was planning a new line of approach, some weeks later, Sir Alfred sent for me and said he had been thinking the matter over regarding my domestic life and thought he might be able to help. He was negotiating with an attractive young Frenchman who had agreed to take over in a month's time. I never had the pleasure of meeting that chap; I just sent him a message of good luck. The day he opened I was already packed and left early in the morning. Actually it was a good many years later that we met. Nelson 'Bunch' Keys was in a show I had produced at the Piccadilly Theatre for Cis—*Folly to be Wise*—and in a curtain speech, having done all the thank-you-for-being-such-a-wonderful-audience stuff, Cis continued:

'Tonight I have the greatest pleasure of introducing that brilliant and delightful French star, who is adored as much in this country as he is in his own—'

She did not have to say any more and Maurice Chevalier stood up in the box and waved to them all. He had to stand there quite a time before he could speak and then he thanked the audience with that irresistible French accent.

He then went on to say, 'I don't know why people who impersonate me think I sing like this,' and he gave an impersonation of Nelson Keys impersonating Maurice Chevalier. The audience loved it. It was then that I met him for the first time when he came backstage. A delightful chap and well deserving the international impact he made by the sterling quality of his performance. A wonderful artiste.

11

Those last depressing weeks in Paris created an ecstatic build-up to my homecoming. Cis and I had a grand reunion and our mutual joy was a striking comment on the massive bond of friendship and affection that defied destruction. Dear old André came back into my life in a big way on my return from Paris. I was engaged immediately for his new revue. He agreed to my doing *Une tasse de thé*, which had succeeded so well in Paris. When I pointed out I was entitled to a royalty as the author he didn't think so. I wasn't surprised but it was worth trying. We compromised. He suggested a flat fee for the sketch and any writing that might be required for the revue. It was a question of how much. I said £250. He said £100. I took it. Great things can happen from small beginnings.

So much for the writing, but I soon found myself in the directing department, in a do-it-yourself situation, directing the stuff I had written and creating my own dance routines. This put the idea in my head of taking up directing seriously. But that was not to happen yet. Rehearsals started round about the end of June. As we had let our flat furnished during our Paris trip, and as our tenants were still in occupation, Cis and I rented a service flat next door to the Prince of Wales Theatre in Coventry Street which was very convenient. During the rehearsal period I never stopped working. Here was a great chance of getting back to where I had left off before joining the Army.

Guv's paternal love for his artistes was a great help, creating a happy atmosphere. The show was called *Bran Pie* and the cast included the Two Bobs, Odette Myrtle, Phyllis Titmus and Beatrice Lillie. I missed my dear friend Phyllis Monkman, I had hoped we would have been

98

playing together again, but unfortunately she wasn't available. And so, on an eventful evening in August, 1919, a very fashionable crowd of First Nighters gathered in the foyer of the Prince of Wales Theatre to take their places in the stalls and dress circle. When the show ended they re-entered the foyer and a large section made for the Savoy Grill. Their verdict immediately went out in all directions by some mysterious bush telegraph. The message was one of wild acclaim. *Bran Pie* was a hit, and as I had played a big part in its success I felt very gratified. It was thanks very largely to Guv' who had allowed me to include a lot of my own original stuff and he got as much pleasure out of making me happy as getting the stuff for nothing. Anyhow this was far better than suffering the tortuous methods of some unscrupulous business man.

But the fact that Guv' approved my stuff gave me confidence. There was nothing he didn't know about intimate revue. His successes could be largely ascribed to his love for originality. He would have no truck with the old hide-bound routine of musical shows. The innovation of intimate revue made the name of André Charlot famous in the twenties. The show after several months was still playing to packed business but Cis was still playing to packed business on the halls, which put her well ahead in the supremacy race although I was beginning to catch up.

Back in Portland Court again we were enjoying the amenities of our first home. Father was still in the Army and my poor mother, who had been ill for some time, was staying with us. I knew in my heart it could not be much longer, my only consolation was that she loved Cis like her own daughter and that I was successful on the stage again which gave her untold happiness. Sweet woman. So young when she died—only in her early forties.

Although I was not fortunate enough to be playing with Phyl Monkman, Cis and I were with her a lot and our friendship continued to flourish. The three of us had supper at Ciro's, the fashionable dining and dancing club, after the show on countless occasions and we also met at André's Sunday night parties at his house in St John's Wood. Eventually Cis was compelled to stop working as her figure was no longer suitable for an officer's uniform.

A few weeks at home in the flat and suddenly the doctor was called urgently. Cis and I both suffered. She was in the bedroom and I was in the dining room. Mercifully, it was not for long. They all said it's a beautiful baby. I agreed heartily, I don't know why, babies all look alike to me. I suppose because it was mine. She was named Pamela Rosemary—the latter was a combination of the two names of Cis's mother and my mother.

Having been given a great reception on her first entrance, in the subsequent weeks she began to cause anxiety. The question of weight —not too heavy but far too light and gradually getting lighter. Nourishment seemed impossible. Everything was tried. The doctors were baffled. It was serious; one morning Cis was in tears. There seemed to be no hope, then along came Mrs Kennedy and everything changed. Mrs Kennedy, what a splendid woman! What a character, entirely illiterate but unbeatable in the instinct and common sense bracket.

'Mellens Food,' she insisted, and would brook no argument. On the job she could be quite imperious. From that moment Pammie went straight ahead and never looked back. Mrs Kennedy was a children's nanny before the war and then joined up as an army nurse. She had been married to a sergeant who was killed on the Somme. She was slightly wounded herself which accounted for her pushing the pram round Regent's Park with a slight limp. Illiteracy in most people can be tedious and boring but with this lovable character it was sheer delight. And the more people laughed at her the happier she was.

We were all strolling along the front at Eastbourne one Sunday and looking at the Wish-Tower at the end of the promenade when she gave us an interesting piece of information: 'That there round thing on the top of the 'ill was because of Napoleon—one of them Marsh Mallow towers all along the coast, but that didn't stop him. They weren't no good but they pinched him at Waterloo, and the station now stands on the spot where he was captured.'

When answering the question on a military paper (What is your religion R.C. or Church of England) she wrote—Prostitute, She was a woman in a million, an expert at getting things wrong, always great fun to talk to. Eternally shall we be grateful to her—she saved Pammie's life.

Cis, having now given her finest performance, was very proud, just as I was, and I had to admit that put her further in the lead despite the fact I was catching up nicely, and within five weeks she was back at work. André was very keen to have her in one of his revues. He caught her act at the Victoria Palace and immediately became a fan, but Cis was tied up for months on the halls, so nothing could be arranged.

Bran Pie had now reached the summer of 1920. The mercurial Seymour Hicks, the charming light comedian with many musical successes to his name, rang me up one morning right out of the blue inviting me to lunch at the Garrick. As he was another of my favourites I accepted with alacrity. On arriving at the club I waited in the hall while the porter went off to find the great man. After a few seconds I heard a madly excited voice away in the distance approaching rapidly.

'My dear fellow, my dear chap, I do so want to meet you. I am delighted you were able to come.' His voice got louder and louder as he approached—the whole club must have heard him. And that was the kind of effervescent character he was, bubbling over like a bottle of champers when the cork flies up and hits the ceiling. I could not believe this was his normal way of greeting a guest; something special must be on his mind. In an access of enthusiasm he revealed some interesting information: I was the greatest thing that had hit London in years. The show he was working on would be an assured success if I played the part. It needed an engaging personality, a man who could sing and dance and give it that light touch which sends the audience into raptures of delight eight times a week at the Prince of Wales Theatre. The build-up went on mounting. 'With a man of your stature, it would be ideal casting.'

But, as I departed from the Garrick and escaped from the spell of this amazing man, the whole thing seemed suspect and my better self counselled caution. It all sounded too good to happen. Just settle for an entertaining lunch and let it go at that, I told myself. But it was difficult not to be excited.

Almost as quickly as I was able to descend from the clouds and restore my mental balance I received another letter—not from Seymour Hicks but from another famous actor, Cyril Maude, who was playing in *Lord Richard in the Pantry*, a big success at the Criterion. Would I consider playing his part for a month as he was taking a holiday? André was very understanding when I saw him and I felt if I pressed it I could persuade him to release me, especially as *Bran Pie* was due to finish in a few weeks.

Then to my great surprise I received a second phone call from the mercurial Seymour Hicks. Could we meet to settle a few details—dates and money, etc. Yes, we could and the dates fitted perfectly. Rehearsals would start soon after the suggested month at the Criterion. The money seemed excellent. When I got home I conferred with my financial adviser; she named a larger sum. 'Just insist and you'll get it.' And I thought, yes after the laudation and eulogy at the Garrick lunch, why not? So I had a go and pulled it off. Dear old André played ball, which enabled me to accept the generous offer made by the management on behalf of Cyril Maude, so I opened at the Criterion in July before going into rehearsal for *The Little Dutch Girl*.

Lord Richard was a very long part and I must have been a bit heavy and ponderous in the first act, the laughs were not coming as they should but, as often happens in real life, a chance remark from a humble person can save a serious situation. It came from an old stager —the property man. He whispered in my ear, 'Bustle it a bit, Guv'.') That phrase has stuck in my mind ever since. Fortunately, I had enough sense to grasp the full significance of the proffered advice. The rest of the show was quite different, it began to move. After a few nights I settled down and enjoyed every minute of it. But the wisdom of that kindly old property man saved me on the first night.

Rehearsals of *The Little Dutch Girl* started the end of October. It was something of a revelation to see a consummate artiste like the dynamic Hicks start bringing the show to life. Zeal and authority combined with the disarming Hicks' charm brought out the best in everyone. It was an excellent cast, headed by the attractive operatic star with the golden voice, Maggie Teyte.

The show was just about the last of the Continental importations and followed the familiar lines the public had grown accustomed to expect. Judging by the way it was acclaimed, they got what they wanted—a love story of royalty in Ruritania. The Prince and Princess sing the big stuff and take care of the romance, with a lesser pair singing and dancing to take care of the lighter stuff. I think the author must have been an ardent fan of Oliver Goldsmith because the lady of high rank assumes the role of a Dutch serving maid and stoops to conquer her reluctant lover. It was rather a lot to expect from a polished operatic star but she looked a picture and sang divinely.

I was one of the lesser pair taking care of the lighter stuff and singing funny duets with Cicely Debenham, a most engaging and talented soubrette. I had an ace of a part. I entered the magnificent palace, the home of my boss, the Royal Princess, in immaculate white tie and tails, covered in dust from head to foot, having walked some twenty miles from a state ball at the palatial country residence of His Royal Highness the Prince. No transport was available owing to a general strike. The song I sang was about being tired and fed up, followed by a slow lazy dance. Unfortunately, the dance routine I had worked on for several months, before all this happened, was a very energetic one and I could not possibly invent another in the time, but Hicks suggested a flunky should cross with a tray of champagne and I should take a drink without stopping the dance and instantly reviving, go straight into the fast routine. It worked. Good old Hicks.!

Laurie de Frece completed the Continental pattern by being the comedian, dressed in funny clothes, making the character unbelievable and being stuck with that make-up all the evening—an embarrassing handicap, I thought, but hide-bound tradition dies hard. Hicks was at his best with me. All kinds of gags and bits of comic business issued from that fertile brain. He would have been marvellous in my part had he been twenty years younger. Never since the early days at the Shaftesbury, with the Governor, had I received such inestimable direction; my part was getting funnier every day. Then suddenly it all stopped. Hicks disappeared. What happened I don't know. He was always unpredictable. All kinds of rumours flew around. Business in the city. Working on another show. I could only hope he had given us enough to get on with and would return later to give us a bit more. And that is exactly what happened.

One morning we were all on the stage running through the first act and at the end a voice in the darkness from the back of the stalls, a replica of the one from that famous meeting at the Garrick, shouted with tremendous enthusiasm, 'My dear boys and girls, well done, terrific. I'm proud of you—my congratulations. Break for lunch—back at 2.30.'

Not a word of explanation. Most of us were surprised that he showed up in the afternoon, but he was there on the dot and in three hours he had made some vast improvements. We sailed along happily for a whole four days and then the elusive Hicks disappeared again. As far as I was concerned he had improved my part so admirably that all I had to do was to play it. Consolidating what he had set and rehearsing meticulously could best be accomplished without his being present, provided his absence was not too prolonged.

It was all rather unorthodox, unethical perhaps, but interesting.

After a few days, as mysteriously as he had departed, he returned. Once again out of the darkness from the back of the stalls came the familiar sounds of enthusiasm and excitement. Seymour was so delighted with the scenes we had polished in his absence that we all received an invitation to lunch at the Café Royal. Diffusion of charm and abundance of wit, in addition to the sight of good food after a strenuous morning's rehearsal, put us all in the best of humour and our host was so amusing he had us all in fits of laughter. Lowering his voice for a moment and speaking confidentially with a 'don't-look-now' glint in his eye, he said, 'We must all appear very happy about the show. There's a rival manager sitting in the corner. Keep laughing everybody and spoil his lunch.'

That was my short but whirlwind encounter with the volatile Seymour Hicks, a great theatre personality in his day. And thanks to him, my father-in-law, Charlot, Cyril Maude and the kindly property man, I got a footing in the West End. His faith in *The Little Dutch Girl*, with his erratic but brilliant production, was amply vindicated.

12

My dear friend Phyl Monkman, in company with several fellow artistes, had created a novel and tremendously successful entertainment called *The Co-optimists* which become one of the great landmarks of the twenties. Phyllis Monkman, Betty Chester, Elsa Macfarlan, Davy Burnaby, Gilbert Childs, Melville Gideon and Stanley Holloway were the interesting personalities in the cast. For years the public flocked to see them. I was happy to see dear Phyl distinguishing herself again and Stanley, in addition to his excellent character sketches and singing, surprised the audience with first rate impersonations of some of his fellow artistes which never failed to please. They never failed to please me, including the one he did of me. I told him so. He presented my peculiarities in such a funny way. I pointed out that it was so beautifully done he must never discard it. Thank you, Stanley. It did me a power of good. Excellent publicity!

Marie Blanche, who was Cis's cousin, and Ivy St Helier were a very successful act on the halls and Marie asked us to join them in a similar show to *The Co-optimists* on the same co-operative basis. I thought it would be a good way to get Cis back on the West End stage so we had a go. The Marie Blanche–Ivy St Helier act was highly successful and Cis's act, especially the male impersonation, also scored, but even those coupled with the grace and charm of Phyllis Dare's singing and dancing and the duets I had with her, plus the excellence of the dry comedy of Eric Blore, did not make the show any better than what the critics said about it when we opened at the Royalty Theatre in Dean Street. We all played in the sketches, some of which went exceedingly well, but there was a slight difference between us

105

and the Co-optimists. They were a smash hit and we were a dismal failure.

In spite of making drastic alterations and obvious improvements we were sinking deeper and deeper into the red. Flying in the teeth of disaster, we struggled on bravely. Then, without warning, a fortuitous descent from the clouds and a golden angel stood in our midst in the guise of an all-in wrestling promoter, a complacent man with money, the sort of big spender it is always a pleasure to meet, and he thanked us for our magnanimous offer to let him in on our organisation. Changing the weak items and transferring to the Vaudeville, a theatre much better suited to our kind of show, failure turned into success. Cis and I, and the rest of the company, loved playing the Vaudeville— it was the old one, of course, before it was rebuilt, a small edition of the Haymarket. We did very good business and continued there until Charlot's tenancy started with his new revue *Pot Luck*, taking a big chance with yours truly as the star. So *Ring Up* had to finish and Cis went back on the halls.

Although we were both grateful to be earning a good living, it was not the happiest arrangement. If a young married couple possess a home of their own, it is not surprising a strong bias in favour of living there asserts itself. But for the time being Cis, as she spent the week living in provincial hotels, had to count the days through to Saturday night. Had she realised that the invaluable experience gained as a music hall star was creating a strong and solid foundation for any type of future entertainment she might have felt some reassurance, but a future crammed with the most appealing possibilities could not alleviate the pangs of loneliness and a longing to be with her baby daughter. Cis wanted to be at home, and that was exactly where I wanted her.

Something had to be done. It was up to me. It was only fair that the real struggle for supremacy must be fought out on the playing fields of the West End. I would have to create a new show of my own and put her in it. These were the thoughts that were rushing through my head. I was beginning to throw my weight about. *Pot Luck* was in high favour with the public and as this made four in a row my lofty thoughts about the future were born of success.

It does one good to think big occasionally, to aspire to great things. It may end in failure but at least one has had the fun of trying. What I had learnt since my initial undergraduate performance in *The Pearl Girl* eight years ago was, in my case, that success could only be achieved through assiduous application—which was no hardship because I loved every aspect of the job. Cis was a shining example of success through diligence. She had reached the heights—on the halls. Now for the West End. Had I been a good business man I could have exploited that manifest potential. But no, poor Cis. It could only be done the hard way.

When *Pot Luck* finished at the Vaudeville we were offered the provincial tour. I assumed indifference but inwardly I was bursting to accept; here was a golden opportunity to practise stage production. I made it a condition that I should reproduce the revue for the tour. This was agreed, and it was then that I started producing all my own shows. The man who made the offer was an agent called Paul Murray who eventually became a close friend. We opened at a small theatre in Boscombe outside Bournemouth and I think by the time we had finished the tour we must have played practically every town and city in Britain.

We engaged a young chap, rather small and attractive, called Bobby Howes to help with the comedy. He was part of a music hall act called The Gotham Quartet which he joined on leaving the army. We also engaged a very attractive girl called Patricia Malone to help with the singing, which she did with charm and efficiency. The rest of the people in the cast were most affable and friendly and as time went by we became one big family party. It was then that we realised that having a happy show was a matter of paramount importance.

To revel in the company of the engaging Pat Malone was sheer entertainment. Her sense of humour was delicious. Cis and I found her enchanting and so did the little comedian Bobby Howes. His involvement was irrevocable. One look at her and he was in the fields of Elysium. But in spite of the disparity between the two characters Pat Malone held similar romantic views. To watch the development of an affair is always a source of great interest. We were intrigued day by day. It only needed some little thing to clinch it and sure enough it occurred when the four of us were motoring through the Lake District one weekend.

We stopped off for lunch at a most inviting place, in a garden of summer flowers basking in the sunshine, radiant and refreshed after recent rain. The scent of roses and the sweet smell of a newly cut lawn sloping gently down to the lake made an idyllic scene for romance, and the birds in the surrounding laurel bushes and trees were doing their utmost to give a rousing and cordial welcome to the young lovers.

At the end of a most convivial lunch a suggestion that they should spend the afternoon alone was rejected out of hand by the tirelessly energetic Bobby who suggested tennis. So tennis it had to be—rather a big word for the kind of stuff we were doing; pat-ball would have been more appropriate. If occasionally the ball did get over the net it was seldom returned. Bobby decided to liven things up and after trying a couple of Wimbledon shots, which greatly disturbed the friendly birds high in the trees, he took a mighty swipe at a full volley which landed right in the eye of his beloved Pat. Consternation! Stricken with remorse, he would have willingly jumped into Lake Windermere, would it have been of any avail. However, beyond presenting his adored one with a beautiful black eye, nothing more disastrous followed; in fact it did the trick, the engagement was announced. After a short time the tour had a week out which enabled the young lovers to get married and spend a glorious two days' honeymoon in Paris, black eye and all.

From this humble beginning a most fascinating story started to unfold and, over a span of half a century, it produced a series of incredible and exciting events. There were events, sometimes humorous and sometimes tragic, in the course of his brilliant career; he was a most talented and endearing clown, adored by the crowds he attracted to the theatre. His success story was the stage; his private life was slightly different. Not easy to live with, I imagine—erratic and impulsive—but a splendid father to the two kids he adored as much as they adored him. Peter is now a well-known clarinettist and his sister an international star of outstanding talent. She has her mother's delicious humour and much of her father's stage technique. We are very happy, and indeed honoured, to be called Uncle Jack and Auntie Cis. It recalls so much of the laughter and fun we had together in the twenties and early thirties. It is not surprising we are great fans of Sally Ann Howes.

Pammie's radiant health testified to Nanny Kennedy's autocratic supervision. It solved the problem of what to do with her while we were away on tour. She could not have been in better hands. A lot of the time she stayed with her grandfather, the illustrious Robert, at his farm outside Hatfield and subsequently at Leighton Buzzard. The Governor, always quick to appreciate strength of character, took a fancy to Nanny at once. He had met his match. She could do no wrong and with Pammie now beginning to talk, he was happy to have his grand-daughter with him as he truly adored her.

There was a smart fashionable show running at the Little Theatre, John Street, just off the Strand, called *The Little Revue Starts at Nine*, for obvious reasons. Edward Laurillard was anxious to follow it with another and asked if we would be interested. I was seized with a mad desire to kiss him on both cheeks and shout 'Long Live Laurillard!' Would we be interested? He didn't realise what he was saying. When we discussed terms I had no difficulty in fixing myself as the director. Since *Bran Pie* in 1919 I had waited for this chance.

Being in sole charge of the creation of an entirely new West End revue should have been a daunting prospect. The responsibility it incurred never entered my head; all I could think of was the end product and success. The ideas I had worked on during the recent tour began to fall into place. There were sketches from different authors and dresses designed by Guy de Gerald and made by Worth. I took tremendous trouble in selecting the right girls for the chorus: the prettiest I could find, irrespective of dancing ability—*that* could always be improved. A pretty girl dancing is a joy to behold but twelve pretty girls dancing is a joy twelve times greater. I placed myself as an ordinary paying member of the public sitting in front and asked what such a man would want to see. An intriguing line-up of pretty girls with vital statistics, dressed in glamorous costumes, darting about the stage in a series of attractive movements. So with those requirements fulfilled, the show was more than half way there.

The Little Theatre, which regrettably no longer exists, contained the audience on one floor. It was like a large Embassy drawing room in Belgrave Square with a stage at one end. It was all very patrician and *beau monde*, so much so that poor nervous Laurillard feared the vulgarity of the Plumber's Honeymoon sketch and the broad comedy of an oratorio based on *Yes we have no bananas*. I tried to convince him that the élite were as good an audience as any for broad comedy. In fact these two items and the Undertaker's Party were the three items that certain members of the royal family, including H.R.H. Prince Edward, the then Prince of Wales, enjoyed to the full.

Cis and I, Pat Malone and Bobby Howes formed the nucleus of the cast, but we wanted a nice-looking young actor ro play the juvenile and some of the character parts. A chap called Harold French, who had made a success in *The Blue Lagoon*, applied for the job. He looked just the type, said Cis. Laurillard was uncertain. I hesitated. His agent was positive: 'He's great—just the man you're looking for. Don't miss this great opportunity.' The agent's recommendation was compelling. Had I made a wrong decision, Harold French might never have become one of our oldest and most valued friends. Agents have their uses.

So frequently the whirligig of time comes up with the unpredictable in a variety of ways. As I used to direct Harold French in the early twenties so *he* came to direct me in the late sixties, and jolly good he was too. Years of experience of stage and screen had shot him into the first flight. He inspired confidence. He knew only too well how an actor responds to encouragement. He was seldom wrong in his appraisal of a script, quick on story value and appreciative of good writing, being no mean writer himself, as shown in his autobiography *I Thought I Never Could*. But he certainly can. He recalls his strange experience of working under my direction with deliciously subtle humour—everything held up while 'the thinker' standing on the stage stares up at the flies seeking inspiration. I knew exactly what he was getting at, the crafty old so-and-so, but I have to admit he was right. I can only plead inexperience in extenuation of my regrettable habit of relying on the spur of the moment. One of my many failings.

The Little Revue had now fallen into shape except for one spot

in the second half between two broad comedy items—something in
sharp contrast was required with colour, charm, sweet music, girls
looking their prettiest. Ballet perhaps, though there'd have to be some
excuse for it, some twist. Suddenly the idea came. I was excited, I
shouted across the stage, 'Cis—come on—lunch.'

'Where are we going?'

'Just along the Strand—Simpsons.'

'Lovely, darling.'

She suddenly appeared looking very stylish, as she always does for
that matter, which is right for the public image, and for me too. I love
all the different outfits and I am reminded of the 'you-might-tell-me-
so-sometimes' and the 'a-woman-likes-to-know' complaints difficult
to dismiss without a tiny sting of compunction. Knowing where
you're wrong is the first step; the next is trying to put it right. I shall
go on trying.

Sitting in one of the cubicles we waited for the carver to come over
with his trolley. I looked at Cis admiringly.

'Nice that coat and skirt. Suits you well. I like the saucy hat.'

'Oh, thank you.' There was a note of surprise in her voice.

'I mean it.'

'What's cooking, chum?'

It was a sharp discerning mind I was up against. Foolishly, I told
her the idea; I should have waited until after lunch.

'Think of the impact—the surprise—Courtneidge the comedienne
dancing in a straight ballet.'

'Brilliant as some of your ideas may be, you've gone a little too far
this time, Hulbert. I'm not getting up on my toes again, thank you
very much. It's costing me a packet at the chiropodist each week as
it is.'

'Who mentioned toe dancing? Just a few balletic movements with
Harold. He'll be Little Boy Blue and you'll be Bluebell.'

'Now I *know* you're crackers.'

'Think of the beautiful costume you can wear—flowing—in a
delicate shade of blue.' Cis had stopped laughing, a slight change
came over her face.

'I'll ring Guy de Gerald now—he works very fast.'

We rehearsed for several weeks on this miniature ballet and it was all coming out according to plan. I explained to all those concerned that I had a surprise finish.

'What's that for heaven's sake?' Cis asked suspiciously.

'A secret I refuse to divulge,' I replied cryptically.

At the dress rehearsal we struggled to the end of the first half, fighting our way through the usual chaos. Just before the start of the second half they tried again to find out the secret. I was adamant.

'Then how do we finish?' they asked urgently.

'You'll see,' was all they got from me.

The curtain went up on the second half and with all the stoppings and restartings, props missing, lighting mistakes, etc., we eventually got to the Fairy Ballet. I must say it looked smashing. Guy de Gerald had really gone to town—a beautiful splash of colour—just the job for that moment in the show. I'd taken a lot of trouble with the dances and the lighting. The chorus worked beautifully. A scene of abundant charm. Then suddenly came the surprise finish.

A young chap in full evening dress—white tie, tails, button hole, the lot—started applauding loudly from the back of the stalls and in a familiar voice shouted, 'Jolly good—fine—very pretty—I'm glad I popped in—just been celebrating with the chumps—lots of fun— but this is much better.'

The spontaneous reaction of the company was perfect: a complete surprise and bewilderment, exactly what I wanted. If only I could keep it that way. I continued to interrupt.

'I'm not the kind of chap to say no to a good celebration and I don't suppose you are, Miss Courtneidge. I don't go for ballet as a rule but when you do it it's a joy—so funny, and Little Boy Blue looks funny without even dancing.'

When I saw Cis and Harold at the end of the rehearsal they were furious.

'What a dirty trick! And all that just to make fun of us.'

My attempts to pacify them were unavailing. We were opening the next night. It was too late to make a change. I implored them just to reproduce their spontaneous reaction, which they did beautifully. On the first night it was as good and realistic as at the dress rehearsal.

The audience loved it and the ballet got some good laughs. The whole item was a big success, like the rest of the show.

The critics were kind, except one, and he attacked Cis which upset her quite a lot. It was a definite hit below the belt. 'Gilding the Lillie' was the hurtful phrase he used suggesting that Cis was copying Bea Lillie. I was furious. It was a bitter disappointment after that long endurance of the rigours of the music hall. But the disappointment was short-lived. The resilient Courtneidge quickly found her form and as far as the Little Theatre audiences were concerned she had made it. Encouragement seldom fails to inspire confidence; one more show like this and she would be there permanently in the West End. Our planning was proving to be right.

When the excitement of the first night was over and a few adjustments made with a bit of tidying up, we were in the clear with a long run ahead. The warm cosy atmosphere of the Little Theatre created a pleasant feeling of togetherness and intimacy shared equally on both sides of the footlights, but it is quite a mistaken idea that the strain on the artists is lightened; on the contrary, it calls for hard concentration to obtain greater precision and at the same time greater restraint. Far from reducing the tempo if anything it is increased. The volume of voice remains unchanged and owing to the close proximity of the audience, greater care has to be shown in hiding these techniques. It's just as much hard work—but so enjoyable.

We had been running several weeks, when after the matinee one day the stage-door man came to my dressing room and said, 'There's a Mr Green would like to see you for a few minutes.' A Mr Green? Of all the millions of Greens, I couldn't at that moment recall one that I knew. In any case I didn't want to see anyone, I was looking forward to my customary forty winks between shows. The stage-door man added that Mr Green said I had known him at Cambridge.

'Good heavens, of course, show him in at once.'

Dear old Green and there he was looking exactly the same as when I sat in his study twenty years ago in Tree Court with him giving me notes and telling me the essential things to read. It was through his skilful coaching that I scraped through the history exam. I shook him warmly by the hand.

'Very delighted to see you again.'

He came to the point quickly, as he always did. 'I have a son . . .'

I knew all the rest and I had several stock phrases ready to hand out, but in this instance I didn't call on any of them. Good old Green, he went to the door and called out, 'This way.'

I was very interested to know what was about to come in. A pretty girl I could train and slip into the chorus, but what appeared was not so easy to deal with, a tall, thin, gangling youth in his late teens.

'This is my son Laurie,' his father said. 'If you could possibly give him some advice. . . .'

I hesitated but I knew where my moral obligations lay. I took a long look at 'My son Laurie' and gave it up. I was hard put to it to comment on the situation. I wanted to help, for old friend Green's sake, but what could I do. Yet there was something about this rather uncouth, callow young gentleman that I found appealing. I decided to put him on the pay roll for small parts and understudying. So we were all happy and as things turned out in the future I had every reason to be.

I formed a rehearsal club for the chorus open to any of them who cared to join and most of them did, including our newcomer Laurie and several who joined from outside. There was no entrance fee or annual subscription. We did scenes from modern plays and Shakespeare. I cannot claim that the idea was entirely philanthropic; while it gave the members a chance of showing any signs of hidden talent, it gave me a chance of practising in a field I was keen to explore. I made one discovery, a beautiful girl called Celia Glyn who showed great promise. I think she would have made a big name for herself but romance, quite naturally for such a lovely creature, was ever present and it eventually ended in marriage, which curtailed her career after a most promising start.

The club used to meet three or four times a week and we got through quite a lot of work. Laurie Green, playing scenes from *Hamlet*, was one of those rare things that only the fortunate few were privileged to witness. There have been many kinky interpretations by some of the avant garde chaps aiming at the intelligentsia. I once saw a young actor in the middle of the 'To be or not to be' soliloquy climb into a long chest, close the lid and finish the speech inside. I was the only one who laughed. Heads turned in my direction showing disgust at my contemptible lack of understanding. Laurie's interpretation, by no means kinky, was striking in its originality but I could never persuade myself that Shakespeare would have said, had he seen it, 'That is exactly what I meant.' Laurie was the first to agree when we started making a few alterations.

There can be little doubt that directing others, however unpromising they appear, is informative, helping one to improve one's own performance. Only too often one sees mistakes in others that one makes oneself and in trying to teach basic techniques one becomes aware of their great importance and tries to improve one's own. In short, the more you teach the more you learn. So it was fine for me. I only hope the kids in the chorus got something out of it.

The undeniable truth that two and two make four is an axiom we accept unreservedly. Those of us who have the turn of mind to exploit its significance to the full, in spite of donating large sums of money to the Inland Revenue, still remain rich enough to wallow in the lap of luxury. In my case I just accept the self-evident fact and leave it at that. It has never been my guiding precept. Had it been, I would today be worth a packet. But I have no regrets. Financial manipulation has no place in my make-up. An insatiable desire to create—the invention of musical shows and all that goes with it—has been my absorbing interest and that has been a full-time job, but no complaints, I love it. Cis and I have a wonderful arrangement: she deals with the business side, paying all the bills, keeping us on an even keel, and most efficiently running the home, leaving me to concentrate on new material for the future.

I had an uncle on the Stock Exchange who strongly advised us to invest our money in the City. We rejoiced in our good fortune at having a relative as our financial consultant. He was only too happy to assume the responsibility of investing our savings, so after defraying expenses we handed over our money each week. Cis, with her more practical mind, enquired from time to time how everything was going and the answer was most reassuring. We never asked for details, we left it entirely to him. A happy and convenient arrangement, all we had to do was to ring him up at his office at intervals, just to keep in touch.

Then followed a period when we lost contact. He never seemed to be in when we phoned. Being unable to receive the usual reassurance, we began to wonder. Cis, always realistic when occasion demands, insisted on immediate action and one morning I found myself sitting next to her in a taxi on the way to the City. We arrived at his office and walked straight in. The confrontation was so sudden and unexpected that my uncle's confusion and embarrassment confirmed our worst fears. What had happened I shall never know. Obviously the exploitation of the two and two principle had gone slightly awry. Manifestly, he had muffed it.

It didn't make us laugh much walking out of that office, having lost the lot. What do you do? Forget it and start again. That's the only way and be thankful you have the health and strength to do it. Cis, always at her best in a crisis, agreed. Her thoughts became crystal clear from then on. Straight into the bank went our joint savings and into my book of mistakes another item was entered. Cis and I shared the same philosophy, never bewail misfortune, just count our blessings, and get on with it. Easily said, but not so easily said at the time.

We were able to run long enough with *The Little Revue* to produce a second edition which extended the run for another six months. A talented young dancer called Phyl Arnold was my head girl. She drilled the chorus after I had set the routines and figured prominently in the rehearsal club, which enabled me to give her small parts in the revue. Such a nice girl and I noticed Harold French had come to the same conclusion.

As we were getting near the end of the run I started preparing an entirely new show. The cast was to include Betty Chester, Harold French, Charles Courtneidge, Cis's brother, Phyllis Bedells, one of our ace ballet dancers, Toots Pounds, of the famous Lorna and Toots Pounds Vaudeville act, Cis and myself. Unfortunately, Bobby Howes was not available. He had signed to go into *Six Cylinder Love* at the Garrick. The next time Bobby and I met was at the Prince of Wales Theatre in 1927. I was producing a musical comedy called *The Blue Train* for Philip Ridgway. Bobby was heading for stardom and this show clinched it—he was brilliant. That ravishing beauty, the adored pin-up girl of happy Edwardian days, Lily Elsie, was making a come-back.

When we first met, my mind reverted immediately to the past. In a flash I saw myself as a schoolboy standing at the back of the pit of Daly's Theatre, where the Warner Theatre now stands, transported with delight, watching Lily Elsie playing Sonia opposite Joe Coyne as Prince Danilo, a man whose personality captivated not only me but the whole of London. His delicate light comedy was superb and when Lily Elsie, towards the end of the show, made her final entrance the result was breathtaking. She stood there in a large velvet hat, a Gibson creation, and a long, tight-fitting dress of the period, a picture of ineffable beauty. Slowly descending the stairs, with surpassing elegance and grace, the sparkle in her eyes showed her determination to get her man. It was inevitable. Danilo succumbed. He was licked, and who wouldn't have been? To my great relief and joy he took her in his arms and they danced in ecstacy to the lilting strains of Franz Lehar's masterpiece. I came away dazzled, entranced. The impact was overwhelming. Here again was the magic of the theatre. Unforgettable.

Then, many years later, working with Lily Elsie at rehearsals proved she was as charming as she looked. Still a raving beauty but so nervous, so shy. My chief job was to give her confidence and dispel her innate modesty and diffidence. I had constantly to remind her of her triumph at Daly's and as she still looked as stunning as she did, nearly twenty years ago, now in a more mature way, the public still loved her. Bobby's big success in *The Blue Train* put me in great heart and I was proud to think that I had started him at the Little Theatre on a brilliant career as one of our best loved and most original comedians.

I found a title for the show I was working on: *By The Way*. No one liked it but *I* did as it was short and easy to remember. It seems in choosing a title more argument is created than in any other part of the show. Suggestions come from everywhere.

Returning to the early stages of *By The Way*, I had the good fortune of meeting Ronnie Jeans, a writer par excellence. With an economy of words and brilliant flashes of wit he charmed audiences in the West

End for a considerable number of years. Never was it necessary to suggest making alterations in his writing. Although sometimes on paper the material did not seem very funny when it was carefully rehearsed and properly played all those concerned were happy and indeed surprised beyond measure by the laughter that came from a delighted audience. All one had to do was to give it the Bernard Shaw treatment—speak the lines verbatim. To have a man of his ability working for us during the next ten years, when Cis and I played in a succession of revues, made us feel extremely fortunate since he was not only a writer of the highest degree but a true friend to us.

We opened the show in the provinces and then toured for some time to give me a chance to lick it into shape. Charles Courtneidge played the piano rather well so I fixed him in a short musical scene— a noisy party gradually reduced to silence by the strains of *Clair de Lune* from Charles at the piano. The listeners dropped into positions of rapt attention. As the lights dimmed Phyllis Bedells, dressed as a ballerina, gradually came into view through a transparent curtain at the back of the room and with her inimitable grace and charm expressed the feeling of the music.

I worked every day on the show making alterations, adjustments and improving some of the chorus work. By the time we got to Golders Green Hippodrome, our last date before going to the Apollo, I was most anxious to put in a sketch Ronnie Jeans had been working on. An idea I had given him at the beginning of rehearsals, he had been unable to finish it in time. I had forgotten all about it until this moment. The sketch was now complete but it had no finish. Ronnie had written it beautifully and much against his will I put it in. By the audience's reaction, Cis and I knew we had got the best thing in the show.

It was a simple idea—a form master dealing with a boy on detention. The form master was sitting at his desk on one side of the room and the boy at a small desk on the other. In the middle at the back was a large window through which came the unmistakable sounds of a cricket match. Cis played the fourteen-year-old boy and I played the irascible form master with venial relish after my hapless experience many years ago playing the schoolboy in real life. The match was the school playing the old boys and as the hostile form master was an old boy himself he was just as eager to see the match as his pupil. Every time the sound of applause came through the window the boy could not resist having a look but the master had to be content with an occasional surreptitious glance. In spite of the precarious position of the old boys, who were well behind with only two wickets in hand, Greek still had to be learnt. Some of the dialogue I still remember.

'Go on,' said the master, as a gloomy presentiment spread across his face.

'Then he marched ten parasangs.' More applause from outside. 'Only one more wicket to fall, sir.' The voice was high-pitched and jubilant.

'Get on with the translation,' snapped the form master.

'Then he marched ten parasangs.'

'We've done that. Oikoumenen?'

'I don't know, sir.'

'Then you ought to know.'

'Yes, sir.' Then through the window came the biggest applause of the afternoon.

'The old boys are all out, sir.'

And as that was as far as Ronnie had written we just blacked out. Ronnie was so elated by the way the sketch went that he got an inspiration and wrote the finish immediately.

The opening at the Apollo was great and so was the press. This time Cis got away with it. Our plans had finally crystallised—she was now firmly established in the West End. Apart from numerous other appearances in the revue, her schoolboy and the part she took in *Laughing Gas* were outstanding.

On looking back it is interesting to note how those ten arduous years on the halls had provided a solid rock foundation on which to build a career as a top performer in the West End. It cannot be denied that she had learnt the job the hard way. Certainly, stars are born not made, but they have got to be trained.

A big change had taken place in *The Hulbert–Courtneidge Saga*. Hulbert had lost his substantial lead. Courtneidge had reduced it to about a quarter of a length.

13

This was my first venture in management with Paul Murray. Cis and I had an ardent fan, a great big teddy bear of a man from the Yorkshire mills. He loved the theatre and he loved us to the extent of becoming a true and trusty friend. William Gaunt of Bradford, with a heart of gold, was only too happy to divert a fraction of his immense wealth to further our activities. He became our backer.

By the Way was successful enough to make Schubert want it for New York. William Gaunt backed it and Paul Murray fixed the deal. There were no jet planes in those days. Transport to America was a question of bobbing up and down on the Atlantic. The whole company crossed on the *Mauritania*. A most pleasant trip, calm most of the way. We were all very excited and as we approached New York and I got my first sight of the skyline I was duly impressed. Skyscrapers were an unfamiliar sight in those early days. But today how much more impressed one would be to see a skyline without them.

We stayed at the Algonquin on 44th Street. Schubert was anxious we should open off Broadway for a week to play ourselves in. Brooklyn was chosen for our clash with an American audience; it was by no means a happy week. A show designed originally for a London audience could hardly be expected to entertain a theatre largely filled with foreigners who had emigrated to the States from Europe and had become American citizens. Small wonder the cast were depressed, particularly as the week included Christmas Day on which we had two performances in spite of it being the greatest day of the year. The audience remained unresponsive.

I called a rehearsal after the matinee. This seemed harsh on such an

ll the years I've known you, I've never eaten sprouts!' A scene from
Swing with George de Warfaz on the right.

Cis and I playing a scene with Leonora Corbett.

Cis and I in happy mood without a care in the world.

Our dear friend Mickey Balcon—
he did all the worrying.

Sonnie Hale and myself outside the
studio in Neubarblesburg.

Myself as a dragoman, in the desert with Peggy Simpson, discussing a scene for *The Camels are Coming*—1937.

The magnificent Nanny Kennedy—'I've brought you a tin of suggestive biscuits.'

The proud father of the bride.

The roof garden at 43 Curzon Street.

The lovely farmhouse we bought to which we added the annex
on the right. On the bridge, Cis helps me drill my chorus of
ducks.

occasion but the discipline maintained during the long London run had to be continued, as I explained from the auditorium to the assembled company who were right downstage, just in front of the running tabs, which were then closed. I went on to deplore the complete lack of the customary sparkle in the performance that afternoon and said that I much regretted having to call a rehearsal. Then I shouted in my usual hectoring voice, 'Act I finale. Open the tabs.'

The stage manager sprang to it and the tabs opened revealing a large Christmas tree decorated with fairy lights and presents, which Cis had been working on secretly with only the stage manager in the know. For a moment the company were stunned. Then screams of delight and the girls started leaping about for joy. All this was not without a few tears—these kids were miles away from relatives and friends and emotion was difficult to conceal. Grown-ups became children again. With most of us the sight of a Christmas tree kindles a warmth in the deepest recesses of the human heart. A symbol of home and kindness among relatives and friends. The morale of the whole company returned higher than ever. Back to square one. Full of hope again for Broadway.

The following week we opened at the Gaiety Theatre, Times Square. The reception was surprisingly good. After Brooklyn anything would have seemed good. George Graves, that fine British comedian, was in the audience and I think he was responsible for some of the enthusiasm at the end. The undisputed success of the show was the one sketch a couple of American friends in London had advised us strongly to discard. They said cricket at a public school in England would have no interest for an American audience. I backed my judgement on the sheer humanity of the situation, a master and a schoolboy with completely opposing interests, both longing to go out and see the match. International, surely? The Americans got it at once.

The notices for the revue could hardly be described as good, they were shocking. One kind gentleman drew attention to the fact 'that it is a long swim back to Blighty'. Another described me as a caricature of Woodrow Wilson. The blatant hostility of the critics stimulated my determination to prove them wrong. I called the company together and told them my intentions. Their reaction was unanimous.

So we started work all over again. I made numerous adjustments, cutting and tightening, getting to the point quicker, which seemed to be essential with an American audience. The result produced a belated but welcome Christmas present; success in a matter of a few weeks.

New York was exciting, everything done at speed. It made me laugh. In the long run no one seemed to get there any quicker. I found it all a bit overpowering; not so Cis, she was if anything ahead of them, and they were fascinated by a British whirlwind. Cis was O.K. and exploited the fact to the full. Shop assistants would gather round the counter to hear her talk in her English accent. She spent most of her time on Fifth Avenue in the shops and seeing matinees of plays, while I was at matinees of musicals, watching the dancing or doing the same thing at stage shows in the big picture houses.

It was the time of the Charleston. Television was still in its infancy and American dancing in a big way had not yet appeared on the screen. So the dancing I saw for the first time in Broadway shows was quite staggering. There was so much I had to learn to catch up. Several shows I saw over and over again, trying to absorb some of the more effective steps. I began to form new routines for future chorus work and got steps together for a routine of my own. Tap Charleston was the vogue. I had to keep practising what I had collected as, unlike ballet, there is no way of getting these particular steps down on paper, which necessitated spending a lot of my spare time dancing, but it was exciting as the routines began to take shape. I showed a lot of the steps to my head girl, so that she could carry some of the burden. There were dancing instructors available with set routines for solo work. For many strenuous hours I sweated in practice clothes in various studios but there was a limit to my intake and she was getting a bit overloaded with new steps. New York and its environs had to wait for weekends before I could embark on a happy voyage of discovering Manhattan.

For the next show I decided to make a change from revue and go for a musical. I had an idea for a story. I discussed the policy with my partner Paul Murray and he agreed. The question of music cropped up. Cis and I had been to several parties and invariably a young composer and lyric writer would help the evening along by playing and singing some of their compositions. Louis Dryfus, the head of the famous music publishing company, whom we had met in London, explained that there were a number of these teams. Most of them were young chaps just out of college. Dryfus suggested we should meet some of them and listen to their stuff as we might find something for the new show. A date was arranged and it proved a very interesting morning. A couple of young chaps were outstanding and Paul and I both thought it would be a good bet to take them to London. They were only too pleased to make the trip. So Paul got to work and fixed a deal.

Things were going well. Lots of effective steps and ideas for the chorus in the new show were taking shape rapidly and *By the Way* was playing to full houses—a luxury we made the most of and enjoyed to the full. And very wise we were, because when anything really good turns up one starts wondering what's cooking round the corner and sure enough there it was—a beautiful heat wave, boiling hot. We were kaput, snookered. Theatres rapidly closed. One of the few places that seemed able to defy the heat and humidity was Chicago. So off to Chicago we went. The welcome we received was cordial and friendly. Visitors came in large numbers to the theatre and professed to like the 'Little English Revue'. So once again we went singing on our way, enjoying our first visit to a unique city which, in its setting, seemed to suggest a summer holiday at the seaside.

That great stretch of water, with a far distant horizon in front of which ships, large and small, plied back and forth, made it difficult to realise it was a lake of enormous proportions, sometimes calm as a mill pond, sometimes rougher than Brighton at its worst. We were lucky—we had splendid weather most of the time and not too hot. The only snag was that Chicago adopted the continental habit of playing on Sunday. This we found unfortunate. We were not happy losing that day of rest.

When we finished the season we had only one thought—a holiday. It seemed too good to contemplate. We had an inspiration. Instead of going straight home, why not cross the border and see a bit of Canada, then go back to New York and return on an Italian liner through the Mediterranean to Naples and see some of Italy. Being the height of summer it should be a lovely trip. Excellent as these thoughts were, it meant putting off the reunion of family and friends a few more weeks. Not an easy decision to make, we were both yearning to see Pammie again—we had been away nearly a year—but Canada was next door, so we steeled ourselves and said goodbye to the company who went back to New York and sailed to England. Then Cis and I, with Paul and Eileen, left for Canada, not by train but by car.

Vincent Lopez, with his band, joined the cast of *By the Way* at the Apollo in London just before we left for New York. A delightful man, he insisted on lending us his car for the Canadian trip. It had 'Vincent Lopez' written in large letters across the back—well, anyhow it was a kind thought. Seeing Niagara Falls was startling, particularly as it was possible to get right up to them on the Canadian side. But I had not yet seen the Victoria Falls in Rhodesia—they really knocked me for six. The whole journey in the car was most interesting and it was a joy to be able to relax and forget all about dancing and musical shows for a short spell.

We were both very tired but recovered by degrees especially when we sailed from New York on the *Conte Rosso*. The weather was friendly on crossing the Atlantic and through the Mediterranean and as we approached the shore through the Bay of Naples it was easy to admire the Italian flair for putting the right kind of house in the right colour in the right place and creating an ideal picture for the tourist's camera. And there was our first glimpse of Naples—Vesuvius looking majestic and angry, but not as angry as it once did when it buried the popular Roman seaside resort of Pompeii in ashes and volcanic dust. But the resentful mountain, far from achieving obliteration, has very kindly preserved the town for posterity. Some of the minute details of many of the buildings are still intact.

Thrilled by what we had seen of Italy for the first time, we could not resist Venice. As we crossed the Lagoon in a motor boat and cruised slowly down the Grand Canal, I could not make myself believe it was real. I was transported suddenly to the Middle Ages. A medieval city in all its pristine glory. The unspeakable beauty of the Venetian Byzantine architecture. All this magnificence standing on a number of tiny islands in the middle of the Lagoon. I can think of no better summer holiday than staying on the Lido, swimming and sun-bathing in the daytime, wandering about Venice after tea, and dinner at night in St Mark's Square. We have done it so many times since. Each visit seems more wonderful and exhilarating.

The crowds by the Doge's magnificent Palace and everywhere else are no worry to me. In fact, I love it. All those nationalities—all the different languages. Having a drink out in the open and watching them go by. Where are they from? What are they? What is their relationship to each other? Vastly interesting. I'm not the type that likes peace and quiet in the evening, I like to mix with the holiday-makers. London and Cambridge I have always cherished with the deepest affection, now I must add a third. May the glory of the ancient Venetian Empire long continue to dominate the placid waters of the Lagoon—from above, not below.

When we got back to England the show, of course, had to be called *Lido Lady* and the backcloth had to include the Campanile and the Doge's Palace. I had it displayed prominently despite the fact that the scene was a luxury hotel on the Lido and so they could only just vaguely be seen in the far distance. It was immaterial. I just had to have them there. *Lido Lady* was my first attempt at a book show and I was glad to have the opportunity of breaking fresh ground.

The latter part of the journey home via Paris to Victoria seemed to take hours with us thinking of Pammie all the time, trying to figure out what she would be like at five and a half. Would she be as pleased as we were? I recalled the time when my mum and dad returned from Poona, which had me dancing for joy. I had missed them so much. I told Cis but she was far from being reassured. A year is a hell of a long time to be away. Then, as we slowly drew into the station, the woman's instinct prevailed. In an instant all fears and doubts disappeared.

There on the platform was a large crowd of friends and relatives— Claudie and Enid, the Governor and in the middle the magnificent Mrs Kennedy holding Pammie's hand. In a split second Cis was on the platform. There was a mad rush and Pammie got there first. Mother and daughter were locked in each other's arms. Then the rest dived in. Chaos followed—Armistice day all over again. What a jubilant home-coming! I must say Pammie was the sweetest looking kid. I was swelling with paternal pride. Cis looked radiant. The occasional sign of depression I had noticed in America had completely disappeared. Skies were blue again. Not a cloud in sight.

The next job was to find a home. The tiny flat in which we had installed Pammie and Nanny Kennedy was too small to accommodate us all, so they stayed put and Mum and Dad checked in at the Savoy. We had got rid of our Portland Court flat and had stored the furniture before leaving for New York. Back in London again, we started to search for a small house in Mayfair.

My two American college boys did some splendid work, especially with *Atlantic Blues*, sung delightfully by Phyllis Dare, who was the leading lady I engaged to carry the love interest, and *Here in My Arms* which I sang with her. I enjoyed producing *Atlantic Blues*. I made the chorus represent the waves, sometimes rough, sometimes smooth, undulating, rolling and anything I could think of that waves do. Phyllis was a beautiful young woman and brought charm and elegance to the show in contrast to the comedy. Cis's part needed some attention in the writing so we asked Ronnie Jeans to step in and he improved it considerably. In the story she was paired off with Harold French and they sang two duets. Harold now seemed to be on our permanent staff and very pleased we were to have him too. The friendship was beginning to flourish which was just as well because he was playing the amateur light-weight boxing champion and the high spot in the second act was the big fight between the two of us. Here was a chance to get his own back for all the long hours I had kept him rehearsing in the past. A bit tricky, but we treated each other with the greatest respect, in the ring and out.

Lido Lady opened at the Gaiety in December, 1926. Standing at the corner of the Aldwych and the Strand opposite Waterloo Bridge, the Gaiety was the successor to the famous theatre of that name which had entertained generations of playgoers with the world-famous comic operas and musical comedies. After a long and successful run, we eventually came off and within a few years that beautiful theatre was demolished to make way for commercial expansion. Deplorable! Another West End landmark had gone for ever.

At Christmas we took a furnished flat in Devonshire Street where we had a small party on Christmas Day. It was during the house-hunting period that Cis lost her sister Rosaline who died in childbirth. A tragic loss—she was so pretty, so young, barely twenty-three, and an actress of great promise. She had married that lovable character Peter Haddon, whom I adored. Her death was a great blow to us all. The baby lived and has now become a very charming lady, another Rosaline.

Cis and I eventually found a beautiful little Georgian house in Curzon Street, number 43, and the estate agent said its occupant, Dr Dearden, might sell. We made an offer; it was turned down flat. Cis said, 'Go and see him yourself.' I knew she felt it was a lost cause sending me of all people, but it was such a charming little house. I made an appointment. When I arrived I was shown into his study. A for-midable figure with a grim determined face rose to meet me. With cold politeness he invited me to draw up a chair and we sat facing each other. An embarrassing silence was broken by his saying, 'And what do you want to see me about?' I was completely put out of countenance by his callous indifference.

'If it's about the house it's entirely in the hands of the estate agents. As you came in I had just put down the phone. A new offer from an American has just been made which is nearly twice the amount you have suggested through the agents, so I'm afraid you are wasting your time. I'm sorry.' He got up from the chair.

'Not at all.' We shook hands. 'Nice meeting you,' I said in a voice sounding like I couldn't care less. I was practically out through the door when my eye caught something on the wall. I was stopped in my tracks. I gazed at it incredulously. A bolt from the blue, the latter being the operative word. Suddenly the whole scene changed. I was an undergraduate again.

'When were you up?' Before he could reply I was reading the gold lettering on the blade. Bumped L.M.B.C. and Pembroke. Went head of the river 1925.

'That's a grand thing to have. I've got one too. Fourth Division bottom of the river. Who cares? It's a bit of Cambridge. This is great news. Let's have lunch. No refusals. You're coming.'

Three years a galley slave on the Cam. I didn't get a blue but I got 43 Curzon Street.

When the time came for our two young American friends to return home, I thanked them heartily for their excellent contributions to *Lido Lady*, expressing the genuine pleasure I had had in working with two such amiable chaps and wished them the best of luck when they got back to America. It was one of the maddest things I ever did. I'm certain they would have worked with me on future shows had I offered them a contract. I should have signed them up then and there and I'm sure they would have played ball. Once again the two and two make four dictum eluded me. Within a matter of a few years they had revolutionised the world of musical comedy.

Just as I had failed in the past to recognise the genius of Noël Coward I was entirely unaware I was working with one of America's greatest composers and one of her best lyric writers. Having done some splendid work, poor Larry Hart, that dynamic little enthusiast, died very young and Oscar Hammerstein succeeded him. So the team changed from Rodgers and Hart to Rodgers and Hammerstein. What they have given to the stage is beyond price.

I suppose the main reason for my winning the British Championship for long arduous rehearsing was my unremitting search for new ideas, or more likely taking old ideas and trying to present them in a new way. Exciting for *me* but for the unfortunate cast, maddening. Many a time when I would be struggling to get a finish to the big musical numbers with all the principals on the stage. Inspiration, often so obstinate, is almost at hand. Only another five minutes. Then Cis whispers in my ear. I look at my watch.

'Break for lunch. Take an hour. That'll be two forty-five here on the stage.'

The company rush out to try and retrieve their lunch dates, smiling at Cis with a tacit thank you as they make for the stage door. The countless times she has covered up for me, helping me in a diversity of ways, unacknowledgeable at the time, but gradually I began to catch on, and a sense of obligation and gratitude has created feelings of unease and compunction. Originality does demand more time however carefully the prefabricated idea is fashioned; it has to be lowered into position, and final adjustments made before taking its permanent place in the construction of the show. Invariably that takes a long time.

During the run of *Lido Lady* I thought a revue with a theme might strike a new note—a slender thread, a *raison d'être* for a new combination of musical numbers and sketches. I wanted the element of surprise as the curtain rose, something apart from the familiar. I wanted the symbolism of fun and laughter—the court jester, the proverbial clown perhaps? Yes, of course. That was it. I'd got it. In a moment it all fell together. I saw the symbolic figure gradually coming into view as the soft light of dawn began to reveal the land of make-believe and all the little clowns asleep on the enchanted bank in the woods.

I engaged a man with a fine voice and a tall imposing figure, and as he walked towards the audience he explained in song he was in charge of the little clowns sleeping on the bank in the woods. He was about to wake them up and put them through their paces. This became the theme of the show, linking the musical items and sketches. The clowns, including the principals, did their stuff. I saw it all happening so clearly in my mind that in spite of much raising of eyebrows and adverse criticism I had no hesitation in going ahead.

It was what I was always looking for, the magic of the theatre. I was back in the stalls, five years old, sitting next to my father. The curtain went up and there it was all over again—sheer magic. Here was an idea that belonged to the theatre and could only be done in a theatre. All very childish perhaps but aren't most of us children at heart though we don't always admit it? I was very happy with the idea. Optimism is highly commendable in our job but it needs to be tempered with realism. I was quite satisfied on that point.

The testing ground was Golders Green Hippodrome. Breaking the tradition of never opening too near the West End, we got just the audience we wanted. They applauded the clown when he entered, the girls when they awoke on the enchanted bank and the principals as they entered in the same gay clown costumes, dancing with the chorus in a fast moving mass of colours. Then the whole company dispersed, discarding their clown make-up and performed the rest of the show in the normal way in clothes suitable for each item, but returning in the clown make-up at the end to go back to sleep on the enchanted bank in the woods.

The success at Golders Green augured well for the West End and at the Adelphi in December, 1927, to the great joy of all concerned, *Clowns in Clover* did it again. I was naturally delighted because a new form of musical had been born.

A great asset to the show was June, a lady of surpassing beauty; as a stage artist she was enchanting. We had a great time together. We played a scene and sang a duet finishing with a dance. With June as a partner you were home and dried before you even started. She looked a million dollars. Not surprising I did the craziest things. We played the scene outside a petrol station. She would enter in an open baby Austin with engine trouble. Immediately I offer my services but being hopelessly distracted by the irresistible charm of June who sits waiting in the car looking divine, I rush around like a mad thing—lifting the bonnet, shutting it, cranking the starting handle, my eyes all the time never leaving her face, sitting next to her, getting out—all very difficult, the car being so tiny—climbing over the back and sitting next to her again pretending to inspect the controls. This is the kind of part to play—a comedy love scene with a beautiful girl, and every young man in the audience, if he is worth his salt, will be wishing he was up there on the stage doing it himself. The scene got great laughs, I enjoyed playing it enormously.

I got an American dance producer to arrange the dance for our duet, as I wanted to get the best obtainable. Larry Ceballas was the chap and he arranged a cracking routine. I was very lucky to get him as I had so much dancing to arrange for the chorus and ensembles. Admittedly I was able to call on a lot of the stuff I had collected in New York but it all took time arranging the routines, teaching the girls and drilling them. I must say I was very proud of my girls; they worked desperately hard, looked lovely and became a very important part of the show.

Cis took advantage of some excellent material and got every ounce out of it. Amongst other items she had one of the funniest sketches I have ever had anything to do with: *The Great White Sale*, commonly known as *Double Damask*. Rehearsing it was a nightmare. We were at the Adelphi. I was in the stalls and I had the company on the stage.

'I only want those in *Double Damask*—Laurie Green, Bobbie Comber, and Cis. June, you're away for your fitting, see you this afternoon at 2.30. Phyl, you can take the girls to—Laurie, what's the address of the rehearsal rooms?' Laurie, who had now become a very efficient stage manager, starts to explain. 'Don't tell me, tell Phyl. Better break the girls now. Have an early lunch and then on to wherever it is.'

'What time shall we rehearse?' Phyl asks.

'Well, take an hour for lunch, better say an hour and a quarter by the time you've got served. Then take half an hour to get to wherever it is. O.K.? Right.'

Having got that under way, I was anxious to start rehearsing.

'Now. Come on please. *Double Damask*.'

Laurie pops his head round the proscenium. 'Strand Electric on the phone. Do you still want perches fitted up downstage in "Two"?'

'Yes, of course. Six lamps on each side. Now please can we start?'

Lauire relays the message to the A.S.M., who enters from the prompt corner looking puzzled.

'Can I just ask—'

'No, you can't,' I say, shutting him up. '*Double Damask* please. Cis darling, let's go from where the assistant, that's you, Laurie, says "Is there anything further, madam?". And don't forget, darling, you have already asked him about your large purchase of table cloths and linen which establishes your reason for wanting dinner napkins. Right, let's go.'

'Is there anything further, Madam?' inquires Laurie as the assistant.

Cis, with her superb sense of timing, looks at him, pauses for a split second and says with the specious refinement of a class-conscious suburbanite, 'Yes, there is. I want two duzzle dummer damask dinner napkins.' Cis spoke the line as if it were the most natural thing in the world to ask for.

'I beg your pardon, madam.' Laurie looks slightly disconcerted but hides it, or should have done. He goes for a comic reaction and kills it dead. I have to tell him.

'Laurie, don't make it funny. Leave it to the author. He's done a splendid job, just say the line.' I was getting a little tetchy. 'Let's get on. Come to the shop-walker's entrance. Call Bobbie Comber. Oh you're there, good. Right, Bobbie, your first line and make him very polite and suave, O.K.? Let's go.'

'Allow me to help you, madam. You require?'

'I want two dazzen dabble dummusk dinner napkins.'

'Hold it a minute,' I shouted from the stalls. Bobbie's reaction was even bigger than Laurie's. 'No, no, Bobbie, much too broad. You're a grand character comic, but don't try for laughs. Keep it dead natural and the laughs will come. Forget this is a revue sketch. Play it for real. You're in the linen department at Selfridges. Go on, Cis.'

'I want two dazzen—'

'You mean two dizzen, madam. In other words, a double dozen.'

'Yes, that's it, a duzzle dubban of dabble dummusk danner nipkins.'

'Fine. Keep it dead natural, Bobbie. It's coming over beautifully. Just those last two words, Cis. darling. We must say exactly what Dion Titheridge has written.'

'You mean danner nipkins?'

'Yes, it should be nipper dankins.'

'No, danner nipkins.' Cis was adamant. 'It took me three weeks to learn. Too late to change now.'

'Darling,' I protested, 'it only means changing dupple dipkins—'

'Dupple dipkins?' Cis was furious. 'Where's that come from? Dion never wrote that.' She looked at me defiantly.

'You've got yourself muddled and I'm not surprised. Sorry, but I'm sticking to danner nipkins.'

I had to insist. 'Nipper dankins,' I shouted.

'Now let's keep calm. It's no good getting heated.'

'What I am saying is, it sounds funnier when you say the whole sentence.' I was finding it hard to cool off. I shouted, 'I want two dazzle dimmick—'

Cis shouted louder. 'You mean two dizzle dammick—'

'No, no,' I yelled. 'I want two dizzle dammick—'

'Excuse me, sir,' the A.S.M. interrupted. 'Strand Electric on the phone again. They were not quite clear what you want.'

That did it. I saw red.

'Two duzzle dibble dummusk bloody nipper dankins,' I exploded. 'And that's that.'

We toured all the big cities: Manchester, Liverpool, Leeds, Newcastle, Birmingham, Edinburgh, Glasgow. The stimulating effect of success intensified the usual procedure of working every day. The chorus were drilled a little more vigorously and the principals were rehearsed in dialogue cuts and adjustments a little more assiduously. If the audience reception had been unfavourable, we should have worked harder still. My poor boys and girls were in the soup either way. I told them I could give no assurance of success but I guaranteed to create conditions most favourable for bringing home the bacon.

By the time we got to the Adelphi we were slick and polished. If a West End audience like a show they are the warmest and most appreciative in the world. They liked this one. So for many happy months none of us had to worry about 'what do we do next?' Irene Russell, a charming girl, added to the decor with her captivating presence and her talent was distinctive. As for Cis, the show might have been made for her. In point of fact it was to a large extent. The result was that *The Hulbert–Courtneidge Saga* was getting exciting; we were now neck and neck. And so, neck and neck, two clowns happily entered the thirties in search of fresh clover.

14

Cis has two engrossing hobbies off the stage—people and the home. As she is endowed with that special gift of making people like her, we possess a great number of delightful friends and a home, which in spite of always being immaculate, is cosy and comfortable. The adoption of these two hobbies means an even greater expenditure of energy than she displays on the stage. Result, I have the perfect home and a large circle of excellent friends, to whom I am devoted, without having lifted a finger to bring it about. Quite unashamedly and blatantly I disclaim all responsibility on both counts. Leave it to the little woman—she works wonders.

Number 43 Curzon Street exceeded all expectations. A perfect antique, inside and out. Early Georgian, I would think. Probably one of the oldest in the street and just right for the four of us. It was a great joy having Pammie with us again; it completed the home. Cis, of course, never stopped for a second. The furniture had to be antique. She was everywhere. She bought *some*, but to do it all would take time. Meanwhile, she had to use the stuff we had stored, and with new carpets and curtains in no time at all she made the place look charming.

The dining room faced the front and the drawing room, which faced the back, had French windows opening on to a flat roof in Shepherd Market, a most unique and unexpected spot suddenly to stumble across in the heart of Mayfair. It was screaming for a roof garden and that was where I took over. The first job was to erect a low fence to screen us from the pedestrians in the market. As an excuse for a miniature garden I erected a small railway running round the whole area. The press heard about it and the publicity suggested my hobby was model trains. I had no idea there were so many people in the country interested in this form of amusement. I had shoals of letters from people asking for further information. It seemed I was regarded as an expert on the subject.

This beastly railway got me into trouble with the authorities, who sent me an official letter ordering me to take it all down immediately which, of course, meant losing the garden. I saw one official after another. They were all adamant. Eventually I found one who suggested a solution. A qualified architect was to design a roof garden and submit a plan to the local council and if it were passed the roof garden could be built. After an interminable delay I received the architect's plan which was simply a technical blue print of my existing lay-out. The plan was passed by the authorities and the garden remained exactly as I had built it. This was my first encounter with bureaucracy. How crazy can you get!

Cis and I loved the festive season and our first big Christmas party at number 43 started a tradition that has lasted through the years. Father Christmas decided to put us permanently on his visiting list and I arranged for him to make his debut in the much-discussed garden outside the French windows of our drawing room. True to his word he showed up bang on time. I got all the necessary lamps and equipment from the Strand Electric and the property man from the theatre knocked up a small ground row of a wall and chimney pots.

His opening night with the Hulberts had a lyrical quality: suddenly appearing on a musical crescendo from a recording coming from the bedroom window—the flowing white beard—the familiar red hood and robe—picked up by the coloured spotlights above the French windows—exciting—emotional—the symbol of goodwill and good cheer now a reality—living—talking—distributing presents from his sack. Most appealing and moving, so I was told. Unfortunately I didn't see it, being otherwise engaged—I had so much to do.

Finally Father Christmas disappeared behind the wall and chimney pots as the music swelled to a climax, leaving us with a promise to return the following year. And year after year the fairy grotto had to be created with all the paraphernalia of the lighting. But it was worth all the trouble, the kids loved it so much—or was it the grown-ups?

I think they loved it even more. On Christmas night the kids had to be wakened and dressed ready to meet him as he always arrived after dinner, about eleven. With the greatest excitement they awaited his arrival. Some were even frightened, the magic was too much for them. Others who had doubts were baffled by the realism of the appearance but were only too eager to open the presents he had brought in his sack now waiting for them in the drawing room. Great joy for the kids, and even greater for those grown-ups who will allow themselves to escape for a brief spell from the interminable complications of modern life.

He returned continually year after year until the late sixties when I received a letter from him saying that as all the children had now grown up, with great regret he had removed our names from his visiting list but he would be with us in spirit just the same. And in all those years we never met. But the long line of big Christmas parties remains intact and dinner terminates with a prepared funny speech from the host and the humour seems to suggest that a little more work on it would have been an advantage. The little woman just talks and it's great stuff.

One of the sad aspects of gradually attaining the rank of a senior citizen apart from free bus rides and free admission to most places of historical interest, is noticing how the original cast of the Christmas party slowly changes from year to year and how new friends are called in to replace those who have left permanently.

I think our best-ever Christmas party was when it was broadcast by the BBC and that adroit and articulate commentator Brian Johnson was in charge. In attempting to recall this particular incident we must leave 1930 and leap forward many years, just for the time being.

When the matter was first mooted Cis erupted 'Madness—impossible—it will be utter chaos.' I see now what she meant. I thought it was a lost cause. Then suddenly a capricious mood caused a complete *volte-face*. She agreed. As it was now nearly forty years since Father Christmas had first called on us, the show had become a major production which she loved as much as I did. Knowing how keen I was to accept the BBC's offer, she agreed for my sake, as always.

We were living in 15 South Audley Street. The roof was much

bigger, on two levels, one just outside the dining room windows and the other further back, six feet higher. I constructed a woodland glade with a little bridge over a stream, using branches of laurel and fir trees that I had brought up from the country. The timber for the bridge and the rostrums forming a sloping bank I got from a timber merchant in Paddington. Rough carpentry and constructing things were hobbies of mine. I obtained twelve spot lamps, six of which I had made myself, all connected to a switch board and dimmers on the wall in the passage. On the wall outside, above the dining room windows, each spot lamp, from a coign of vantage, lit various parts of the scene. It was a fully equipped stage.

I had been hard at it for several weeks and Christmas was only four days away. I was outside working at pressure. It was cold and raining hard. One of the dining room windows opened and a rather pleading voice said, 'I do think you ought to come in.'

'I'm all right, darling. I've got three sweaters on. I must get the job finished.'

'You know what it is with your voice. Catch cold and you've had it. Then we're all in the soup.'

'I'm watching it, darling, really—'

'That's exactly what you're not doing. Do be sensible and come in.'

'Darling, I can't possibly stop—'

The window shut rather noisily. The incessant rain was making the job much more difficult. My hands being cold with the wet I had difficulty holding the tools. I struggled on, making very slow progress. The window opened again. The voice was loud and compelling.

'I insist you come in at once.'

'But, darling—'

'No buts. I insist. You've got to play tonight. No arguments. Come in at once and straight into a hot bath.'

And that is the only kind of nagging I ever get from Cis—the mother scolding a stubborn child type—quite innocuous, in fact rather sweet. Having had a bath and got myself dressed, I sat down to lunch with her. The mothering instinct persisted.

'Darling, don't you think you're rather overdoing it. I mean you never stop. You'll tire yourself out—'

It made me think, I must be mad. All that time and work. But that was just me—flat out or nothing. In this case it served a double purpose. I was able to indulge my passion for stage lighting, experimenting with different combinations of colours and varying intensities of light. And as a consequence, in the summer evenings we could sit outside taking coffee after dinner with our friends, among the geraniums and pelargoniums on the roof garden with our very own Blackpool illuminations.

Those last few days of preparation were hectic. I think about thirty people were to sit down to dinner. Cis was in her element. The bigger the party the more she enjoyed it, never stopping for an instant. I suddenly got the same feeling about her as she had had when I was so ruthlessly called in out of the rain. In retaliation I ventured a suggestion.

'Darling, don't you think you ought to put your feet up for half an hour?'

'This is no time for cracking gags. You don't seem to understand what has to be done. Just take a look at this dining room—a shambles.' Then followed a blistering attack on outside broadcasting. 'A jungle —cables everywhere—sound equipment—technicians. It's impossible to move and we're trying to set the table. Do you realise in a matter of hours we shall be sitting there enjoying ourselves! How am I going to do it in the time? All the cutlery, the chairs, cards with the names put in the right places—'

'Now take it easy, darling. It'll sort itself out.'

'Thanks, pal, for the good news. And when do I decorate the table, if it's not a rude answer? The silver Christmas tree, the fairy lights, the crackers, the sweets, the fruit, the lot. All festooned with streamers. Will you please tell me that? This BBC lark is making it impossible. I knew it would be chaos.'

These occasional outbursts were a good sign. They meant she had got the whole thing sewn up. When the great moment arrived for the Christmas dinner, all the sound equipment, cables, microphones, etc., were covered up and hidden, ready to be rushed into position the moment dinner was over. It all went perfectly. When we got to the port, the pulling crackers and throwing streamers stage, Cis, in complete control, stood up and in the silence which followed said, 'This party is being broadcast as you all know and we have to stick to a time-table—to the very second. Everybody upstairs, please. We will then call you back here into this room to meet Father Christmas.'

She had them all out at once. I had slipped away unnoticed a little earlier to make the final preparations outside. When the guests were brought down from upstairs and reassembled in the dining room, Cis continued giving orders.

'Everybody crowd round the two windows which we'll open at the last minute. Girls in the chairs and gents at the back. You must all bunch close together.'

I had fitted up a small signal light and gave Cis the all clear from outside. Cis picked up the cue.

'Father Christmas has just signalled he is on his way. Open the window and not a sound, please, from anyone.'

While the lights were beginning to reveal the scene, faintly the strains of *Good King Wenceslas* could just be heard, gradually becoming louder as the light grew stronger. The colour mixing on the laurel leaves and the fir branches produced the most unusual and beautiful effects, artificial but arresting. The music changed to a dramatic move-ment in the overture of *Reinzi* and as it was reaching the climax a light picked up a chimney pot just visible through the woods, the climax came and Father Christmas appeared through the top of the chimney. It was most dramatic and very moving, according to Cis. Leaving the chimney he crossed the bridge and walking down the grass bank towards the audience, saying he had brought presents for all his dear children upstairs. He then delivered his Christmas message, in which he referred to nearly every member of the party. And then, wishing everyone joy and good cheer, the dear old boy returned over the bridge to great applause and shouts of Happy Christmas from the guests in the dining room. Admittedly, it was all very childish, all very simple stuff, but I am convinced most of us love it, a fleeting return to childhood and the happy land of make-believe.

Cis and I once played pantomine, *Mother Goose*, at Wimbledon. Dear Peter Haddon was running the theatre and Noël Coward and Binkie Beaumont came down from town to see it. They came round after the show. They were exhilarated and excited like a couple of happy school kids. They loved pantomine and were genuinely enthralled by it. I love it myself. To see it, not to play it. I've had my fun.

The result of the broadcast was exciting. Brian did one of his characteristic commentaries, giving a vivid picture of the whole proceedings from one of the rooms upstairs on a separate mike. Letters of appreciation came in from all over the country. There was only one dissentient, a clergyman in the Midlands. 'Why do you glorify the pagan side and completely ignore the spiritual?' was the theme of his letter. Dear dear, how sad to think he had missed the point of the whole thing so completely. If Father Christmas had replied he would have made it very clear. I feel sure he would have said:

'Christmas Day is the greatest day of the year. It is one big birthday party being celebrated all over the world and it's my job to help everyone rejoice and make merry. I would like to take this opportunity of wishing you a merry Christmas next year.'

With *Clowns in Clover* swinging along merrily at the Adelphi, we wasted no time in celebrating our good fortune which was easy to do in those days. London in the thirties was ideal, enjoyable and great fun. It had quality and refinement; good manners were still in vogue and held in high esteem. The permissive age had not yet mysteriously wormed its way into society to eradicate the saving grace of good taste. Today anything goes. Nudity, vulgarity—do what you like, dress how you like, behave how you like—so tough on the younger generation. They've never seen the other side of the picture.

Life was smoother and quieter. There was less noise. There was no mad rush. Dance bands played softly, making conversation possible. The volume of sound at musicals was comfortable and by no means deafening. But it seems with the mounting pressure of today life has to be played double *forte* and the youngsters align themselves with this fallacy, never having experienced the ingratiating charm of *pianissimo*. Louder and louder, that's how they want their music and that's how they get it. Sad to think of what they have missed.

Each night that Cis and I walked on to the Adelphi stage it was like being at a party. The white shirt fronts of the men and the bare shoulders of the ladies set the scene. One felt, this is a party—come on, let's have fun. The whole atmosphere was gay and glamorous. The audience had come to enjoy a night out.

Stage life differs in most ways from other jobs. We start work when everyone else has finished. At the end of the show, by the time the make-up has been removed, we get out to a restaurant and sit down to the main meal of the day, when the majority of the public are in the land of nod. The amount of energy expended in trying to entertain an audience creates a prodigious appetite. Invariably, during the last act I am figuring out what I am going to have for the main course. Knowing exactly where to go to satisfy this basic demand presented no problems then. Most of the fashionable restaurants specialised in late night entertainment, which meant white tie and tails, but this was no deterrent; high society contributed gleefully to the gaiety of London. Shows started later and by the time Cis and I were all dressed up and ready to go it was usually after midnight when we set off from the theatre. Mostly we were together, but some nights she would be taken out by one of her boyfriends and I would take out one of the girls in the show.

We were very fond of the Savoy. Carol Gibbons was a pleasant fellow to meet and we enjoyed dancing to his band. Several times a week we had supper there. Some nights it was the Café de Paris in Coventry Street, good food and a good cabaret. Ciro's just behind Garrick Street was one of the bright spots we used a lot together with the Yacht Club Boys and Bee Lillie, whom I adored. It has wonderful memories for us—Phyl Monkman, Cis and I—from way back in the Charlot days. It was the time when our big friendship started. So long ago now but such happy memories never fade.

When I took out a girlfriend it was usually the Berkeley, one of the nicest and most exclusive places in the West End with a band that made you want to dance. A great place for the young deb and her beau. A high spot for the Bright Young Things. But I think Cis and I enjoyed the Savoy the most. It had such a happy atmosphere and was so convenient for the Adelphi. Another spot we used frequently was the Kit Kat at the top of The Haymarket. You could get in there with a black tie and even without one, provided you sat on the balcony. That engaging personality Sophie Tucker, another of my favourites, often appeared there. How many times I have enjoyed her performance on the Kit Kat floor when she was an outstanding success in what was then one of the gay high spots of the West End.

When the Charleston was at its height in this country, C. B. Cochran put up a challenge shield for the best Charleston performance of teams from all the various musicals in London. He took the Albert Hall one night in 1927. The place was packed from floor to ceiling. My girls were wildly excited; they were hot favourites. The team from each theatre consisted of four girls, so a month before the date of the contest I had the difficult job of selecting our four representatives. I set the routine quickly and we practised solidly every day on this one short dance with meticulous attention to detail.

On the night of the contest they came on last. I was watching from the back of a box in a high state of nerves. There was so much at stake. My chorus girls were earning a big reputation for themselves by their looks and their work and now tonight, in front of an enormous crowd of theatre people and members of the public, their prestige was about to be put to the test. The announcement of 'The team from *Clowns in Clover*' over the speakers produced a big ovation, which if anything made me feel even worse, so much was expected. I needn't have worried about my girls. The ovation acted as a stimulus, a spur to victory. Never before had they shown such verve and animation—the dance glittered. There could be no doubt about the result; just over half way the audience started applauding right through to the end and then they cheered. Later, when it was announced the girls had won the shield, they cheered again louder than ever. I hadn't given them the smartest routine in the world by a long chalk. It was the way they did it. They had proved themselves the best chorus in London. I couldn't have wished for anything better.

During the run of *Clowns* I was asked by the Daniel Mayer office to produce a romantic musical *Song of the Sea*. Luella Pakin was the leading lady, an operatic star from abroad. When we started rehearsing I realised that her acting did not match up to her singing. To teach a lady the rudiments of dramatic art in five weeks had me licked. The situation was critical. I was committed and had to face it. She was such a nice woman, too, and mad keen to make the grade. Each day I devoted a portion of the precious five weeks to giving acting lessons or rather a series of short cuts, which I knew was love's labour lost, but I had no alternative. It was an ambitious production with a lot of scene changes. There was a big singing chorus, a ballet and several dancing numbers. Dennis Hoey played the lead and Claudie was the Comedian.

He had come a long way by now since his success in the Footlights at Cambridge in 1920. He had played in a series of musicals in London, including *Fantasia*, *Primrose*, *Tell Me More*, *Kid Boots*, *Sunny* and *O.K.* His greatest success was marrying Enid Trevor, a charming young actress, in 1924. They played together in various shows and in later years Claudie found himself playing an entirely different part as a father, living at home with his family, which he did extremely well. So frequently the most unlikely people make excellent fathers. His two daughters were mad about him.

Claudie's unique humour was individual, something which evolved from his amusing personality. Exploiting it meant surefire success. I couldn't build him up as much as I would like as it was a period play set around Nelson and Lady Hamilton, but in the musical numbers we pushed in some funny stuff which was acclaimed on the first night. Luella sang divinely, looked charming but . . . if only it could have finished at that. Poor girl, she did try so hard. I didn't see the opening night at His Majesty's because I was playing at the Adelphi, but I was told the reception was splendid and the audience loved Claudie. At the final dress rehearsal I thought the production looked lavish and colourful. I was pleased. Poor Luella Pakin never opened in London. Her place was taken by Lilian Davis.

Cis and I seldom had lunch together as she was usually dashing about all over the place and I always seemed to be working. I used Simpson's a lot as it was practically opposite the Adelphi. Having a preference for plain English food, the cut off the joint, the speciality of the house, became the speciality of a hungry actor trying to repair the ravages of eight shows a week. As I sat there eating, my mind wandered to America, the dance studios where I had sweated to learn so quickly, the shows I had visited in search of new stuff, and I thought of a man I had come across quite fortuitously, a chap called Al Jolson.

He just sang a few songs and chatted to the audience in between. It had been a matinee, a dreary revue. I was just about to leave. He started to sing and for half an hour I sat riveted to my seat. I cannot pay him a higher compliment. Just ordinary stuff: popular songs, the Mammie–Dixie type, but the feeling in the voice, the emotion, the sympathy. He was a most intriguing and compelling personality, one of the greatest stars in this particular line.

I don't know what started this train of thought; I should have been thinking of a new idea I was trying to develop for a show to succeed *Clowns*. I was finishing my cheese and biscuits when a chap came up to me and said, 'Pardon me, sir, for interrupting your meal but I want to say I saw you in the show across the road. You were swell, and if ever you want to come to New York and play on Broadway just let me know. My name's Al Jolson.' Before I had time to tell him I was one of his greatest fans, he'd gone. Another fortuitous meeting or was it mental telepathy?

How pleasant it was having that dear man Willie Gaunt calling frequently at the Adelphi and taking us out to supper. He seemed really fond of us and we certainly went overboard for him, not just because he was our backer, it was genuine affection. This big, bluff Yorkshireman, in spite of his great wealth, was a simple, homely sort of chap with a great love of the theatre, especially the musical Cis and I were in.

In addition to the partnership that existed between Paul and myself, a close friendship had sprung up and we spent most of our weekends with him and Eileen his wife, either visiting Temple, near Maidenhead, to play golf or, in the summer, spending weekends at Oatlands Park in Weybridge, driving down after the show with a nice crack at tennis on the Sunday. We had a lot of fun together. The division of our activities in the partnership, with Paul doing all the business and leaving me free to create and produce the shows, seemed to be an ideal arrangement. The time was rapidly approaching for me to be getting something down on paper for a successor to *Clowns*. I wanted another theme idea and the one I had been turning over in my mind suggested an obvious title, *The House That Jack Built*. I decided to go ahead.

When we started to rehearse I worked hard trying to invent a different first act finale. Always a vital spot in a revue. Most of the cast signed on with the exception of June who, unfortunately, was not available. She had left to become Lady Inverclyde. I also spent a lot of time working out new steps and routines for the chorus, who had now become the Charleston Champions. They had a big responsibility, and I made it patently clear I had too. The standard could only be maintained by increased effort. I loved working with those girls, they were so loyal and conscientious. Let it be said that in all the years I was producing musicals the chorus was my pride and joy.

Mayfair at one time was a delightful place to live in, but the invention of the pneumatic drill has in no way added to its endearing charm. Gone for ever is the old method of three stalwart navvies taking a swipe at a large cold chisel, held in position by a fourth navvy with a pair of tongs. This at least was bearable. Sunday morning, when one tries to snatch a little extra sleep, seems to be a special time for a water main to burst at various intervals within a small radius of our home and the pneumatic monster defies any attempt at pretending not to hear it.

The digging of the two enormous holes just outside in Charles Street, which is part of the construction of a tunnel for a telephone cable coming from Green Park to the exchange at the top of Chesterfield Hill, went on for weeks. The noise of the drill that impinged upon our ears was nearly as bad as a pop group in full cry. And now three gentlemen have called on us to see if our present home in Charles Street is strong enough to withstand subterranean tremors a hundred feet below where they are now tunnelling to bring the new Fleet underground railway on its way from Green Park to Bond Street station. I understand they are calling again shortly to estimate the strength of the foundations and when the new line is opened I shall ask them to display notices in each train—

NOTICE TO ALL PASSENGERS
When you have travelled north bound for fifteen seconds from Green Park Station, you will be passing a hundred feet below the residence of Jack Hulbert and Cicely Courtneidge.

It is only fair that we should receive this publicity as compensation for the excruciating noise of all that drilling.

Not that we enjoy tranquillity in the *house*, far from it. Peace and quiet is something we never suffer from. The hustle and bustle starts in the morning gently enough but gathers momentum rapidly, reaching the rush hour just before noon.

After the beds have been made and the bathroom cleaned, Cis proceeds to demonstrate her experience and skill in dust-flicking. Holding a feather contraption on the end of a cane she applies the business end to a speck of dust and with an adroit turn of the wrist it disappears, only to settle, one would imagine, in some other inaccessible place, but this apparently is forestalled by further flicking. Where it goes to eventually seems to be unimportant.

One morning, I was downstairs in the sitting room trying to improve the last act of a show I was working on. I was just beginning to get the gist of an idea. I started writing.

'Good morning, sir.' It was Mrs Coates, one of our daily helpers armed with a Hoover, 'Is it all right if I do the room?'

'Yes, of course.' I went on writing.

She plugged in and started with great enthusiasm—obviously to drive me out, and succeeded. I went up to the bedroom; dust-flicking would be less distracting.

'Jack, will you learn to put your things away? You had three suits thrown over the chair. Were you thinking of wearing them all today, one after the other? Socks and ties, two pairs of shoes, letters and papers all over the dressing table and I have to clear up after you. I've got a hair appointment at twelve—'

The room was completely transformed and looked immaculate. I was seized with a sense of guilt. I must do something about it. I felt determined. Cis rushed downstairs to deal with catering problems—into the sitting room to arrange the new flowers and remove the old ones. The rush hour was in full swing and I felt partly responsible for giving her extra work. She had to hurry to make up time: doing accounts with our secretary, dealing with things concerning Pammie, up and down stairs, never still. In fact, the only time she sits down is at the hairdressers' under the drier, having lunch. With all this grim determination to keep the house in order there is a softness, a great warmth and a high voltage sense of humour, but there is a power cut in the morning until lunchtime and then we're back to normal.

Being in complete agreement with her insistence on tidiness, I try to emulate this admirable quality but experience tells me not to expect too great a change in too short a time. A lot of my job makes heavy demands on the faculty of invention, but the flight of fancy pays scant regard to time and tidying up, being low in the list of priorities, gets little chance of being aired. I would like to be a tidy man. I would like to be a methodical man and I never give up hope.

15

We were very unhappy not having heard anything for some time from dear old Willie Gaunt. That kindly and genial personality was greatly missed. Rumours, infrequent at first, soon became factual. Much to our dismay we never saw him again. When he was forced to make a fresh start he just wanted to be alone, to recover some of his lost fortune.

The House That Jack Built, opening at the new Empire Theatre, Liverpool, drew the crowds. There was quite a bit to be done which I was prepared to face, but what did surprise me was the press which criticised unfavourably the end of the first half—the item on which I had spent so much time, striving for originality. 'This is disappointing,' the papers said. 'Where is the sparkle, the excitement? This is not a Hulbert finale.' A back-handed compliment in a way but I took it to heart.

I scrapped the whole idea and started on another finale built on dancing, the safest bet in the world. My poor exhausted company, not yet recovered from the stresses and strains of the opening night, had to endure another hard grind of Spartan exercise. Before the end of the week the finale was set and into the show it went and even in the rough and ragged state, I knew, in my bones, it was all right. I kept the best step for the finish and as we approached the climax the audience started to applaud. I gave the arranged signal to drop the curtain while we were still dancing. The trick worked. I signalled to take the curtain up and down again. The applause increased a hundredfold. We continued the process until I think the audience were getting as exhausted applauding as we were dancing. And when the curtain finally fell,

148

with what little breath I had left I turned to the company and shouted, 'Thank you, boys and girls. We've got it. Well done, all of you.' It was a simple idea which appealed to the audience. I opened the second half with us all still dancing as if we had never stopped all through the interval. This further intrigued the audience and gave us a good start for Act II.

Having finished the provincial tour and opened at the dear old Adelphi, we were back in business again. Cis was hailed by the press as the Queen of Comedy and we ran merrily for many months.

In the meantime Paul had the idea of getting Sophie Tucker to sign a contract to appear in the next show with me, which I thought was a good idea, and Cis was to appear in a different show with 'Bunch' Keys, after I had got the Sophie Tucker show launched.

Cis and I were now on the crest of a wave, and after *The House That Jack Built* had been running a few weeks I started on the Sophie Tucker enterprise. Douglas Furber, who had done a lot of excellent work for me, helped with the book and we rounded up a strong cast including Sophie, Archie Bascombe, Alfred Drayton, Rene Russell and Claudie. I was delighted to be working with him again because this time we could really go to town with the broad comedy, but I found at once when we started rehearsing that I had a problem in presenting Sophie in a book show, much the same problem as with Luella Pakin.

At the first rehearsal Sophie said to me, 'Jack, you play my part in this scene. Let me see you do it so that I can get the feel of it.' She may have 'got the feel of it' but it didn't show when she read the lines.

Archie Bascombe was great. He was a good actor as well as a good comic. Alfred Drayton, as the menace in the story, was a tower of strength; he had great authority—a splendid artist. As soon as we started rehearsing I could see that poor Sophie, in spite of being a big star in the cabaret category, was far from happy. This was a very different line of country. It was sad to see such an outstanding entertainer floundering and trying to bluff it through. I had a difficult job in store, but nothing like as difficult as poor Luella Pakin, who had the responsibility of the love interest. Obviously there would have to be a lot of cutting and condensing.

Alfred Drayton came up to me in the lunch break, looking rather worried.

'I'd just like a word with you,' he said. I thought he was going to say 'How can I possibly play scenes with a woman who can't act?' and I was ready to retort, 'With your compelling personality the audience will be looking at you all the time.' But I did him a great injustice. It was about himself. He took me aside.

'Jack, let's get this clear. No gags in our scene. Don't you try any of your stuff when we are together. You'd have me in a panic.'

'No, no, of course not,' I assured him. 'Just the script—verbatim.' As a matter of fact I never so much as altered a line, he played with such conviction—so strong and intimidating. He got the laughs for me, all I had to do was react.

On the first night the show was going with a great swing and Sophie's speciality with Ted Shapiro at the piano was a riot, so much so that she took an encore and sang several more numbers from her extensive repertoire which the audience adored, but it literally stopped the show and the last ten minutes of *Follow a Star* became an anti-climax from which we never fully recovered. We did good business for about ten weeks and then we had to make a decision. But Claudie had made a big success; I thought him very funny doing his piano-playing act. Then I did an eccentric dance with him playing a comedy accompaniment. We collected a lot of laughs. It was all great fun. Rene Russell, who had come on with us from *Clowns*, appeared in several scenes to the enjoyment of the audience. With her striking red hair and vital statistics she looked like a cover girl on the front page of *Vogue*—so chic and soignée. At the Berkeley one night, where we were having supper, I had to tell her the sad news that *Follow a Star* would have to finish. Nothing could have been less calculated to make it a happy evening but it had to be said.

I started working on a revue idea for Cis so Paul and I signed up Nelson Keys and Mary Eaton. Finding material for these artistes had to be done quickly as time was short. Cis had a boyfriend called Ivor McLaren, a charming chap who had been with us since *Lido Lady*. He invited her out to supper one evening which she accepted gladly and said, 'We'll go to the second house of the Victoria Palace first.' She was determined to find an entirely new idea for the forthcoming revue. The end of the first half finished with a French dancing act comprising three men and a girl in what is known in the profession as an 'adagio act'. The three men lifted and threw the girl from one to another—she must have had great courage—and all performed in elegant classical style.

Cis came home bubbling with excitement. 'I've got it,' she said. 'A marvellous idea.' She explained in detail and added, 'I play the girl.' I saw the immense possibilities. As far as I knew there was no Society for the Prevention of Cruelty to Wives so the act was booked for the revue. Paul agreed it was a fine idea and arranged the contract stipulating that Cis should play the girl's part.

When Cis and I got down to rehearsals we came up against the language problem. None of the four French dancers could speak English. I could only attempt a few words with a shocking accent, while Cis could only remember a very little from her Lausanne days. André, the big chap, the boss, was a great enthusiast and threw out all kinds of humorous suggestions or we assumed they were humorous suggestions because he kept pointing to 'Madam Courtneidge' and laughing. Failing to make us understand, he resorted to sign language. Then we got it, and were not a little disturbed. He could make the lifts and throws look awkward and clumsy so it would look funnier still for 'Madam Courtneidge'. How could we explain the whole thing had to be deadly serious and the comedy would come from things going slightly wrong unintentionally. How could we muster enough French to explain the subtle difference between trying to be funny and being funny by not trying to be funny?

I recalled the French exercise book of my early school days—'My aunt's pen has fallen in the garden, and the coachman has been struck by lightning.' Hardly very applicable. There was nothing there we could use. We had to get some outside assistance. When spoken to intelligently in his own language, André cottoned on at once. He knew exactly what was wanted and then never deviated one iota. He turned out to be a very splendid man.

Cis had set herself a hell of a task. The physical strain was enormous. For the first couple of weeks it was torture. Muscles were forced to function with unaccustomed violence. André, a man of great physical strength, picked up Cis and threw her around as if she were a young teenager. I began to worry. It was agony for Cis to move and she had other dances to rehearse as well. Beyond all question the adagio would be a knock-out. And that was it. Would it knock out Madam Courtneidge? I put it to her frankly.

'Darling, are we doing the right thing? Do you think we ought to turn it in?'

'Are you crazy? Turn it in, after all this agony? Not on your nelly.'

With these echoes of the early music hall days I felt constrained to let it rip and hope for the best. No one could have been more concerned about the safety of Madam Courtneidge than the stalwart André but, ironically, it was his iron grip on her limbs and waist that was chiefly responsible for the bruises and the pain. One could only hope it would diminish as the rehearsals progressed. Apart from this, being lifted high in the air frightened her considerably and was becoming a very strong deterrent until one morning, in a small basement room of a dancing school, André lifted her high in the air as usual and she was able to touch the ceiling, which immediately gave her confidence and she felt entirely different. The nervousness had gone for good. Strapping cushions around her middle helped to palliate the distressing effect of André's two strong hands. There was no doubt about it; apart from jolly hard work, it had become an endurance test.

Cis and 'Bunch' Keys got on splendidly together. He was a charming little man when handled properly. Cis had, of course, played with him in *The Arcadians* twenty years ago. They had always got on well together.

I thought Cis would be funny as the average wife of the average professional man singing one of those 'I want to go back' Dixie songs in vogue at that time. *South is the place for me* was the song I got the authors to write, the theme being the irresistible charm of Bromley. Finishing it with a dance, which was strenuous enough in itself, and wearing carefully padded stockings to make her legs twice the size greatly added to the burden but when she danced it certainly looked very funny. So with that, plus the adagio, it was a bit much. What we suffer for art's sake—and money!

I got hold of a lovely sketch for Cis: two middle-aged English ladies travelling alone, entering a sleazy French café, ordering 'Tea for two with biscuits' and getting involved in a murder. The police arrive, the murdered woman is put in a chair next to the two English ladies and the two thugs sit on either side of them, making it look like a jolly drinking party as they prop up the body and talk in their own dialect. I was able to use the three adagio dancers who, of course, spoke authentic French and a breath of reality was added to the scene. Cis was at her best in portraying the imperturbable *sang froid* of the cultured English lady.

As I never went in for snap decisions if I could help it, I amassed a large amount of problems waiting to be solved which I had to deal with in my spare time, and that was nil. The working day, being first thing in the morning to last thing at night, could not be extended so several things had to be done at once. Cis and I were at home. It was early evening. Darsey, my stage manager, was trying to get the designs for the girls' dresses settled. He was carrying a large number of dress designs by Berkley Sutcliffe.

'Lay them all out on the floor,' I told him. 'Let's have a final look.' While he laid them out in order I said to Cis, who was rehearsing with Rose, the rehearsal pianist, 'I want Rose to play over these numbers. Tell me what you think, darling.'

I handed over a number of copies and several were played but Cis said, 'Let's hear that one again about *The King's horses, the King's men*. I'm rather in favour.'

'But I'm definitely not in favour of this red and gold set.' I was holding one of the designs Darsey had now laid out in sets covering most of the floor.

'What do you think, Cis?'

She started singing again.

'Darling, this number's jolly good. Listen.' She sang with enthusiasm, '*The King's horses, the King's men*'.

I broke in. 'I'm sorry I don't agree. And I'm asking you about this red and gold set.'

'Oh darling, it's delightful,' Cis protested. 'Noël Gay at his best. Play the chorus again.'

Rose complied by banging out the tune, which made me like it even less.

'It's definitely out. Let's hear some of the others.'

'I think you're wrong Hulbert, but still—'

Rose was just finishing the chorus of *Three little words*.

'Now this is good—just right for Ivor McLaren and Mary Eaton. Play it again, Rose,' Cis said and started to sing it.

'Do you agree we should scrap the red and gold?' I was determined to get something settled.

'Three little words . . .' Cis started the chorus again.

I raised my voice. 'Do you agree about the red and gold dresses?'

'Darling, you must take this number, it's cute.'

'All right, that's a bet. Now please—the red and gold. No good, are they?'

'No good? You must be mad.' Cis was amazed. 'They're beautiful.'

'I can't see it.'

'Put your glasses on—oh, for heaven's sake.' Cis was so insistent I deemed it inadvisable to flout a woman's instinct.

'Right, Darsey, mark them O.K.'

'Rose, play *The King's horses* again.' Cis started singing.

'Just a minute, darling. One thing at a time. We must decide on these designs. Now this black set—very effective for the finale . . . Darling, do listen. Do you like—'

'I hate them,' she shouted and stopped singing for a moment.

'The girls would look stunning—oh, do shut up, that number's out. We've scrapped it. I've got to settle about these dresses tonight—'

'Jolly good luck, Hulbert.'

'What's wrong with them?' I demanded angrily.

'Just not right for a finale. You want something light and gay. But don't worry, little fellow, the good fairy is here to help you,' and doing a couple of graceful ballet movements she gave me a smacking kiss on the cheek. 'My magic wand will help you choose,' and the magic wand pointed to the rose pink.

What did I do? Go hopping mad? No. Reluctantly I gave in.

And on the opening night at the Picadilly the rose pink finale dresses which replaced the black, got a round of applause. As if to emphasise

still further my erroneous judgement *The King's horses* was one of the
big hits of the show. In the immaculate uniform of two guards officers
outside Buck House, complete with grey overcoats and Busbies, Cis
and 'Bunch' Keys made a perfectly matching pair. They worked it
beautifully. The item became so popular that years afterwards she was
asked to do it with me at a Royal Performance at the Palladium and
quite recently Keith Michell made a special request to sing the number
with her on one of his T.V. appearances. That's why I detest snap
decisions. I've made too many mistakes.

Before coming into the Piccadilly I produced the show at the big
theatre at Streatham so that I could play the last few performances of
Follow a Star at the Winter Garden. I had a lighting bridge built to hang
in the flies big enough to carry four electricians which enables me to get
some novel lighting effects. I never saw the show at Streatham. I had to
get back to the Winter Garden, but I was able to rehearse and make
adjustments during the remainder of the week.

On the opening night at the Piccadilly I had a seat at the back of the
dress circle. I couldn't sit down, I couldn't stand up, I couldn't walk
about—nothing would calm my nerves. Always in the past on a first
night I was up there *with* them on the stage, facing the audience, concentrating hard on my own performance, but now I was out in front
watching them and worrying. So much could go wrong: the lighting
cues, the music cues, the scene changes. It was a far more agonising
ordeal. I was so obsessed with these searing thoughts that for a moment
I hadn't realised the curtain had gone up. It was a very representative
first night audience, expectantly waiting for a show well up to
standard—the very thought gave me cold shivers. It was my very first
experience of watching one of my own productions.

The scene depicted a street corner in a typical London fog. Dimly
visible in this murky gloom, a policeman was helping a man who had
lost his way. 'Keep on straight ahead, just follow the curb. It's not so
thick further on. Anyhow the fog's lifting.' And here came the first
laugh of the evening. Stupidly, that was the cue I had given to fly the
gauze and the audience watched the fog rising greatly amused.

The next morning that was one of the first mistakes I corrected. I
used the gloom opening to heighten the dazzling brightness and vivid

colours of a gay fantasy opening. The audience enjoyed the combination of Bunch and Cis, particularly in *The King's horses* and went for it in a big way. By the end of the first half we were home and dry. I ought to have been delighted. I was, I think, and yet . . . there was another hour and a half to go. Could we keep it up? With my lot playing as they were doing, most certainly—and the best stuff was yet to come—Bunch's impersonations, Cis in the French sketch and of course the adagio. A formidable line-up.

A normal person would have rejoined the audience after the interval with the utmost complacency and abandon, but not me. Why? What was the worry? The speed and animation—that was it. They must keep it up. Hadn't I been round and told them? Yes, possibly but . . . The curtain rose on the second half. I could feel the warmth and enthusiasm in the theatre and I didn't realise I was sitting down, that my stomach was no longer turning somersaults.

Still I managed to line up a new set of worries. Had I done the right thing for Cis? Had I got her the right material in the best kind of show I could invent? It was her first time ever in a musical playing without me. I felt an overwhelming responsibility and I was walking about again. The French sketch started. Cis was away. The audience loved the character. She never missed a laugh. I was sitting down again. I laughed, myself, for sheer joy. The French dancers surpassed themselves, they did everything I had asked them to do. The audience laughed themselves silly—and the adagio was yet to come. Bunch had made a big hit, the chorus were superb and looked lovely.

Then for me the big moment arrived. I was no longer in a panic—I was in a state of intense excitement. On the programme the item was called simply 'The Adagio Dancers'.

The rather grandiose orchestral prelude crashed in on the applause of the previous item, enhancing the dramatic effect of the unconventional lighting which revealed what appeared to be three statues—two men standing on two low pedestals each holding a girl on their shoulders with a third man with outstretched arms in a striking attitude in the middle of the stage. I left the audience to decide what it meant. *I* had no idea. I just wanted to arrest their attention. The back lighting on the statues slowly moved to the front. As it changed colour a soft tremolo from the violins, accompanied a slight movement of the statues striking a different posture. The rapid colour changes increased until the whole scene was a blaze of Strand Electric 7 pink and 51 gold. The two girls still poised on the men's shoulders were identical in dress and make-up, black wigs and all. The soft tremolo continued as the statues struck a new position once more and remained static. Now came the dénouement. Everything was dead still and the girl on the left scratched her leg. The magic spell was broken. The audience laughed and from then on they began to get the idea.

The dance proceeded as if this untoward incident had never taken place. The girl on the right disappeared and the three men concentrated on the girl on the left. André grabbed her, hoisted her in the air, threw her to the second man. He in turn threw her to the third who returned her to André. After this had been repeated several times she was looking like a centre forward playing extra time in a cup tie and if anyone deserved to be capped for England it was Cis. She had invented a wonderful bit of business. Every time André put her down she made for the exit. He hauled her back, lifted her high in the air, turned her upside down, swung her around his body then over to the second man who returned her to André via the third man. Cis made for the exit again. By this time the audience were hysterical. It became one long uninterrupted yell.

I must admit I was laughing myself. That business of trying to escape and being hauled back. I became just one of the audience. Worry and responsibility vanished. I've always been an admirer of her work, but it was the way she acted in that hopeless attempt to escape, that's what got me. After all she had been through. That laughter was the crowning glory, the perfect reward. It was pretty good going for a woman in her middle thirties. As a producer it was only right I should show my supreme admiration and as a husband nothing will ever stop me doing exactly that.

Bunch made a big success and it was one night a few weeks after the opening that Maurice Chevalier came to see him doing his famous imitation, as I mentioned before.

There was much rejoicing in the Hulbert ménage as we settled down for a nice long run. Cis, with her inherent compassion, turned her attention to her husband, who she said looked tired after the strain of playing every night at the Winter Garden and producing two shows running. Much as I hated the idea I had enough sense to take her advice and have a rest. Claudie was also looking tired so we decided to join up on a cruise to the Canaries and North West Africa.

When we got on board Claudie told the Purser I was on a rest cure, suffering from overwork, and he'd come to keep me as quiet as possible and away from social activities. I, in turn, informed the Purser that it was my brother who had to be watched and protected. He got the message. Our fellow passengers behaved with considerate restraint. It worked beautifully. Hardly anyone spoke to us until we spoke first. So we were able to pick and choose—the only way to avoid getting stuck with the wrong people.

Claudie and I wondered how long we could keep up this pretence of mental and physical exhaustion because in about a week we were feeling fighting fit. A contribution to one of the ship's many entertainments seemed inevitable. There was a sports day coming up so we settled for the obstacle race, deciding to do the funny stuff, make a meal of it, give them the lot. Trying to negotiate the hanging buckets of water would present the perfect opportunity.

When the day arrived we did everything wrong. We tried to crawl underneath, tried to climb over the top; we upset the buckets, got soaked to the skin, slipped on the wet boards of the deck, got up, fell down, staggered and collapsed, exhausted. Claudie tried to pull me towards the winning post and collapsed himself in the effort. I staggered to my feet and tried to pull him forward. We were now both as wet as if we had just come out of the sea. From the time we started getting wet and slipping, right to the finish, the laughter never stopped. We put in everything we'd got; we went on until we were beaten to a standstill. I whispered to Claudie, 'This is it. Come on.' We helped each other to our feet, linked arms and hurried to the finishing post . . . going the wrong way.

It made a definite exit to our entirely impromptu knock-about act and it got a hearty cheer from our fellow passengers. This sudden and totally unexpected outburst of energy gave the lie to two men suffering from excessive fatigue. The passengers laughed so heartily that it was all forgotten. But what a price to pay! We could barely get out of bed the next morning. The pain from bruises and aching muscles made it almost impossible to move. I must say, it surprised me considerably that it should have hit us so hard. Claudie was an acrobatic dancer who specialised in stage falls and I was completely limbered up after dancing for months on end. Surprise or no surprise, it was nearly a fortnight before we fully recovered.

<h1 style="text-align:center">16</h1>

We enjoyed some very interesting places on the cruise. Casablanca, Rabat, Freetown and, on the way home, Algiers and Gibraltar. Claudie and I got an idea for an act describing some of these places we had visited, which gave us a successful programme on radio called *The Hulbert Brothers* which we launched soon after our return. It gave me pause to think back over the years, when Claudie and I first worked together as a couple of kids at Bath in our Christmas pantomime in the big drawing room.

On coming home, I think we both felt the same excitement as we did when we met our parents coming back from India. As the train pulled up at the station we spotted our respective wives on the platform. A terrific 'Jack! Hello, darling' came from Cis. I yelled back, so did Claudie. Enid couldn't understand why two Oriental visitors, each wearing a fez should be so familiar. A leap on to the platform and we were both hugging them. Enid was delighted to see Claudie looking so well, it had obviously done him a power of good, and Cis was equally delighted with me. Conversation was meaningless. The noise made it impossible.

Cis took over. 'Porter, this lot please.' She grabbed the stuff I was holding. 'The rest must be in the van. Come on, darling, let's go and find it.' For one brief moment two blue eyes looked straight into mine. 'Are you pleased to see me?'

'Am I? Let me tell you—' but the hissing noise of escaping steam made the rest inaudible. We said goodbye to Claudie and Enid and then . . . home at last. It was worth going away just for the exquisite joy of that moment.

'And how are you, my darling?' I asked, hoping to get the answer that meant so much to me.

'Fine,' she said, and I was greatly relieved.

'And how's the show?'

'Fine,' she repeated unhesitatingly but I had a feeling there was something wrong—were we about to play once more the scene we had played years ago when we seemed to be on top of the world?

'Tell me about it darling.'

'Oh, I'll tell you later.' She hurried on. 'Did you have a lovely time on the cruise? You look so well, so sunburnt—'

'Cis, something's wrong, what is it?'

A moment's pause then the tension snapped, a flood of words came pouring out.

'You know Bunch is filming in the daytime. Well, two weeks ago he invited me down to the studios to have lunch. It was all very nice. I enjoyed it and when we were having coffee he said, "Cis, I want to talk to you about something. I don't know quite how to say this. Jack is away, so you are the only one I can talk to. Please don't misunderstand me but ... Have you been getting your money?" Money? I was so surprised I said, "Yes of course. Why?" Bunch said, "Some of us haven't been paid." '

'Not paid!' I was horrified. 'I just can't believe it.'

'Neither could I, but let me go on telling you. Then I said to Bunch, "Now I come to think of it I did have a couple of cheques returned from the bank and they were marked R.D. I didn't know exactly what that meant so I sent for Paul and asked him. 'Oh, it's just the bank being stupid,' he said. 'Let me have them. I'll fix it.' Then I was paid in cash. Out of the box office I expect." Bunch said, "Yes, there have been rumours about it. I got a cheque returned marked R.D. then later on I was paid in cash, hence the rumour about the box office. It was the same with Mary Eaton. The same thing happened to her." '

'Darling, this is shattering. It must have been blowing up before I went away—why on earth didn't Paul tell me? If I'd known—if I'd been warned—I'd have cancelled the cruise immediately. Perhaps that was the reason. He hoped to put things straight while I was away. Why hasn't he rung me? He knows I'm back. What an appalling mess. I don't know where to begin or what to do.'

'You must find out the truth at once.' The astute business woman was now in charge, displaying that same ice cold logic as before, a surprising facet in a woman of her volcanic nature.

'Who is the solicitor for the partnership? Moverley Sharp, isn't it? And Willie Gillespie does our income tax?'

I nodded in agreement.

'You must see them at once—now—get on the 'phone. I'll get the numbers.'

Moverley Sharp was out, Gillespie was in—I went round to his office in Regent Street and saw him right away. He was a dear man with whom we had, over several years, struck up a warm friendship, a man of integrity, a great believer in the truth, in fact a real gent, a safe bet you could put your shirt on. The orderly appearance and tidiness of his office seemed to reflect his mind. Tidiness—that admirable quality I was still trying to acquire. As soon as I entered I told him how appalled I was by the situation and he was equally appalled when I told him I had nothing to do with the business side other than signing the contracts.

'But surely you must have discussed money, the accounts, how did—'

'No, that was the whole idea. I didn't want to get involved. I had too much to do, producing and playing in the shows. I needed someone to run the financial side. I just signed the contracts. They were in our joint names.'

'But, my dear boy, surely—'

'Willie, either you trust someone or you don't. I trusted Paul implicitly. So there it is.'

'And what does Paul Murray say?'

'Nothing. I haven't heard a word from him.'

'We must get the facts and figures at once. Who is the solicitor?'

'Moverley Sharp.'

'Right, the four of us must meet at once. My dear Jack, I'm terribly sorry, but we'll tackle it together—without delay.'

A meeting was arranged immediately in Moverley Sharp's office and it was in that dingy back room on the third floor of a business block in Shaftesbury Avenue that my whole future was changed. Moverley

Sharp, a humourless type, was elderly and as dry as the dust on the documents and papers cluttering up that stuffy and depressing little room. Willie, mentally alert, with much charm and urbanity, described my distressing situation accurately. Moverley Sharp, with his uncongenial manner, did nothing to dispel the gloom and made heavy weather of the meeting. Although it was the first time we had met since my return, Paul remained completely silent. Moverley Sharp began a long-winded introduction.

'Gentlemen, we are here today to evaluate the regrettable liabilities incurred in a theatrical venture that augured well for future prosperity. It is my unhappy task to reveal that what appeared to be a flourishing partnership is now deeply in debt. The initial success—'

He was all set to go on for ever. He had to be stopped.

'Oh, for heaven's sake. Please—let's come to the point. Why wasn't I warned? You had the figures, Mr Sharp. Paul, why didn't you tell me?' I looked at my partner, waiting anxiously for him to speak for the first time. He was silent. 'Paul, I appeal to you. What happened?' Again complete silence. Why? What did it mean? He was a friend—a close friend—I was completely nonplussed.

Sharp intervened. 'Perhaps Mr Murray would like to postpone the meeting and consult—'

'No, I want the truth now, this moment—Paul please.' But nothing —not a word from him. His silence was driving me up the wall. I gave up trying. 'Mr Sharp, what exactly do we owe the creditors.'

He picked up the balance sheet and started to read the items—I couldn't stand it anymore.

'To hell with all this shilly-shallying. Mr Sharp, please cut out the details, what is the total amount?'

He read out the figure. I was stunned. I can't remember what it was. It is now more than forty years ago but it had me reeling. A snap decision was inevitable because it was the only possible one.

'Every penny has got to be paid if it means working day and night for months—'

'But, Mr Hulbert—' Sharp tried to interrupt.

'Every penny and I mean exactly what I say.' And with that I dashed out of the office. That was the last time I saw Paul.

As I hurried along Shaftesbury Avenue in the direction of home, I couldn't understand why, with the outstanding success of *Clowns in Clover* and *The House That Jack Built* to say nothing of the present show at the Piccadilly, we had incurred this heavy loss. Admittedly, when I had the Adelphi with Paul for a couple of years we had it dark for one week—that was expensive—and in the last weeks of *Follow a Star* we probably lost some of what we made at the beginning but with all that we should have been sitting pretty. I had made an unforgivable mistake in dividing the partnership in two. I had been so happy to be free of the business end and able to devote all my energies to creating and producing that I had felt sure I was doing the intelligent thing. I see now only too well how wrong I was. The financial side had been badly mishandled but why was I ignored, left guessing! I was his partner, his friend. The humiliation increased my distress.

When I got home I told Cis about the meeting and Paul's unaccountable silence.

'If only he would have told what happened, but never a word. So I had to cut him right out and face the music alone. I'll never be able to rest until all these debts are liquidated.' When I told her the amount she could hardly believe it but her reaction was sympathetic and calm. The practical mind got to work immediately.

'Willie Gillespie, at once. He must advise you about the next step.'

'Agreed, but you see, darling, the various gentlemen in the past who have looked after our expense allowance on our joint income tax have been so inefficient that we never got anything like the allowances we were entitled to and, as you know, just before I went on holiday, we sent the Inland Revenue another cheque—'

'Large enough to pay off most of the National Debt,' Cis said. 'And that means there isn't much left in the kitty. I know all that. So how are the creditors going to be paid? We need a kind fairy godmother.'

'Darling, you're not to worry.' I tried to sound reassuring.

'No, of course not, I just keep going at the Piccadilly and you start all over again. Simple—nothing to it.'

'Those chaps have got to be paid, and at the earliest possible moment—'

'I'll have a look round,' Cis continued, 'and if I find a half-witted millionaire who wants to throw away his fortune on theatre business I'll keep you posted.' This light-hearted approach defied despondency, which made it easier to think straight. Cis was never at a loss. 'Get Willie Gillespie to call the creditors together. Have a proper meeting and tell them you are going to pay back in full.'

That afternoon I was in his office in Regent's Street. Not only did he agree entirely with the plan, but he decided to notify each creditor separately the date, time and place of the meeting. He was fully aware of the seriousness of the situation.

'It's the only proper course to take to try to stave off bankruptcy.'

'Bankruptcy.' The very name was abhorrent to me.

'It's a slender chance I'm afraid,' Willie said, 'but we must try. So much will depend on what you say and how you say it. But if you fail to win them over . . . well.'

'Willie, I've *got* to pull it off. I'm determined to pay them back in full, but I must have time to earn the money, to fight the slur of insolvency. You must see that.'

'I do. But you must make *them* see it.'

I forget where we had the meeting but it was in a large room with chairs arranged in rows like a lecture hall. Willie and I walked round from his office and got there ahead of time to see that everything was in order. Gradually the creditors began to drift in until the room was filled. Apparently everyone had answered the call to attend. Willie handled the whole thing with perfect ease and good humour. This is where he excelled. It was all very formal which increased my nervousness considerably. Here was I about to play to an audience who, far from paying for their seats, had come to claim large sums of money that I owed them for services rendered, so I did not expect to get a rousing reception. Willie started the proceedings with an opening speech telling them I was a man of impeccable character, which seemed entirely incompatible with the jam I had landed them in through my negligence. I expected angry protests. He continued in this eulogistic vein which was making me more and more apprehensive and then finished by saying, 'And now let Mr Hulbert speak for himself.'

I never felt less like giving a performance. I had to nerve myself for the ordeal. I started. They listened in rapt silence. I said I would pay back every penny if they would give me time to earn the money. The rapt silence continued. At least they were listening. I spoke to them as man to man. I was getting worked up. I forgot the formality.

'Give me the chance and you'll get every penny. I make this solemn promise to you all for two vital reasons. Firstly, to avoid bankruptcy and, secondly, I could never rest until I paid back everything I owe.'

I've no recollection of what else I said. I just went on talking without pause. I didn't want to risk angry interruptions. I had no idea how it was going. On the stage I can tell at once by the laughter and applause, or lack of it, but all this was in deathly silence. I just went on talking as I felt and meaning every word of it. Then I suddenly caught sight of Willie. He was beaming. So I sat down quickly and got a round of applause. Willie jumped to his feet and asked for a decision. The answer was unanimous.

Willie said after it was all over, 'Frank, straightforward and honest. Well done, You said exactly the right thing. Now, how are you going to earn the money?'

'By taking every job that comes along,' I replied.

'Good,' said Willie. 'We'll open a special account at the bank.'

But not with that truculent establishment that didn't even have the decency to show up at the meeting. They just sat tight and demanded their pound of flesh. When I think of all those chaps we'd just been addressing, trusting me to keep my word and willing to wait indefinitely for their money, I despise the callousness and complete lack of goodwill, the pay-up-or-else attitude from a bank that's big enough to know better! It's most unfair. They can afford to wait. Some of the other creditors can't.

When I got back home to Curzon Street, Cis was delighted to hear about the success of the meeting and that only the bank had repudiated the suggested terms.

'Probably the manager saw you in *Follow a Star* and didn't laugh, but presumably Basil Dean went to the show and *did* laugh.'

'What's that got to do with it?'

'He's just been on the 'phone. He's in charge of the stage shows at the Leicester Square cinema and wants you to produce one to go on in a month's time.'

'I'll do it!'

'Spoken like a true Hulbert!'

'I'll start tomorrow. I'll get Claudie to write with me—'

'And this is where I am going to laugh,' Cis said, intensely amused.

'Why?' I didn't quite follow.

'You and Basil Dean working together.'

'What's funny about that?'

'He's not easy.'

'Neither am I.'

'Exactly, that's why it's going to be funny.'

'I think he's a brilliant man. I'll learn a lot from him.'

'*Good afternoon.*' Cis said this with an incredulous smile.

'Don't you think he's great?'

'Of course. I can't wait to see you both at it.'

The next morning I went to see him in his office at the cinema. He was charming. I got a very good contract to write and produce. He gave me an office to work in, a stage carpenter was at my disposal and a manager to organise the dresses and decor, etc. He told me he had the highest opinion of me as a director of musicals and I assured him with enthusiasm that the feeling was mutual.

He continued, 'There is only one snag. I am going away and I shall not be back until after you have got the show in. So I am afraid I shall have to leave the whole thing to you.'

It was a little time before I could recover from the staggering blow but I assured him I would do my best to struggle on without him.

When I related all this to Cis she expressed her disappointment.

'Oh dear, how sad, I shall now have to wait for five weeks for the big laugh.'

I was a little indignant after the delightful interview I had experienced with Basil Dean and I made no attempt to hide it.

'There will be no big laugh. He repects me as I respect him.'

The star turn of the show was Harry Roy and his band and I brought them into view playing their opening number on a specially built revolve. It made a very striking entrance. With some good effective dancing from a well-drilled chorus and bits of comedy in between, the show became a very popular feature of the cinema. True to his word

Basil Dean returned soon after we had opened and he expressed his admiration for the work I had done.

'Splendid, dear chap. I am very pleased. Now we can get down to working together. There are just one or two alterations I would like to make—'

'Alterations?' I said, surprised. 'I don't want to alter a thing. It's all been worked out meticulously. We can't risk upsetting the balance—'

'There are three items that must be changed at once—'

'No items are going to be changed.'

Tempers rose to boiling point as we stood glaring at each other.

Cis was just leaving for the Piccadilly when I got back. 'Hullo, darling. Well, I've just *had* my big laugh.'

'How on earth did you know?'

'Nowhere does news travel faster than in the theatre. What a pity Basil Dean came back. I wish I could have been there to see the meeting.'

I thought afterwards what a fool I had been. I should have swallowed my pride. The show was a success, I should have stayed put and started on another show in conjunction with Basil Dean, quick money was the objective. Now I had to look elsewhere. I couldn't afford to waste time. What was I to do? Write a new musical, produce it and play in it —that was the long term policy. It was the short term job that had to be found. Like these new talking pictures. That would be ideal. Something immediate with good money. But how do you crack that one? There wasn't a soul in the film business that I knew. Hopeless. Have to think again. It was then that the telephone rang.

I was in the bath. I'd missed it in the morning having to rush out to keep an appointment. I had been thinking earlier on of the disgusting rapacity of that stinking bank and the cheque I had just been compelled to send. What was now left in the kitty was minimal. I was happy to slip into a hot bath, and forget. But it stimulated thought—the riddle of Paul's silence. I supposed a determined effort would reveal the truth. But why waste time? The debt had to be paid. Be thankful for the good will of the creditors, number one priority. Keep that in mind. Pay them in full at the earliest possible moment.

The phone bell rang so persistently that I had to get out of the bath.

Wrapped in a towel and dripping wet, I picked up the 'phone. The message I received was incredible—bewildering. I dried off, dressed and hurried to the theatre. I felt I must break it to Cis. I shot through the stage door down to Cis's dressing room.

'Cis, I've got something I must tell you at once.'

'Have you, darling? Nellie, give me a couple of minutes will you.'

The dresser promptly obeyed.

'Darling, it's happened.'

'What?'

'Pictures. I got a phone call from Herman Felner—old Herman. He said, "Hullo, Jack, would you like to make a picture?" '

'Darling, how wonderful!'

'It's unbelievable.'

And from that phone call I started an entirely new career. For the next ten years I left the stage and was making pictures. It enabled me to pay off the debt in a shorter time than I had ever hoped.

Herman came along in the morning and was very happy to see us again. Cis rushed up to him and kissed him. 'The fairy godmother disguised as Herman Felner.'

Anything less like a fairy godmother would be hard to imagine. He was a Polish Jew, a good six foot six, with a capacious chest and middle that made him resemble an all-in wrestler. His clothes looked as if he wore them in the ring. Admittedly not an easy shape to fit, his trousers were too short and he was about the only man in London wearing boots. But with all that he had a charm endearing him to all who were lucky enough to know him well. His main job was buying and selling the rights of Continental musical comedies. He had done a lot of business with the Governor but now he had entered the new world of talking pictures. What ever possessed him to choose that psychological moment to get me out of the bath to talk on the phone will remain unknown to the end of time. Dear Herman, a friend in need, he will always be remembered with gratitude.

The film was *The Ghost Train*, an adaptation for the screen of Arnold Ridley's play. I was suggested for the light comedy lead and to my great delight Cis was to be in it too. It was to be made by Gainsborough Pictures, directed by Walter Ford and produced by Michael

Balcon. In due course I received a call from the studio. Could I come along tomorrow at 10.00 a.m.?

Next morning I arrived ahead of time being so eager to get started. A chap who introduced himself as an assistant director met me at the entrance and took me on to the studio floor which seemed to contain a huge quantity of lamps of all sizes, some on stands on the floor and others on the gantries above, concentrating on a small set representing a modern drawing room with a camera focused on a settee in the centre.

The assistant said, 'Now what are you going to do?'

'You tell me. I'm a new boy.'

'Just do your stuff and we'll turn the cameras on it.'

'What stuff?' I asked, completely mystified.

'All that funny spontaneous stuff you make up on the stage each night.'

'Let me tell you, sir, that all that funny spontaneous stuff is the result of weeks of invention and rehearsing.'

'Well, just repeat some of it now. About three minutes. That's enough for a test.'

'Test? What's all this? You've seen me on the stage.'

'Ah yes, but we want to see what you look like on the screen.'

This got me worried. If the test wan't satisfactory it could cost me the job. I'd have to try and get some laughs, but I had nothing prepared.

'Well, what do you want me to do?'

'Anything you like. Say anything.'

'Anything?'

'Yes.'

'Who's going to see this?'

'The boss Michael Balcon tomorrow morning. It will be joined on to the end of the rushes of the current picture we're making here.'

While the camera man was making a few lighting alterations I got a sudden idea, risky but worth a try.

'Sound O.K.?' a voice asked. 'Fine, quiet in the studio. Right roll 'em.'

The assistant spoke into the mike. 'Screen test. The Ghost Train. Jack Hulbert.' He then turned to me. 'Right.'

I forced myself to imagine I was playing to that audience of Michael Balcon with his studio staff and technicians watching this test tomorrow morning in the projection theatre. I tried to make it sound natural and easy. I said something like this:

'I understand that the boss of this outfit is a chap called Balcon. His name means nothing to me. Korda, yes, he's O.K. But Balcon—never heard of him. And if he knew anything about making pictures he wouldn't be wasting time looking at me. I'm a song-and-dance man and if he's thinking of casting me for the hero in *The Ghost Train*, he must be raving mad. Do you mind if I sit down? Thank you.' I vaulted over the settee and landed plumb in the middle lolling back among the cushions.

'Thank you. That's more comfortable. And let me tell you, Mr Balcon,' I leant forward to address him, 'film making calls for a high degree of intelligence and efficiency. I suggest you try something else. Thanks for the use of the studio which obviously I shall *not* be seeing again. Good afternoon.'

Even the hard-boiled assistant was laughing when I finished, which augured well for tomorrow.

In the early afternoon of the following day Herman Felner rang me in a great state.

'Jack, what have you been up to? The whole studio was in an uproar. Whatever made you do it?'

'I was playing for safety.' My hopes were fading rapidly. 'I was hoping the test would get a good laugh and I'd get the job.'

'Laugh, you should have heard them. They loved it. The whole thing was tremendous.'

This was a great relief. So the insult gag worked. It seldom fails. Poor Micky had to laugh too and that's how I landed my first job in pictures. Some forty odd years ago it happened. Rather difficult to remember all of the details. Sir Michael Balcon, who is now one of our oldest and dearest friends, showed in those days he had a keen sense of humour—and he needed it, working with me for the next ten years.

17

Starting a new career was thrilling. The future now depended on success in my first picture. If I could get away with it . . . well, immense possibilities.

The money was agreed and the contract signed. It was a great day for me and the creditors. A moment of relief and exhilaration. Where we had previously failed to make it, good old Herman had broken down the barrier.

Cis was exempt from the test ordeal and *The Ghost Train* started almost immediately. The meeting up with the Fords, Walter and his wife Cully, was not entirely happy. We seemed to have little in common. Cis got on better than I did. The humour of Walter and Cis seemed to harmonise, but mine was going to take him a little longer to get used to and yet after only a few days he asked me to rewrite my dialogue scenes which, of course, I was delighted to do, and that was how I started as a writer, as well as performer, in pictures. When I saw myself on the screen for the first time I couldn't believe it. Good heavens it can't be true, I thought, where was the image I had fondly nurtured of the dashing, rather romantic young comedian? What I saw was most depressing. Why had they bothered even to make a test! In fact I was beginning to think that what I said about Michael Balcon must be true. But as time went on I began to get used to it, and in the end when it was accepted by the public with pleasure and laughter I was a happy man.

When we rehearsed and shot a scene in the studio we always had an audience of two, Mr and Mrs Walter Ford—very inhibiting. One or a crowd, yes, but two—it was like giving an audition—it gave me an

'Alice in Wonderland' complex. I was expecting any minute to hear 'Off with his head', from the ruthless 'Queen of Hearts' who also had an unfortunate knack of signalling her disapproval surreptitiously to the 'King of Hearts' during a take—a slight shaking of the head which I always managed to see out of the corner of my eye and found rather disconcerting. But, being a new boy, tolerance seemed essential, so that I could concentrate entirely on how to play the juvenile lead in a medium I knew nothing about. The wisest course seemed not to try anything new, but stick rigidly to what I had been doing on the stage since I began. So my first picture had to be a musical comedy performance. It was a gamble but isn't that the whole thing about show business—hit or miss all the time?

Walter Ford said very little after a take and went straight to the piano that he insisted on having just behind the set. The music he played expressed his mood. *H.M.S. Pinafore* signalled success but *Tosca* meant things were pretty grim. Expressing despondency, or happiness by playing odd bits from great composers must be a very satisfying way of getting back to an equable state of mind, particularly if one played well, and Walter Ford did, having had a lot of practice at the start of his career in the orchestra pits of cinemas showing silent pictures. With the soft gentle strains of *Hearts and Flowers* he enhanced the rapture of romance and with a dramatic switch to 'hurry music' he warned of the impending danger of the rapidly approaching menace. He seems to have been in every form of show business from knock-about comedy to working in the cutting room. Mr and Mrs Ford were expert cutters, which I found out later was one of the criteria of an ace director. Up till now all I could appreciate was being in very good hands. I never got to understand this unique husband and wife team until the third picture we made together.

All those concerned with the making of *The Ghost Train* were high in their praise of the way it was turning out, particularly Michael Balcon with whom I struck up an immediate friendship. In appearance he was a direct contrast to dear old Herman. Nothing ponderous or heavy about him. I would think he was a good ten stone lighter. His movements were brisk and agile, like his brain. He thought quickly and talked quickly and what he said was well worth listening to.

For the exteriors of *The Ghost Train* we went to an old disused railway station at Camerton just outside Bath. We had a shot where I had to run in front of the train to cross the line immediately to deliver an urgent message. Here was a chance, I thought, to make it sensational. The train was gathering speed, I ran along with it, neck and neck, then I accelerated and crossed the line within inches of being hit by the engine. The women screamed. They thought I'd had it, but I emerged laughing to be told by everyone it was a crazy thing to do and when I reflected I began to think they were right. But it was worth the risk. It should be a hair-raising sight in the screen. When I saw the rushes it meant nothing at all, just an odd-looking young man running in front of a train—all that risk and nothing to show for it—but it had a very salutary effect on my thinking. No more dangerous thrills for me. It could all be faked and look much more convincing.

I got Claudie to come down to Camerton for a few days because we had started our radio series *The Hulbert Brothers* and there was just the little question of writing the next programme. He duly arrived and we talked about doing some work between the shots when I was not actually filming and that was as far as it got. I was always a great one for hobbies and I think that, starting from boyhood, I must have had every hobby under the sun. Butterflies, birds' eggs, stamps, fretwork, wood carving, photography—a list that goes on and on. I suppose the absorbing interest of these hobbies when I started my professional career until the present day has saved me from going nuts with all the work I was doing. The particular hobby that kept me very busy at Camerton —when I was not risking my life running in front of trains—was geology. Next to the derelict railway station there was a disused coal mine and the underground waste that had been brought up from the tunnelling below contained the fossilliferous formations above and below the coal seams.

Round the edge of this old slag heap I picked up, among the softer rock formations, some excellent fossils of tropical ferns and fossilised portions of palm trees. Interesting to think that there were large tropical swamps in the country at one period of geological history. I brought my treasures back home to London by car at the weekend. In my study at 43 Curzon Street I had a show case built to cover the whole of one wall and I had it full of most interesting fossils and various rocks going back to the igneous rocks of the earth's cooling-down period. I just managed to find room for my latest acquisitions.

When we were doing night shots at Camerton we had quite a large audience. Some enterprising transport firm was running coach trips from Bath and Bristol. Such was the interest in film-making in those days.

On the way home on Saturday evening in the car, which was weighed down by the valuable cargo from Camerton, Claudie and I were sitting in the back and I suggested this was a good opportunity to get on with the urgent job of writing our broadcast for Monday. Claudie gave a big yawn and agreed. We'd been up all night doing night shots. I continued with my suggestions.

'I think it would be a funny idea to start the broadcast by saying . . . by saying . . .' When we both woke up we had nearly got to Reading and all we could think about was food.

There was still quite a bit to do on the picture when we got back to the studio. Cis's part was coming out beautifully and she was very funny as the frustrated spinster, caught up with the gang in the derelict station. She was not with us at Camerton as she was very busily caught up with another gang, being thrown about the stage at the Piccadilly to the delight of the public who were still packing in which enabled me, in addition to my salary for the filming, to make a good start in taking care of the creditors.

As the rushes were assembled into a rough cut a wave of optimism swept the studios and when it got to the trade show we were in business. Mick Balcon was delighted. Mr and Mrs Ford had done a grand job. The innovation of a musical comedy performance in a dramatic picture proved surprising but popular. Thank goodness I had enough sense to plump for that and I can see now where Walter Ford had added to and elaborated a lot of the things I did and said, so he must have thumped out more gay tunes on the piano than I realised. Cis's work was excellent and came in for high praise, and between us we collected a goodly quantity of laughs at the trade show. Of course, we didn't know what the public would think but when the boys in Wardour Street are enthusiastic—that's it. On the strength of it, Mick Balcon gave us both contracts for more pictures immediately.

My next job was to play the comedian's part in the translated version of a German film. I thought Cis should have a rest as she had such an overwhelming job at the Piccadilly, as well as filming in the daytime, and Mick agreed. The part I was to play in the German film was a comic janitor of a bank and when they ran the original film for me to see I thought it was charming. Renate Muller was the Berlin star and she sang *Today I feel so happy* with the chorus joining in, leaning out of the windows of the houses across the street. It was the first time singing on the screen had been attempted in a big way. I thought it had tremendous possibilities. This, of course, was before the advent of the big Hollywood musicals. Everything was fine except the comic janitor and I thought he was the end. Every time he came on the screen, as far as I was concerned, the film was on the floor. Mick, Victor Saville, who was directing, and the boys in the script department thought him very funny and this is where my trouble started.

'It's such childish humour,' I protested. 'Do you honestly, as intelligent gents, think it's funny when he passes a fishmonger's shop and smacks a cod's head and says "naughty fish", and that silly gag when he tries to shut the door of the bank manager's office and finds he can't do it because his foot's in the way? It's just kid stuff. Have you thought what an audience would do to that in Liverpool, Bradford, Leeds, Wolverhampton, or any provincial city. I can tell you, if you want to know, I've played those cities over and over again. They're marvellous audiences but you've got to give them better stuff than that.'

I think this shook them a bit but they were far from convinced. They were so enamoured of the whole film. I thank my lucky stars for all those months I had, playing in the provinces and finding out first hand what they like and what they don't like. But it was too late to change the plans. Renate Muller had been engaged and most of the other artistes. I was in despair. The first few days we did some shots where I had practically nothing to do and then the picture came to an abrupt stop. Poor Renate got ill and the film had to be suspended for a couple of months. I was very sorry for her but indirectly she did me a great service. It gave me time to make adjustments and think up some ideas.

I won the day eliminating all the fatuous comedy and making the janitor a more likeable and believable character, instead of a complete idiot. Renate Muller eventually recovered and the day she returned, while we were all waiting for her on the set, and I was all ready, dressed in the janitor's clothes and wearing a wig of close-cropped hair in the German style, I started fooling around. I went up to Victor Saville who was on the set and said,

'Good morning, sir. Mr Victor Saville, I believe. Do sit down, sir. Let me get you a chair, sir. I trust you had a pleasant vacation, sir. You're looking extremely well, sir, and, if I may say so, a little stouter.'

Dressed in this very German outfit and with this Teutonic wig it must have looked funny because all the chaps on the set were laughing, and Victor Saville most of all.

'If I could play Harsel like this all my troubles would be over,' I said.

And he replied, 'Why not? It would be perfect.'

So that's how I played it—Jack Hulbert with a wig on. I was happy. Victor was happy. Mick was happy and thank goodness the audience were happy and it turned out to be the right treatment for a film that came to be known as a 'happy picture'. The great charm of Renate Muller's engaging personality and her singing of *Today I feel so happy* at once struck a note of gaiety in a Continental setting. The peculiar combination of Hulbert and a German make-up had no difficulty in getting laughs as I found out on the second day's shooting.

The scene was a beer garden with a hundred or so crowd artistes sitting around drinking and listening to the band. The janitor Harsel had brought Renate Muller, who was playing Susie, because she had fallen for the bank manager and Harsel was fixing a fortuitous meeting. He had several beers in the process which produced such a happy mood that he jumped on to the little stage with the band and did an impromptu act singing *I've got an Aunt Eliza* and finished with a dance. The constant laughter of the extras showed the idea of the character worked and I was able to build up this impromptu act on account of their natural and encouraging reaction to my fooling. I had a smashing day and I had found, thanks to those dear crowd artistes, the right way to play Harsel the janitor, whose job in the story was to further the romance of the bank manager and *Sunshine Susie.*

That lovely actor Owen Nares was the romantic lead and I was very lucky to have several scenes with him. Before we started shooting the picture I happened to be in the room with the casting department and the writing boys who were discussing the merits and demerits of the man I revered and respected as one of our finest actors on the legitimate stage. Apparently failing to get anything better he had been rather condescendingly engaged for the picture. To hear these young chaps derogating from this great man's reputation as a performer of sterling worth was sacrilege. But I held my peace and sat there burning with indignation. I'd never known such cheek. Ignorant, young—but they'll find out in time. Experience is slow but invaluable. I have always held the legitimate theatre in the highest esteem; Owen Nares occupied a prominent place in that august institution and deservedly so.

I waited eagerly each day for his arrival and then one morning there he stood, the famous matinee idol. After a delightful chat he asked me if I would like to run through our scene. I found it hard to realise at first I was actually rehearsing with a man whose work I so greatly admired. I started very cautiously not knowing how my broad approach to the scene would be accepted. He was word-perfect, I was just winging it. With a minimum amount of movement he took off his hat and coat and hung them in the cupboard. I was fascinated by the neatness.

'Now, Jack. May I call you, Jack?'

'Good heavens, really. . .I mean…I should be hon…Yes, please do.'

'Now, Jack, would you say your line "Anything you require, sir?" as I am hanging up my hat. Then I will turn and say "Thank you, no".'

We went through it again, observing the exact timing.

'Was that more or less what you meant?'

'Yes. Exactly. All right for you, Jack?'

'Yes.' I was game for anything. I wanted to learn this legitimate stage stuff.

'Shall we continue?'

'Certainly, Mr Nar—Owen.'

'I think it's your line.'

'Yes, it is,' I said eagerly. 'Can I have a word with you, sir?'

'Forgive me,' Owen said politely. 'I think the "sir" comes first.'

'Yes, you're probably right.'

'So, if you pause after "sir" I can give you a quick glance and your reaction of embarrassment can be much smaller.'

I got the message and he was dead right. I tried it. I said 'sir' with a big smile and on receiving the look from Nares, which was one of slight annoyance, I merely removed the smile. Owne said 'Fine' and laughed. And it got a big laugh at the rushes the next morning. So did the rest of the scene played on similar lines. The neatness and accuracy of all that hanging up the hat and coat stuff was most effective. Owen Nares had pointed the way—a new approach to comedy. Stand still and don't move a muscle, let the audience see in your face what you're thinking. A minimum of movement and a maximum of thought transference. Well over ten years it's taken me to find this out. Dear Owen, my thanks for revealing the high priority of precision—'I remain, yours sincerely, an ardent fan.'

Victor Saville did a splendid job directing. The charming Renate made a notable success and dear Owen, with his artistry and professionalism, made even the prosaic bank manager a romantic figure. Thanks to all concerned and Micky Balcon, my success in pictures was consolidated. Was I pleased? Deliriously.

My behaviour in the first two pictures had been exemplary. But this was not to last. From now on I became a nuisance. It wasn't that I was throwing my weight about, it was due to the simple fact that the more experience one gains the more one realises pitfalls and the necessity to avoid them. It becomes imperative. One doesn't know exactly how success has been achieved, but one has a pretty good idea of how easy it would be to fail in pictures—a few bad mistakes and you're out on your ear. So, in the relentless battle for survival, one quickly earns the reputation of being difficult to handle. Even with a brilliant man like Micky Balcon promoting my career, I had to do a lot of hard thinking and all this time Cis was being turned upside down and thrown about the stage at the Piccadilly eight times a week. How she stood up to it so long I shall never know, but I was eternally grateful that she eventually emerged unscathed. Yet she loved every minute of *Folly to be Wise* and revelled in the show, the peak of her success, which I proudly state, husband or not, she so richly deserved.

18

My third picture was *Jack's the Boy*. Back to square one with Walter Ford directing and it was here I got to know him not only as a brilliant director but as a sincere friend. It happened suddenly one afternoon after we had been shooting for a couple of weeks. A period of unease. I was conscious all the time of an aloofness and mistrust. It was not a happy atmosphere. The blow-up was no surprise. I walked on to the set a couple of minutes late. He glared at me.

'I am not accustomed to being kept waiting,' was the cordial greeting I received. I looked at my watch.

'Two minutes. I'm sorry.'

'That's not the point. You should be here on time.'

'Who the hell are you talking to?' I could no longer keep my cool.

'You.'

'All right then, I'm not sorry.'

'A man in your position should know better.'

'Is that so.' I was furious. 'Then let's call the whole thing off.'

'Right,' he shouted angrily.

'Right,' I shouted back.

We stood there glaring at each other both red in the face with fury. A moment's pause. I don't know whether he laughed first or I did—probably simultaneously—and here the friendship started which has stood the test of time, all through two fully grown men behaving outrageously, like a couple of silly, big boys. I got Walter in the right perspective. I saw him for the first time for what he was, a brilliant man at his job and I think he saw me as a man dedicated to my work. The barrier of unfriendliness and frigid indifference was broken down. We now had a perfect understanding of each other.

I was in on the writing again, thanks to Walter, and it was now made permanent so that by working with the other writers I was able to get things more or less to conform to what I wanted. Micky Balcon had some excellent chaps in the script department who were bubbling over with ideas. Here was something that I had never experienced before, working with young chaps equally enthusiastic. I was learning all the time and being paid for it.

After the success of *Sunshine Susie* the introduction of singing and dancing was inevitable. It meant a lot more work but when you're young and enthusiastic you don't even know you're doing it. I was tickled to death anyway. Another string, why not use it? So composers and lyric writers were engaged and I worked overtime with Philip Buchel on dance routines. I think this was the first time the hero and his girlfriend sang a duet together and finished it with a dance. The innovation pleased the public so it became firmly established in my subsequent pictures. I was delighted to be the first in the field and thus breaking fresh ground, I had it all to myself. Everything was going splendidly until some chap called Fred Astaire suddenly appeared on the screen. Things were different after that. I'd never seen such dancing. I was enthralled. It meant working harder than ever. Poor Philip Buchel, I bullied the life out of him.

'We've got to improve, we've got to do better.' And I must say Philip came up with some splendid stuff, but who could dance like Fred Astaire? No one, and no one ever will. He goes into the same category as Hawtrey and Du Maurier—my three gold medallists.

The rushes of *Jack's the Boy* were very funny. Walter was in top form. Cis, playing a character part again, was bang on so I had no worries there. Walter's ace piece of direction in the film was what we called 'the ladder sequence.' I was playing a policeman in the story and I was on point duty controlling the traffic in one of the busiest parts of London. We did it on the lot at Welwyn Studios. They had a London street built outside, which Gainsborough Pictures hired for this particular sequence. They also hired London taxis, buses, all kinds of vehicles and a large amount of crowd artistes. A tremendous turn-out.

As I am holding up the traffic, two men carrying a long ladder, one on each end, start to cross the road. They discover they are going in the wrong direction and try to turn round but there isn't room—the ladder's too long and the traffic too dense. The result is chaos. I move the people back. I stop the traffic. The two men with the ladder get one end wedged between a taxi and a bus. I am helping them to pull it free when a small part actor comes up to me and says, 'You'll never do it.' I just give him a look and walk away. At least, that was the intention but it was necessary to make a slight adjustment. Walter had his hands full giving instructions to the drivers and getting the traffic moving in the right place. I took the little man aside.

'Very funny,' I told him. 'I can tell you this it's going to be the big laugh of the picture. It's not so much the line, it's the way you say it.'

'Oh, thank you very much.' The little man was delighted and very surprised.

'I can see you're an expert at the dead pan stuff.'

'Well, I don't know. I wouldn't say that.'

'Oh, but you *are*, and jolly lucky we are to have you. Any other actor would have said, "This is my big chance" and given it the works, but your subtle approach, your restraint, it's so funny, so unexpected and the quieter and more natural you are the more the audience is going to laugh. The situation is yours, and I want to see you take it.'

'Well, I'll do my best,' the little man said, quite overcome.

'Let's try it again.'

He had a go. It was still grossly overdone but not quite so outrageous.

'It gets funnier every time you say it. Now you have to say it three times in the take. I'll give you a look each time. That'll be your cue to speak. Don't alter your intonation—the same flat voice and the same dead pan delivery. Once more for luck. Right.'

This time there was a great improvement. If I could get him to stand still . . . .

'Better and better. One more thing, don't move a muscle when you talk. Good, the audience are going to love it. It's beautiful. It kills me.'

'Stand by for a take.' Walter was ready. 'All set. *Action*,' he shouted.

I started trying to get the ladder clear. I gave the little man the cue.

He said the line beautifully—flat voice—dead pan— the lot, and he did the same the second and third time.

'*Cut*,' shouted Walter. 'Print that one.'

When the film was finally shown, so many people said, 'That ladder sequence and that funny little man who kept saying "You'll never do it". I laugh every time I think about it.'

From what I saw of the rushes the picture was going to be far and away the funniest of the three. Cis, as the comedienne, doubled the amount of laughs. Her character of a frightened woman working with me in the story was most effective. When we got into dangerous situations, trying to unmask the crooks, it presented great opportunities which she grabbed with both hands. I was most anxious she should make it in order to follow up her success in *The Ghost Train*. If she could hit the high spots once more she'd be all set. As far as the rushes were concerned, all the stuff was getting big laughs.

Winifred Shotter looked beautiful, which was just as well because she had to take care of the love interest with the dashing, romantic comedian. The duet we sang, followed by the dance in the squalid surroundings of a damp gloomy cellar, seemed to gain considerably in effect by being in such an unexpected and unsuitable place. Then there was the dance I did as a policeman in uniform complete with helmet and overcoat, finishing with a series of pirouettes right into a hole in the road. I had high hopes that the public would be amused by the sentimental policeman patrolling Piccadilly who could not resist dancing to the music coming from the Berkeley restaurant because he was not in there himself dancing with the beautiful Winnie Shotter. Altogether we seemed to have the makings of a good picture. Cis and I, Walter and Cully were very happy but Micky was not very happy. On the contrary he was extremely worried.

He sent for me and told me so. For some unknown reason he had lost confidence in the enterprise and felt he would be compelled to cut his losses and call it a day. I was shattered. I couldn't believe my ears.

'Why for heaven's sake? What on earth's gone wrong?'

'It's the style. I just feel it's wrong.'

'Walter's doing a great job—'

'I just have that feeling. Excellent things in it, but the style—' He pursed his lips and shook his head. I could only think that comedy was always difficult to assess and that the innovation of singing and dancing not seen before in an adventure story on the screen was an undeniable risk which, of course, it was. Any new departure, any original idea, is always a risk. I pointed this out and told him why I had implicit faith in the picture; the story was good with a strong basic idea and after playing to audiences in the provinces as well as the West End, I assured him that this was the kind of stuff they go for. Had it been anyone else talking I wouldn't have worried, but I had such confidence in Mick's ability. I fought like a tiger trying to convince him, but the best I could get was a temporary postponement of any drastic action.

How interesting today to reflect on this unexpected crisis. Paradoxically the very thing that Mick seemed afraid of was to make him famous—British comedy.

Having won a reprieve, Walter, Cully and I agreed to work as fast as possible to finish the picture before we suffered another alarming upheaval. But there was no need to panic, we were in the clear. I don't know what it was that won Mick over. It may have been after seeing the ladder sequence on the rushes, and the little man saying, 'You'll never do it.' It could either have made him laugh or made him accept it as a challenge. Anyhow, what did it matter? After the trade show he was just as enthusiastic and happy as we were.

When Cis finished shooting she went off to Monte Carlo with some of our chums to change the black and blue on various parts of her body to a nice brown tan and if anyone needed a holiday, she did. She'd had two years without a break in *Folly to be Wise*—all that work plus filming in the daytime and the worry of our second financial collapse. She must have been terribly tired. What a relief when she decided to go on ahead of me. I was straining at the leash to follow her out as soon as possible but a fortnight's work still had to be done before I could say goodbye to Cully and Walter. Two days before I left, His Master's Voice rang up and asked me if I would make a record of one of the numbers I sang in the picture: *The Flies Crawled Up the Window*. I told them I was very sorry but I was off to the South of France in a couple of days.

'It can be done in one session,' they urged.

…aring for the greatest day of the year.

All dressed up for our first entrance . . . not the Palace Theatre but the Buckingham Palace Garden Party.

oud husband and proud daughter get in the picture as the
woman displays her CBE decoration.

The telegram we shall always treasure.

Cis in the front row with Arthur Macrae on her right and Manning Sherwin, left. Harold French (with glasses) is second from right. Also in the picture, back row from right, Jack Buchanan, Idair, Firth Shepherd, Harry Green and Collie Knox.

The first anniversary of *Under the Counter* at the Phoenix.

Myself and Cis in the front row with Harry Green, Dot Dixon, and Thorley Walters, standing behind me. In the back row at the right are Bobby Howes, Dorothy Ward, Peter Graves and Sandy Maxwell.

Forty years on—forty years too late for that matter—still, by paying a bit more, I eventually claimed my MA. Cis happened to be performing at the Arts Theatre and for her benefit I performed at the Senate House.

'Look at the camera, please'—and 'Wilson' did.

This is what Binkie Beaumont and Noël Coward saw when they motored down through the snow to Wimbledon—and they loved it, so we were all happy. *Mother Goose.*

St Valentine's Day 1966 . . . and the little woman's still smiling.

'Sorry, fellas, the moment the picture's finished I'm away. Thanks all the same.'

They rang again. 'We hear the picture's good. We want to get the record out at once.' They tried hard to persuade me but I was adamant.

Sea, sunshine and fresh air had made a splendid job of Cis. I was delighted to find on arrival that all signs of strain and fatigue had disappeared. She was in cracking form. It didn't take me long either to yield to the treatment: the crisp sparkle of the blue Mediterranean inviting a swim in the crystal clear water, then back to the golden sand to absorb the healing rays of the sun as it sent cordial greetings from its path across the heavens. Paradise. It was a scene of ineffable beauty except for the blemish of naked humanity reclining ungracefully on the beach, looking like bodies cooking in a slow oven. So many people look better with their clothes *on*. But a tired film actor with a skin the colour of a freshly peeled potato was equally responsible for this blot on the golden sands of the Mediterranean.

After four days of unspeakable bliss I was just coming out of the water when I heard one of the hotel porters shouting from the beach.

'*Monsieur 'Ulbert, Monsieur 'Ulbert. Deux Gentilhommes arrivant de Londres, désirent de vous voir.*' And sure enough the two gentlemen representing His Master's Voice were standing just behind him.

Greeting me warmly they went on to say, 'We're all fixed up in the ballroom of the hotel—all the equipment and a four piece band. You'll be back in the sea again before lunch.'

'Well,' I said, 'of all the—'

'Come on in just as you are.'

Such enterprise and keenness was impossible to refuse and still dripping wet I said, 'Right. It's a bet.' It was so hot that by the time we reached the ballroom I was bone dry. I walked into the temporary recording set-up they had arranged wearing nothing more than the briefest of bathing slips much to the the amusement of the technicians and the four French musicians who had been engaged for the band. In that gay atmosphere, naked as I was, I did an impromptu act. Out came the schoolboy French again and I treated the whole thing as a bit of holiday fun.

The record has been played a lot on radio but, as far as I know, it was never explained to the listeners how, when or where the recording was made. The story behind it was the most important thing. Being entirely on the spur of the moment, only two takes were necessary and I was back in that crystal-clear blue water in just under the hour.

The picture opened while we were still on holiday and got a heart-warming reception. It was shown at Peter Robinson's in the Strand, or rather, on the spot where Peter Robinson's now stands. The cinema was called the New Tivoli which had replaced the original famous music hall of that name.

On the success of *Jack's the Boy*, Cis and I landed a big contract. Micky Balcon was so delighted at the way things had turned out that he wanted to keep us working for the company for the next three years. The terms were excellent. Cis and I had no desire to make a change. Staying with Mick was infinitely preferable. Without hesitation, we signed the contract. To us it was a fortune. For the next three years we were sitting pretty.

And also following the success of *Jack's the Boy* a fantastic offer was made for my services at the Palladium. I showed complete indifference. Preferring the sunshine of the South of France I turned down the offer. I must have been mad. No, I was right, I didn't need the money. The creditors had been paid in full, and that was what really mattered. Which goes to show how important it is to be successful.

I was the Golden Boy of the exalted hierarchy of Wardour Street. It was red carpet, champagne and 'Jack's the Boy'. But one bad film and I knew my name would stink. That's why being a success becomes a great worry; a standard has to be maintained. The greater the success the more difficult it becomes to find a worthy successor. The script boys in the writing department seemed to have the answer: *Jack Ahoy*. Coming on the heels of the story of an ordinary policeman, that of an able-bodied seaman in the Navy seemed to be the natural follow-up. Walter, who was going to direct, was enthusiastic and Mick gave us the go ahead.

Just as Mick was building me up as a picture star so he was doing the same for Cis. She had Albert de Courville as a director. I could not help her much as naturally it was none of my business, but the script boys had apparently written her a good part and she seemed quite happy, and that was all I really knew. We were living in a different world, leading a different life—getting up at five or six in the morning and then a long drive to the studio to be made ready to start shooting at 9.00 a.m. It was just the opposite to what we had been used to, but no complaints. After all, it was exciting. Working in the same studio did not mean we saw a lot of each other. We belonged to entirely separate units. Our hours of working seldom coincided. Even to and from the studio we were frequently driven at different times. And then there were words to be learnt when we got home ready for tomorrow's shooting, a quick meal, then bed. Not much time to find out about each other and how we were doing. I was constantly worrying about Cis. I only knew de Courville as a stage producer, and knew he was excellent as such, but as a film director I had no idea. I saw some of the rushes. They were pretty good and Cis seemed happy so I could only hope for the best.

The spectacular setting of life on a battleship fulfilled its promise. Although quite different to *Jack's the Boy*, it had the same flavour, the same mixture of comedy and romance. When I was a kid there was a popular magazine called *The Boys' Own Paper* and each week it contained a story of the adventures of a young hero. It was very popular in those days and that's how these films were developing. Tough adventure and a hero doing mad things, but coming out on top in the end. Being in on the writing, I always insisted that the comedy should evolve naturally from the situation and never be fatuous. The hero must never go for laughter by being silly. The audience must always be sorry for him and laugh at the things he does to get out of a jam, because by sheer bad luck they go wrong. The boys agreed.

Claudie wrote the words of the song *The hat's on the side of my head* with an American composer which I sang on the battleship thereby violating the sanctity of the Quarter Deck. I even went further and danced—we had to assume that the admiral and the entire crew were otherwise engaged. I finished the routine by slipping on the deck and sliding overboard into the sea, cutting to a shot of me in the water, laughing and singing the last line of the song and pushing my hat on the side of my head.

All this was shot in the studio at Islington except for the water shot.

That had to be an exterior so it was left for a later date. In fact, it was late November when we all tripped gaily down to Weymouth for me to jump off the quay into the ice-cold English Channel. We had to have sun to match the Quarter Deck lighting. It was one of those 'in and out' days. We were all waiting for the sun to appear suddenly through the clouds.

'Stand by. Here it comes,' said the camera man, looking at the sky through a piece of smoked glass.

'O.K. sound? *Camera*,' Walter shouted.

I jumped—a drop of about ten feet. Before I hit the water even, Walter shouted, 'Cut.' Too late—I was swimming madly for the quayside. The water was icy. A tent had been rigged up on the top with four lots of sailors' clothes ready if required. Wringing wet, I climbed up and had to change into a perfectly dry set and come out to do the shot again.

When I was ready the camera man, looking at the clouds, said, 'Stand by—no, it's going in again—no, we're all right.'

Walter Ford shouted, '*Camera*,' and I jumped. The water seemed colder. I looked up hopefully. No, the sun went in again at the crucial moment. Another climb up to the top of the quay, another change into a dry set of clothes and then another wait for the sun.

It came out and stayed out. I jumped. We got the shot. A beauty. No, the camera had jammed. The water was colder still and so was the wind, which had got up suddenly to join the fun. This was the last chance. I was putting on the last dry set of clothes. I came out shivering, waiting for the sun. The clouds were much heavier, threatening rain. The situation was desperate.

The camera man, looking at the angry clouds, said, 'There's a slight break coming. We might just have enough—stand by. Here it comes.'

'O.K. sound? *Camera*,' Walter shouted with a ring of determination in his voice. I jumped. Then a great cheer came from the top of the quay and Walter's voice rang out, 'We've got it. A beauty. Now we can all go home tonight.'

<h1 style="text-align:center">19</h1>

The publicity agent for the company was very keen that we should go on the air and talk about the pictures we were making. It was a bit much on top of the long hours of filming but, as I pointed out to Cis, they would have to give us time off away from shooting, so we'd get a bit of a rest. The result was we found ourselves sitting in one of the BBC studios having a preliminary discussion about what we were going to say with a young man who seemed rather pleased with himself, a pleasure I was unable to share. He was to ask us about our respective films, that seemed fair enough, and then a few questions about our married life. I was grateful for the warning. He started off by saying, 'Now I would like to try and make this sound natural and spontaneous.' A very fatuous remark, I thought, to two people who earn their living by trying to do just that. Cis was about to point this out but her self-control prevailed.

Having been in radio since the far off Savoy Hill days I have had the pleasure of working with some delightful chaps but this young interviewer didn't happen to be one of them. With great condescension Mr Smug said, 'I would prefer not to rehearse anything, I rather favour the unexpected.' As he turned to speak to the engineers working the sound panel Cis whispered in my ear, 'This is going to be fun. Stand by, comics.'

We were sitting at a big table with a mike just above our heads. The interviewer sat opposite. Having taken a sound test of our voices and adjusted our positions, relative to the mike, a voice from the recording room said, 'If you're O.K. we'll go. Ten seconds from . . . *now*.' We waited, the green light flashed and we were away. The interviewer started.

'We are very happy to have Miss Cicely Courtneidge and Mr Jack Hulbert with us in the studio. In your long experience in show business, Miss Courtneidge, what was the funniest thing that happened to you?'

'Marrying Jack.'

'And she's never stopped laughing since,' I added.

Mr Smug was slightly disconcerted, obviously preferring the clichés and the old tried and true stuff.

'How long have you been married?' he asked, trying to recover. And I knew exactly what was coming next.

'How old were you when you first—'

Before he had time to finish I gave Cis a wink. She got the idea and crashed in immediately.

'My first picture was directed by Albert de Courville. The world famous tennis star Suzanne Lenglen was engaged and in the story I had to play against her. I took a mighty swipe at her service and missed, and all that sort of thing, but if I did connect I hit it so hard that it landed in a field a quarter of a mile away. On one occasion we were filming on the court, I was waiting for her service and it came over the net like a shot from a gun and my return had to be just the same, but miles out of court. The umpire, Hay Plum, sitting on a pair of steps, registered the wildness of the shot by jerking his head back as the ball flashed past his nose. This effect was obtained in a separate shot. Lenglen came over to where I was standing and hit the ball as hard as when she served. With incredible accuracy it passed within inches of Hay Plum's face. De Courville shouted, 'O.K. one more—and closer.' Lenglen repeated the shot with the same amazing accuracy. De Courville shouted again. "O.K. one more—and closer." The tennis professional who was coaching me in a few elementary technical points went up to De Courville and whispered, "If he gets hit by that ball it could kill him." De Courville said, quite unmoved, "I'll risk it." Apart from that he was rather nice and a clever director.'

'Most interesting,' I said turning to Cis. 'Please go on talking, Miss Courtneidge, I'm fascinated.'

'Thank you, Mr Hulbert, I certainly will.'

Mr Smug's expression suggested the broadcast was developing on unfamiliar lines. He tried to get back to normal but we weren't going to have any of that.

'Now, Miss Courtneidge,' he chipped in very quickly, 'I would like to ask you—' But he wasn't quick enough for Cis, she beat him to it.

'I must tell you about Sam Hardy, a glorious man I had with me in the film *Sally*. What a lovely sense of humour that man had—quite mad. He would walk on to the set in the morning and say, "Hullo, Cis. Well, it's getting rather late so I think I'll call it a day. Goodbye." He brought his wife on the set one morning, a delightful lady, and when he introduced her he would say, "This is Mrs Sam Hardy," and then quietly in your ear, "I'm thinking of making a change." *Sally* was not my favourite picture but Mick and the boys were all very pleased.'

Cis was now in top gear. She knew as well as I did a good interview depends on being asked the right questions, giving one a chance of saying something interesting or amusing. So we were forced to take the initiative.

'Now *Bulldog Jack*,' she said enthusiastically, 'that really was something—'

Mr Smug tried to cut in. 'I think if we had—'

'A cup of coffee. An excellent idea. How nice of you to think of it.' Cis then turned to me. 'You'd like some too, wouldn't you?'

'Yes, indeed. Now you were going to tell us about *Bulldog Jack*.'

'Oh yes—trouble—stand-by comics—situations not funny—lines not funny—all that la-di-da. You tell them Jack.'

'No, you tell them.'

'We'll both tell them. You go first, Mr Hulbert.'

'Right. The time now is eight and a half minutes past seven and here's a post card from Mrs Peters of 9 Eversley Road, S.W. 10, wishing her husband a Happy Wedding Anniversary at Brighton whoever he is with—'

That was the moment for Cis to enquire, 'Is the coffee on its way?'

'Yes, of course.' Mr Smug was completely deflated. 'Shall we—'

'Yes, let's.' Cis was off again. 'They wanted you to play a straight-forward Bulldog Drummond part. Right? Very wisely, you refused. Right? They were determined. So were you—deadlock—last minute suggestions made by Mr Hulbert—may I call you Jack?'

'Please do.'

'Thank you. Jack said, why not a compromise. The real Bulldog Drummond is about to do a job but doesn't show up, because he's got flu. Being a great fan Jack offers help. Drummond accepts so Jack does the job for him which immediately puts him, a comic, in a dangerous adventure story. Drummond gives you an address. Jack goes along and takes Claudie, his brother, another comic, to assist. Jack rings the bell—the door opens. Two thugs grab Jack and Claudie, pull them inside and bolt the door. What could be more exciting? Two comics dealing with it all absolutely seriously and all that sort of thing. Directed by dear old Walter at his best. Result, very exciting and very funny picture. The best scene was the menace, the mad criminal trying to escape, rushing down the spiral staircase of an old disused tube station with you and Claudie in hot pursuit, tobogganing down on a couple of tea trays trying to catch him. He jumps into the driver's cab of a train in the station, knocks out the driver and seizes the controls. You and Claudie jump into the nearest coach as the train shoots ahead. Every time it passes a station, Claudie, petrified, tried to get out but fails—the train's going much too fast. And who was the madman driving the train? Sir Ralph Richardson. Stand by comics, only the best is good enough in a Hulbert picture. What a tremendous help. He's come quite a long way since then.'

Cis paused to take breath.

'Now, Mr Hulbert,' Mr Smug said quickly, 'your next picture *Love on Wheels* was the story of—'

Cis was too quick for him again. 'A shop assistant in a big West End store. Leonora Corbett was the girlfriend. Every weekend for six weeks by kind permission of the owner, Selfridges was used for the store shots which gave reality to the picture plus the amazing performance of Jack.'

One last desperate effort from Mr Smug to regain control. 'Perhaps Mr Hulbert would tell us in his own words—' The studio door opened very quietly.

'Ah, here comes the coffee. It's all right, Bring it in, my dear. Thank you. Now Mr Sm—er—sure you won't join us?'

He shook his head miserably. 'No, thank you.'

'Right. Now let's get back to Jack's new picture—the *Love on Wheels* la-di-da. Unfortunately, Jack's best performance never appeared on the screen. Rushing about like a mad thing he raced down all the steps of the staircase to the basement at a tremendous speed but left out the last one and broke his ankle. The poor darling had his leg in plaster so the rest of the film had to be shot waist high. He had to walk with a stiff leg without moving the upper part of his body—a brilliant performance never to be appreciated by the public.'

The hapless Mr Smug managed to squeeze in on the act by changing the subject.

'You two have been happily married for quite a number of years.'

Here we go again, back to square one. I could see by Cis's expression she had the same thought.

'What's the secret?'

'Picking the right woman.' I gave him an immediate answer.

'How did you do that.'

'He had a little assistance.' Cis finished her coffee.

'What are the qualities you look for in a man, Miss Courtneidge?'

'Quick thinking, quick action and quick decision and I'm still looking.'

'But you have a perfect understanding?'

'We don't talk in the morning—it would be dangerous, but after lunch try and stop me.'

'She's an expert talker and I'm an expert listener.'

'And I'm an expert trainer.'

'Outstanding. I'm learning all the time. A bit slow perhaps but willing. At the moment I'm concentrating on tidiness. It's coming gradually.'

Cis continued, 'We don't argue. We never quarrel.'

'Exactly,' I agreed. 'It's all a matter of give and take. Toleration.'

'What was that again?' Cis wasn't letting it pass.

'Toleration,' I said innocently.

'You mean you tolerate me.' There was strong resentment in her voice.

'I never said so—'

'You implied it,' she snapped.

Poor Mr Smug was completely flummoxed. He couldn't be sure if this heated exchange of words was on the level or not so the interview was summarily concluded. I like to think by now he has renounced his arrogance. Outrageous behaviour on our part but what fun it was. I only hope the listeners enjoyed it as much as we did. At least they got something different.

'Thank you, Miss Courtneidge and Mr Hulbert, for joining us. It's been a great pleasure.'

Cis whispered in my ear, 'Stand by, comics!'

20

In another of Cis's pictures *Things Are Looking Up* she played with a young American star, William Gargan. Part of the story was set in a girl's school and some of the girls were beautiful, especially one. Cis asked who she was. A girl called Vivien Leigh. Just one of the girls who became a world star.

Cis's favourite picture was *Soldier of the Queen* in which she played a double role, herself and her own grandmother. Douglas Furber, just as he had done in *Jack's the Boy*, came up with an excellent idea centred on the Marvello family, long established in theatre history. It was from the viewpoint of the grandmother watching the grand-daughter carrying on the family tradition. Cis was most enthusiastic about one of the cast.

'We've got that darling man Edward Everitt Horton,' she told me. 'Wonderful to work with, just as funny off the screen as on. His camera technique, superb. He knows the lot, I'm learning all the time.'

Here was the Owen Nares situation repeated by an American expert. As I was not filming myself at that moment I was able to be on the set watching. And here I became a nuisance again. Cis had a splendid story and with good direction a fair chance of doing something big. So I appointed myself an unofficial supervisor. Maurice Elvy was an experienced director but it needed a little something out of the ordinary for Cis to hit the high spots. Mick begged me not to interfere but I explained how desperately important it was for Cis to take advantage of the excellent part. Anyone else would have ordered me out of the studio but Mick was always so kind and co-operative. We began to get some good stuff in the can but it was not the happiest way of working.

195

Noël Gay wrote a special number for Cis *There's Something About a Soldier*, which was a big hit and looked great on the screen. This film was probably her best. Playing the dual role, the grandmother and grand-daughter was most effective, especially when the two characters met on a split screen.

Me and Marlborough was a costume piece, a story of an incident on one of Marlborough's campaigns. A good picture with Tom Walls as the great general. Noël Gay wrote another soldier song for Cis, *All for a Shilling a Day*.

My next job was *Jack of all Trades*. This I was directing myself with Bob Stevenson. We couldn't make the picture without Cecil Parker of course. This was the period when he seemed to be in everything and mighty glad we were to have him, he was a smooth and polished actor. I enjoyed the scenes we played together. A dear friend of mine, Robertson Hare, was a great asset to the film. He only had to appear and it was a laugh. Dear Bunny, one of the best on and off the stage.

That man Fred Astaire, I couldn't get him out of my mind. Philip Buchel worked hard on my dance routines and I worked equally hard learning them. Fred's dancing was perfection. Drawing level was out of the question but dropping too far behind had to be avoided at all costs. I was forced to find a plausible reason for a dance in the film and had to invent a dance which had something to do with the story. Anyhow, it all helped to make life more interesting.

I had a whale of a time with one of the ideas I got, dancing along a street specially built on a lot in Northolt. I danced all night, three nights running. Disguised as a chimney sweep I had an excellent song written for me by my friend, the young composer Vivien Ellis, called *Sweep All Your Troubles Away*. I sang the song as I walked down the street and then into the dance. For technical reasons it had to be done at night. The singing part was easy—that was disposed of in three takes—but this dance, why did I ever think of it? All night—just crazy—three nights running. By the end of the third night I was completely danced out. What a job Fred or Gene Kelly would have made of it! Thank heavens I thought of it first, but it served its purpose being something new on the screen.

Some people never learn. I suppose I was one of them. In a subsequent picture I thought of winter sports as a background. Micky liked the idea. I worked with the script boys on a story and we went to St Moritz on location. Cis was in it too, and with Bob Stevenson, who was directing with me, we were all enjoying the hospitality of the Suvretta House. Three weeks in St Moritz is fun. Three months is a mistake, especially when the thaw sets in.

We saw the magnificent ice rink belonging to the Suvretta House gradually collecting large puddles of water. We saw the snow losing its pure whiteness as it disappeared unevenly on the ski slopes. We had to have snow collected and laid down where we were shooting to cover up the ravages of the thaw. We had to be careful to avoid showing dripping trees in the picture. When we first arrived after Christmas, it was ideal, just as I had anticipated when I first suggested the idea to the company. We had always enjoyed our winter sports holidays in Switzerland and now that we were in the process of making successful pictures my suggestion had been diplomatically accepted. Great fun to start with it then became a long tedious grind.

Before arriving on location I was working with one of the script writers in a search for originality and I arranged that the heroine, played by Tamara Desni, a young actress of great beauty, should be an amateur skating champion so that I could attempt to win her favour with a display of skill and agility on the ice. It seemed a very promising idea. The inevitable question arose: could I skate? I should have said I could only just about stand up, but in order to avoid lengthy arguments I told them figure skating was one of my hobbies. So on that assurance we went ahead. The first thing I had done on arrival at St Moritz had been to engage the skating instructor for daily lessons and I suppose my sense of balance as a dancer enabled me to make fairly swift progress. Falling presented no fears—I had done all that for years on the stage. I treated my 'programme', as the instructor called it, as a dance routine and I arranged with Bob Stevenson, my co-director, that I would get as far as I could in performing the routine and when I fell, which was bound to happen sooner or later, he would cut to Tamara Desni laughing. I also got him to take several shots of her looking at me that he could cut in just before I crashed, which, when it was finally put together, looked exactly as if her sudden glance in my direction was the cause of the catastrophy. All that was fine but learning all those spins and loops and jumps was another matter. We left the shooting of the skating sequence till the end to give me as much time as possible to practise. I had roughly six weeks.

Directing and playing in the film reduced considerably the amount of time left to skating practice—not that I *could* have skated any longer. I had to have a masseur to work on my leg muscles every evening as it was. Tamara Desni's exhibition skating was performed by a professional girl skater of the same figure and shape which, of course, had to be in long shot, and the looks in my direction and the laughing when I fell, was Tamara herself in close up. In the final cutting it seemed worth all the trouble. The crashes looked real and spontaneous—which is exactly what they were.

In the chase scene, in the last reel, we went for laughter and excitement. Cis and I were trying to rescue Tamara from the clutches of the menace, excellently played by Garry Marsh. I was on skis and Cis was on a toboggan. The menace was driving a sleigh, with the captive Tamara aboard, at a furious speed down the mountain road and every time we got near one of us crashed and the sleigh forged ahead. Finally, Cis took a wrong turning and got on to the fast toboggan run and finished up shooting through a ground floor window into the hotel, which got big laughs from the audience when the picture was shown. Continuing the chase, I reached the sleigh but couldn't stop and went shooting past. All this took a devil of a long time to shoot but we got it in the end—only just. We had reached the shifting-the-snow period as the thaw had set in. It was the only time that Cis and I were glad to leave the winter sports and go home.

After the big success of the adaptation from the German, *Sunshine Susie*, it seemed a feasible idea that Micky Balcon and Gaumont British should be working in conjunction with Ufa in Berlin. *Congress Dancers*, starring Conrad Veidt and Lilian Harvey, had already been made in London. Cis and I were sent over to the studios in Neubarblsburg to make the English version of a film called *Happy Ever After*. Lilian Harvey and Willie Fritch were the German stars. Lilian Harvey was making three versions—German, French and English—which meant every scene had to be done three times. The story was rather a neat idea centring round two window cleaners, both pals, in love with the same girl. A romantic setting for Lilian Harvey and Willie Fritch. Charming but not quite *our* cup of tea. The boys at home gave us the rewritten version before we left for Berlin and they had done quite a good job. Of course, it did not work as far as we were concerned. The difficulties we had in trying to fit our humour into scenes already established were insuperable. Mick came over with a lot of the London press to appraise the value of the scheme.

Cis took Mick aside and told him in her quiet gentle manner that things were not going quite as smoothly as we hoped.

'Coming all this way over here indeed, and no one has the foggiest idea who we are even.'

'Absolute nonsense.' Mick was furious. 'I was talking to Pommer two days ago. He thinks you're both great—'

'Oh well, Pommer, he's only the boss. It's this man Martin, the director. Believe it or not he doesn't speak a word of English and doesn't understand a single word we are saying.' Cis continued to expand on the subject in her own characteristic way. 'Stand-by comics. That's a lot of help when you're trying to be funny. I ask you. I was doing a scene with Jack. I was stopped. A lot of hurried talk went on in German then Vexler the interpreter said, "Mr Martin wants to know why you are playing the part this way." That started me seeing red. "Tell Mr Martin it is because in England I am expected to be be funny." A lot more jabbering in German and Vexler has another go. "Mr Martin says why do you have to be funny?" "Because it's my job. I'm a funny woman, that's what I'm paid for, I'm a comedienne." Then Vexler told this to Martin who said, "What is comedienne?" ·

'Oh, for heaven's sake! I don't know what goes on. I really don't. Anyway, I tried again: "Me—funny—say funny things—make people laugh—do funny things. Tell him." This translated into German sounded most peculiar then Vexler came back to me and said, "Mr Martin says please show him the funny things." That got me crawling up the wall.'

Poor Mick was most concerned and saw the fatal mistake of having a director who did not understand English comedy or even understand the language. He went off to see Pommer at once.

What would have made a novel and very funny picture would be a bewildered German director trying to make a film about the oddities of a country he knew nothing about and trying desperately hard to understand the intricacies of an English joke through an interpreter. At least that might have given us a success.

Apart from the frustration of having to play in a picture we knew was not right and never could be, we had a most enjoyable time in Berlin. Ivor McLaren, who had now become one of our particular friends came over and motored us around when we had a day off or were not wanted at the studio.

After many years of inventing dance routines for the chorus and producing a number of full scale musicals, I felt a compulsive urge to get a piece of land somewhere and dig. A yearning to escape for a brief spell from the stress and complications of stage and films. The joy of a garden, growing flowers, the simple delights of nature. The call was irresistible.

I told our secretary Beaufoy Lane—'Beef' as he was fondly known—who joined us in the early thirties, and Laurie Green who was still working for me to go out into the country and procure a small piece of land, a corner of a field, anything, somewhere just outside London, preferably north, off the old Roman road. There was less traffic that way and it was easier to reach. Beef, excellent at fixing things, called on Lord Salisbury's agent at Hatfield House who took him to *West End Farm* and found the very thing. I went down to see it, an ideal spot just outside the village of Essendon. The farmer was only too glad to do a deal. I went into Hatfield immediately, bought a spade and a fork, returned to the farm and started digging. I then bought a few plants and stuck them in the ground. In a matter of months I rented the whole field. Again the farmer was delighted, especially as I hired a room in the old farmhouse. Within a year I took over the entire farm and kept him on as manager. I was now up to my neck in it. I had become a farmer. Needless to say, I lost money being a new boy but it was worth every penny for its therapeutic value. When people rang up 43 Curzon Street on business they were told invarably, 'Mr Hulbert has gone to the farm' and that was the end of that. Indeed I was down there whenever I could reasonably get away.

In addition to acquiring a passion for gardening, I did every kind of job on that farm: mending gates, repairing fences, cutting down trees for posts, construction work as I made a small barn for storing part of the hay crop, a large shed for the tractor, a stable for the horses. It was a new world for me—a world I loved. Back to nature in the open air. It was hard work physically but such a healthy recreation.

I employed my property man Jim, who had worked for me for many years in the theatre. Since being saved by that genial old property man on my first night at the Criterion, whose name unfortunately I have forgotten, I have always regarded 'Props' with the highest esteem. But Jim could tackle anything. There was not a job he could not do. He was outstanding, both as a technician and a man, and I was particularly fond of him. He built a large workshop which I had fitted up with a circular saw and a planer. Over the years he built a large barn with a tiled roof and five large greenhouses. I had plans later on to go in for market gardening concentrating on flowers. He had never made a greenhouse in his life and these were perfect. He was brilliant and a delight to have about the place.

When I first took over the farm, it was oil lamps and candles. I tried to get the Electricity people to wire us up but they refused. Later I gave permission for pylons carrying high tension cables to be erected in one of my fields. While I was away in Hollywood they went ahead with the work and cut down the trees in a little copse in the corner of the meadow. It was one of my favourite spots on the farm with lovely old oak trees, which were a dominant feature of the landscape. When I returned and saw the havoc they had wrought I demanded compensation stating clearly in my letter that I had not given permission for this copse to be destroyed. They met me with cap in hand full of apologies and asked what reparation would be acceptable. I said for them to get a line from the cables to the house. They willingly agreed. And that's how I got electricity laid on for nothing.

21

In the mean time the script boys had come up with an exciting idea for a story based on the British Air Command in Egypt. It was a good adventure story involving Luxor, Karnack, and the Valley of the Kings. 'The story called for a certain amount of skilled horsemanship,' the script boys informed me. 'But that should be right down your street,' they said. Again I should have confessed but such an attractive location with Cairo and the pyramids thrown in was not to be missed. I immediately got the address of a riding school run by a chap called Captain Phillips somewhere near Bishops Stortford. I put on a pair of riding bags and leggings I had used for skating and drove down right away. It took a bit of finding, being off the beaten track but from the owner's point of view it was worth it. A charming little Georgian house with a walled garden and with the arena, or covered-in school, hidden behind a little wood. Captain Phillips' short-clipped military moustache caught my eye. We shook hands. I told him what I required and I was at it right away on a beautiful grey horse.

'Keep your heels down and grip with your knees.' he said as the horse walked gently round the ring. 'Hold the reins through your fingers and keep your elbows into your side.' Just walking, all this was easy. Trotting was another matter.

'Lean in slightly as you go round. No, no, the other way,' he shouted as I nearly came off. I managed to recover and we continued on our way.

'Grip with the knees. Heels down, elbows in. Good. Lean in slightly. That's right, you're getting it. Check the reins very gently and the horse will walk. Good. Check a little more and you'll stop.' We did

202

and I finished up with my arms round the horse's neck. The animal had excellent manners and ignored this familiarity.

'Now we'll turn and walk round the reverse way. Pull slightly with your left hand—good. Now into a gentle trot. A slight kick with the heels. Oh, I'm sorry about that. Are you all right? You kicked a little too hard so the horse thought you were in a hurry.'

Captain Phillips helped me to remount and said, 'Let's start again. Remember a very gentle kick.' That, I was not likely to forget.

'Good. Now into a trot and about turn. Very gentle pressure with the heels. Good. Bend slightly inwards—go with the horse. Good. Now let's reverse the direction. Turn him round. Pull the right rein very gently. Good. Into the trot, that's right. Don't bump along—rise and fall. Take it all very easily—lean slightly—the other way—*the other way*. Are you all right? Sorry about that. I'll help you remount. All right to try again? Good. It's all a question of balance and don't forget, heels down, elbows in.'

I was back in the circus act again, trotting round the ring. I had so much to remember that when Phillips shouted 'Lean' I'd forgotten which way, so I had to take a chance. 'Oh, my dear chap, I'm so sorry. Are you all right?'

'It's this leaning business that foxes me,' I said remounting, which I was now pretty good at.

'Put it another way,' said Phillips. 'Balance—just go with the horse.' I did and fell off at once.

After a couple of days I felt I must approach the problem a different way. I persuaded Phillips to let me play around in a field and practise on my own. This worked wonders. I only fell off once. I now had a mad ambition to jump. Phillips had a paddock fitted up for this purpose. He was in his element. It gave him more scope. 'Go with the horse,' he said. 'As he jumps lean forward.' The first couple of times I stayed on by sheer determination, but the third time I scrambled to my feet wondering what went wrong. I was still harrassed by so many does and don'ts. I just felt I wanted practice. I told Phillips I would like to go out hunting. He thought I was fooling.

'It's exactly like my job,' I assured him. 'The only way to learn it is to do it.' In the end he was persuaded. 'Well, I think it's crazy but if you're determined the best I can do is give you a horse that will take you over safely if you can manage to sit there and let him negotiate the jumps without interference. Just leave him to do it on his own.'

I had some clothes made in record time and turned up in a complete outfit but not a top hat. I thought a bowler would be less conspicuous, because I looked more like a groom than one of the elite hunting set. I chose the 'Old Berkeley' as it was fairly near London. Captain Phillips met me as arranged at 'The George and Dragon' having just driven up.

Opening the door of the trailer he said, 'He's a first rate hunter—loves it. He knows exactly what to do. Leave it all to him. Don't try to stop him. When you come to a jump just leave it all to him. His name is Steve. Talk to him. He likes it. See you back here at three.'

The meet was just outside the grounds of an old seventeenth century mansion belonging to one of our peers—the perfect backcloth to the colourful scene of men, some in hunting pink and top hats, others in black with yellow waistcoats, mounted on horses of quality and breed. The women were similarly clad in black, looking both glamorous and charming. It was a delightful glimpse of the England of yesterday. My only previous experience of mixing with ladies and gentlemen of high society, parading in the traditional splendour of the Hunt, was in the first act finale of a musical comedy. My arrival at the 'meet' caused quite a stir, the very last thing I wanted. I found myself hobnobbing with the aristocracy of the hunting world, sitting on a horse which, unlike the embarrassed film actor on its back, was on familiar ground and thoroughly enjoying every minute of it. I would have liked to have stayed in the background and avoided the greetings and social chat but not Steve—he took me right into the thick of it and remembering Phillips' last words I deemed it unwise to interfere.

'Good morning, Mr Hulbert, nice to have you with us,' came from all kinds of people.

'I am Mrs Egerton Russford,' came from a lady of striking appearance in a dark well-cut suit complete with top hat. 'So pleased you have joined us.'

I don't think Steve liked her. He walked away immediately so all our conversation had to take place on the move. I was so afraid she might think I was trying to get away from her.

'Steve,' I said firmly, 'stand.' He just shook his head and walked a bit faster. Mrs Egerton Russford followed suit.

'Full of beans, isn't he? Very wise to keep him moving. Now you simply must meet the Master. Charming man—he's just over there behind us. Shall we do an about-turn and go over and meet him.'

'Well—yes—delighted.' I couldn't possibly refuse, what was I to do? Playing for time I said feebly, 'Come on, Steve, about turn—the Master.' To my amazement, he obliged and turned swiftly. Then I saw what made him do it. The whole hunt were moving off. Mrs Egerton Russford was most concerned.

'Too late—I'm so sorry. Some other time.'

'Please don't apologise.' I raised my voice. 'I shall look forward—' But Steve had taken me well ahead. He knew the drill. He wasn't going to be left standing. The cavalcade moved along briskly.

'You've brought the right kind of weather.' This came from a gentleman in 'pink' with a well-trimmed grey moustache growing on a face of many hues, mostly blue and purple, with a black top hat enhancing the colour scheme. 'Scent should be good.'

'I wouldn't be at all surprised.'

'Nice and damp—no wind.'

'Perfectly splendid.' I daren't get involved in conversations of this kind and I was trying to concentrate on all the points Phillips had told me.

'They're going to draw Felgate Wood—almost certain to find—good place—plenty of foxes—suggest slow up and wait.'

But Steve was not in agreement. The advice was ignored. We continued to move forward and I saw the first jump coming up. The people in front were already going over. As we drew nearer I could see it was not too formidable.

A familiar voice behind me said, 'Would you like me to give you a lead?'

'Oh, thank you,' I replied, not understanding.

Mrs Egerton Russford sailed over with the greatest of ease.

'This is it, Steve,' I said. 'It's up to you, Good luck'. He increased his speed slightly. I saw the hedge coming at me. A few more strides and he took off. I bent forward then leant back as we landed and stayed on. Steve seemed as pleased as I was. He raced forward to catch up with those in front who were now jumping the second fence. I made no attempt to interfere. Once again I saw the hedge coming at me—a little higher than the other, I thought. 'It's all yours again, Steve.' He took off, I leant forward and leant back as he made a perfect landing. 'Well done, boy. I'm proud of you.' I patted his neck affectionately. He seemed pleased. I felt we were now two very good friends. I was gaining confidence fast.

We were a little to the right of the crowd which gave me a chance of escaping from a lot of the social stuff. Normally it would have been fun and I envied those experienced riders who made it all look so easy. Hunt etiquette could not be assimilated at one sitting and without it the utmost caution had to be exercised. So with that and the does and don'ts, only scant attention could be given to social chit-chat. The more I could keep away from it the better. Unfortunately, Steve's temperament would never allow him to miss an opportunity of joining the crowd so he took a left incline and we were right in the thick of it.

'That certainly is a nice horse.' I turned quickly. As I thought, Mrs Egerton Russford again. 'Had him long?'

'Er—no—not very.'

'He seems a good strong jumper. Just what you need. It gets a bit tricky farther on.' She hailed a rather distinguished-looking rider.

'Puggie, come here. Mr Hulbert, I don't think you have met Lord—' But I missed the name as the wind removed my hat, which was saved by the cord attached to the brim.

'Always nice meeting you film chaps, what?' A broad grin wrinkled his classic features. He was one of those excessively gay types. 'Thanks for all the laughter. Don't know how you keep it up. Good show. Plenty of laughter and pretty women. That's life, what? We're all intrigued to know why you favour the bowler and not the top hat. Do tell us,' he said with a charming smile.

I knew I'd made a mistake. I felt most uncomfortable. Suddenly the sound of repeated blasts from the hunting horn in the distance changed the entire scene. I had no idea what it meant. Steve knew exactly. The hounds were in 'full cry'.

'We're away,' shouted Lord Whoever It Was. The whole field went off at a gallop. This was obviously the moment Steve had been waiting for. He shot forward at a cracking speed, scattering a herd of cows that were grazing in the meadow. The riders in front were already jumping a formidable hedge. Evidently this was the beginning of the 'tricky part' recently mentioned. One horse refused, the rest were getting over.

Mrs Egerton Russford goes into the lead. Steve's not standing for that. He catches up—passes her—fifty yards to go—the hedge gets bigger—a matter of seconds—bigger still—we're there—it's enormous—like the Grand National—Steve takes off—a beautiful jump —we're over—what a thrill—a perfect landing. But in my excitement I forgot to lean back. Steve, getting rid of eleven stone twelve, forges ahead.

As I picked myself up from the mud, several members of the hunt shouted, 'Are you all right?'

'Yes, fine, thanks. Just made a bad landing.' And there I was in the middle of a field covered in mud with no horse and wearing a bowler. In the distance I could vaguely see someone had caught Steve and was bringing him back. As that someone got closer I could see who it was. My humiliation was complete. I thanked her profusely and remounted —that and falling off were the only things I could do with certainty.

'Pecked on landing I suppose,' Mrs Egerton Russford said in her irritating way.

'Yes, exactly.' I could only guess what she meant.

'Shall we try and catch up with the field?'

'No, I think I shall call it a day. He's slightly out of condition and I don't want to work him too hard.'

'Quite right. Hope to see you out again.'

'Yes, rather.'

'Next week perhaps. Very nice to have met you.'

'Same here.'

'Goodbye.' And she galloped away.

Steve had no intention of letting her get in front and started off in hot pursuit. This was the moment to assert my authority. I pulled on the reins. It had no effect. By pulling one side only we started on a wide circular tour round the field. Get him tired out, I thought—make him go faster. I applied the spurs very gently. We immediately got into a mad gallop, circling the field. On the second time round a few stragglers of the hunt stopped and watched in amazement. As I passed them on the third time round I shouted, 'A little exercise. He was far too fresh.' The plan was successful. When I pulled on both reins we dropped down to a comfortable trot.

'I thought you said he was out of condition and you were taking him home.'

'Oh, hullo.' So there she was again. I might have guessed it.

'I just came back to see if you're all right.'

'Fine, thanks, and so's Steve.'

'I couldn't make out what was happening.'

'Just a little test, you know. Point to Point season getting near.'

Steve rescued me from any further conversation. He'd had enough of that woman. Away we went at full speed again. I could only shout apologies.

'Sorry—suddenly remembered—horse van—' I was shouting louder and louder. 'Three o'clock. Hope to see you.' But by now we were too far away.

'Steve, you're a grand chap. We've had a great day.' I was patting him affectionately on the neck. 'You've taught me so much. Sorry about that third fence—entirely my fault.'

The second time out, which was with the Enfield Chase, Steve and I, complete with top hat, had a clear round. Suddenly I could ride, thanks to the incomparable Steve. I was very sorry to say goodbye to him, but the hunting territory of the Enfield Chase was adjacent to the farm and as I got friendly with the honorary huntsman, a chap called Tim Muxworthy, who was a farmer-cum-riding master with several horses, he mounted me on one from his stable.

The long-term contract we had signed for making two pictures a year each, which enabled us to enjoy the fruits of prosperity, made a pleasant change from the never-ending worry of stage production.

Not that I failed to enjoy every minute of it but enough was enough for the time being.

I think we'd had practically every make of car since 1919 when we started with a second-hand Daimler chassis, without a body. We sat on a couple of soap boxes. It took a long time to get a body made in those days just after the First World War, but it was ours and it went quite well. That was good enough. Claudie, who was living with us for quite a time, was an excellent driver. I was appalling. Years later I rendered a signal service to my country by resigning from the driving seat. We finished by travelling up and down the country in a Rolls, which was the best of the lot.

It was my job to take the Pekinese for a walk whenever I was available, a duty I dodged if I possibly could. On one occasion Cis said to our chauffeur, 'I haven't time to take Peekie for a run today so I would like you to take him to Hyde Park this afternoon.' The intelligent chauffeur drove round Hyde Park twice with Peekie sitting majestically in the front seat.

Pammie, now sixteen years old, shortly to leave her school in Harley Street, destined for the stage, showing great promise as a dancer, expressed a strong desire to hunt. I felt insulted. A kid of sixteen with no riding experience, just a bit of hacking near the farm, talking to her father, who had been trained in a riding school at great cost and fallen off more times than anyone in the country!

'I love you dearly, my darling, but that's going a little too far.'

But she persisted, her mother's tenacious spirit showing itself, and the next thing I found was that the three of us, Pammie, Muxworthy and myself, were with the Enfield Chase in full cry near Northaw Wood, jumping everything that came in sight. With mixed feelings of wounded pride and a paternal admiration for her natural horsemanship and courage, I had to admit she was 'born to it'. We had some very happy outings together. On a murky grey December afternoon the unfrequented parts of the English countryside just beyond the fringe of industrial development touch an emotional chord in the heart by their exquisite beauty. Had it not been for the excellent schooling I received from dear old Steve, which enabled me to ride to hounds, I might never have known that this heritage of beauty

existed in our homeland. After all this hard training in horsemanship
and adventure in the hunting field, what I rode in the film in Egypt
was a camel.

About two years previously I had persuaded the studios to build a
dancing platform in a corner of a field in a secluded part of my farm
at Essendon and three carpenters and two loads of timber were sent
down. In the course of a week a perfectly good practice stage had been
created. It served an excellent purpose. Instead of sweating in some
stuffy London rehearsal room, Philip Buchel and I were enabled to
take some healthy exercise in the invigorating air of Hertfordshire.
With a gramophone in place of a piano we did most of our work in
those ideal surroundings. The grazing cattle in the adjoining meadow,
undisturbed by the noise, regarded it as another of Hulbert's mad
ideas. When not in use a large tarpaulin protected it from the weather.
After I had finished in pictures I knocked it to pieces and used every
scrap of the timber for making fences and all kinds of repair work
on the farm. I also had this in mind when first suggesting the idea
to the studio.

22

It was becoming patently clear that Cis and I would not be able to spend all our time together in the course of our respective film careers. There would be times when I would be working in one part of the world and she in another. It was inevitable. And sure enough I found myself filming *The Camels Are Coming* in Egypt while Cis was in London, and later Cis would be filming in Hollywood and *I* would be in London.

Working in Egypt on location was sensational—scenes near the Pyramids and in the desert for weeks on end. A memorable experience but a long way from London. Then right up the Nile to Luxor where we photographed some of the action of the story in front of the magnificent ruins of the temple. We would leave our luxury hotel each morning, cross the Nile in a small boat and drive a short distance to ancient Thebes to marvel each day at the fabulous great temple of Amun with its towering columns, some of it so well preserved that the pictures cut into the stone of the massive walls representing the glories of Egyptian conquests are as clear and well defined today as they were thousands of years ago. It was all so incredibly interesting that I had great difficulty in concentrating on the scenes we were shooting, trying to escape from the villain in those august precincts. The glorious weeks in Luxor and Karnak, never will they fade from my memory.

In the early days of filming in the desert we had great difficulty with the light. Each day the sun was hazy. The camera man suggested trying to shoot at dawn. This meant my sitting in the make-up chair at four each morning so I'd be ready to catch the dawn, but that was also a failure. We then received orders from London to bring back the camel I had been using to repeat the shots at home. On our arrival the chaps got busy painting a neutral backcloth and covering the studio floor with sand. I repeated all the same business of trying to mount the camel and falling off each time it got up off its knees and then trying to get on to its back when it was standing up. When we saw the rushes the whole thing looked absolutely real, whereas before, the shots we took in the desert looked flat and unnatural because there were no shadows. All that trouble in the desert for nothing. That part of the job had to be scrapped.

Just after I got back Cis went out to Hollywood to make a picture called *The Imperfect Lady*, starring with Frank Morgan. Micky Balcon had a tie-up with Metro-Goldwyn-Mayer. Cis had a special clause in her contract covering the expenses of a companion. The companion of her choice still had a few more days to go on his picture and as soon as he was clear he hopped aboard a Cunarder and then on the Santa Fé to join her in Hollywood. Cis had an apartment in Sunset Towers on Sunset Boulevard. The companion went straight there and the reunion was most cordial. From the true Courtneidge flood of words I gathered things were not going well and it was not surprising when I heard the full story.

'Oh, darling, I'm so glad you're here. It's all such a mess, I don't know what goes on, I really don't. When I arrived I got a lovely welcome—red carpet—V.I.P. treatment—the lot. It couldn't have been nicer. Then the producer arrives and from then everything seems to go wrong. D'you know, after all that ballyhoo in the press, he didn't know who I was? And he's in charge of the picture! One of the M.G.M. producers. I ask you. Isn't it marvellous? I saw through him at once, watching him handle other people and bluffing his way through. But he wasn't going to do that with me. Oh, no. "Come into my office," he said, "and let's talk things over."

' "Now, Miss Courtneidge, what d'you do?" he asked, which annoyed me intensely.

' "Get the tea, make the bed, do the room, wash up, go to the hairdresser and if there's time have lunch."

' "No, no. What do you do when you're on the stage?" This annoyed me even more.

' "Count the house. What would you do if you were on a percentage?"

'Not a smile from him—he got louder and more emphatic. "I mean do you sing, dance, act, play comedy or tragedy—"

' "The lot." If only he'd stop trying to impress me with his importance, we might have got somewhere. "It may be of some help to you if I mention the fact that I was asked to go to my own tailor in London and have a military uniform made, which I was asked to bring with me." That really tied him up.

' "Whatever for?" he asked in that soft caressing voice of his.

' "Probably to work a number," I suggested.

' "Oh, you sing?"

' "Divinely. You've heard of Covent Garden of course—" '

Having delivered this glossy panegyric on the producer's merits, Cis reclined on the settee for a few brief moments, just long enough for me to ask 'What does Mick say?' before she was off again. I cabled Mick and he phoned M.G.M. immediately about this appalling lack of organisation. Then Cis continued.

'Louis B. Mayer sent for me. I was shown into an enormous room rather like the audience chamber in Buck House, and away in the distance I could just see a man sitting at a huge desk. It seemed ages walking to meet him. When I got near he rose from his chair very politely—a nice change from the producer's lack of manners—and said, "Good morning, Miss Courtneidge, I am sorry to hear you are unhappy."

'I told him the producer knew nothing about me at all and Mayer said hadn't he seen my pictures and when I told him no, the fun really started. The director was removed and another was installed. The producer, I never saw him again. The authors started madly rewriting and the whole picture is being remade.'

Cis was naturally fed up and instead of Hollywood being an interesting and edifying experience, a golden opportunity to learn, the only golden thing about it was the salary. We had fixed to have a holiday in Miami, but the shooting went so far over the scheduled time that we had to cancel the plans and go back home to make our own picture with Gaumont British which was *Take My Tip* with that grand character actor Frank Cellier. The script boys had been working at it all the time we were in Hollywood.

We had been away from the stage for nearly ten years, and were both yearning to get back. Plans were being made excitedly to this end, but, as so frequently happens in our business, they were held up.

For a long time it had been my ambition to become an international star which, of course, meant Hollywood. Harry Ham, a well known agent who worked over here and in California, assured me he would pull it off sooner or later and sure enough he called me up to say Selznick wanted me for a picture and I was to go over to Hollywood at once and meet him. This was startling news. Once again I made the journey. Harry Ham met me over there and took me to R.K.O. Studios to meet Selznick. He greeted me rather like Seymour Hicks did when I lunched with him at the Garrick years ago.

'Come in, come in, delighted to meet you, I'm still laughing. I've seen all your pictures. You're so funny. Please forgive me for laughing now I look at you. I'll get the writers working at once. Sure we'll turn out a swell picture and a lot more to follow. I'll talk to Harry about a contract at once.'

I left in a state of wild excitement. I was jubilant. At last the fulfilment of my ambition was in sight. I wanted to celebrate. I would treat myself to a jolly good dinner. Myself? Where was Cis? On the other side of the Atlantic. I must be crazy! I went straight back to my hotel and booked a night flight to New York the next evening and a passage to England on the *Aquitania*. Six thousand miles away from England. I thought, one picture, two pictures, even more, it would take months—might be several years—all that time in Hollywood away from the London I loved. Why? What for? To hell with being an international star. There is something else far more important. I got on that plane and the *Aquitania*, leaving Hollywood for good. I've never regretted it; to this day I know in my heart I was right.

Cis was on holiday with friends in Monte Carlo. I went out there at once and we had another grand reunion. Cis was as happy as I was. Lots of people thought I was mad to give up such an opportunity, but not Cis and that was the all-important thing. We had a smashing holiday and returned home to start work on *Take My Tip*.

We both thought the script for *Take My Tip* was very well written, with excellent parts for the two of us, and as we had to play most of our scenes with that delightful actor Frank Cellier we were very happy. Coming out of the story I got a couple of ideas right away for two dance routines. Philip Buchel started work on inventing the steps and in a short time he provided me with two excellent routines. It meant a hell of a lot of rehearsing, especially in the scene where I had to throw valuable pieces of china to that talented comedian Rob Wilton, who was playing the furniture remover. I was at one end of the room dancing all the time and picking up each piece of china in rhythm and then throwing it to enable the startled Rob Wilton, at the other end of the room, to catch each one on the last beat of each phase of the music. I blame Fred Astaire entirely for all this strenuous exertion.

Mick was away, steeped in the M.G.M. tie-up. *Take My Tip* was the last picture to be made at the old Gaumont British studios at Lime Grove, Shepherds Bush; the whole place was packing up. When I went to the studios I was met by the chap who was left in charge—I forget his name—and in his office, after some desultory conversation, he came straight to the point.

'We have another film lined up for Cis with a part we think—er— much more suitable.' He was obviously ill at ease.

'But this is madness—'

'Not when you consider the situation. To put it bluntly, the part in *Take My Tip* must be played by a woman who is much more glamorous.'

'But surely the comedy is far more important.'

'We feel it would be kinder and more tactful if her husband were to break the news.'

I knew the film story they were suggesting. It certainly was excellent and a great starring vehicle for Cis. Perhaps they were right. I found Cis immediately and we sat down together in my dressing room. Once Cis has made up her mind it is not easy to shift her.

'Darling,' I began, 'I'm a little worried about your part.'

'Why? I think it's terrific. The comedy—'

'That's it, I'm just wondering—you don't think your style will be rather cramped—I mean—she's got to be—well—so appealing —prepossessing—so—glamorous.'

'Exactly—that's what makes it such a stunning part. That make-up I had in Hollywood—well, you saw the rushes and told me I looked smashing.'

'Yes, I know. You don't think it will be a little restricting?'

'On the contrary, the part calls for restraint and subtlety. Jack, why not come straight to the point and say what you've been told to say— I'm not glamorous enough.'

'You mean you knew all the time what I was leading up to?'

'Darling, don't be absurd—after all these years.'

'What are you going to do?' I asked, feeling greatly relieved.

'Fight them.'

That's my girl. I thought, but I didn't say so.

'Who told you they'd decided you were not glamorous enough?'

'Herbert Mason, our director. He thinks they're all up the pole.'

'Werb' Mason I knew well, he had stage-managed so many shows in the West End. He said to me, 'Lie low for a bit; they'll never find anybody to replace Cis, she's ideal for the part.'

And sure enough, after a couple of weeks, Cis was overwhelmed with apologies. But she was in no mood to let them off the hook. In despair they asked me to intervene. I said, 'No, thank you. Not again. It's up to you chaps.' Cis flatly refused to play the part. But knowing her as well as she knows me I had no worries.

In spite of having little experience in films, Werb did a good job directing. We found him a great help and at the end of it all everyone was happy. Cis and I felt it was one of the best films in which we had played together.

And now, almost sooner than I had hoped, came the happy swing back to the stage, hastened by the enthusiasm of a delightful little American called Lee Ephraim. With his quiet ingratiating manner he really got things done in the theatre world. We had to refuse his offer of the two leading parts in an American musical *On Your Toes* as I was preparing a musical of my own called *Hide and Seek* to be produced at the Hippodrome with Cis and our old friend Bobby Howes. Lee Ephraim willingly came in on the venture and took over the financial responsibility. We had a good success which marked the beginning of a long and happy association. Lee's wife Betty, a sweet lady of excellent taste, had a superlative gift for dress designing and created some beautiful costumes for *Hide and Seek* and the subsequent shows Lee and I did together. Her sense of colour and style was a valuable asset to the show, and our future productions. Lee was a dear man to know and a joy to work with. Cis felt the same about him as I did. Practically anything I asked for Lee would be at great pains to procure, which help me considerably in striving for new production ideas.

It was dear old Lee who found me the most efficient and reliable stage manager I ever had, a chap called Pat Hillyard. He made my job as producer fifty times easier. At last I had got the ideal assistant. We opened in *Hide and Seek* in Glasgow prior to London, but unhappily, during the week, Pat collided with some electrical equipment in a stage black-out which put him out of action for several weeks and that was where Laurie Green took over in his absence. Pat Hillyard eventually came back but after a short time asked to be released to join the BBC which was experimenting at the Alexandra Palace with a new form of entertainment now known as television. He saw great possibilities in the development of this new technique.

I tried to convince him it was a waste of time. I told him about what I had seen. The Boat Race—two cardboard models moving jerkily forward pulled along by an invisible thread indicating the relative position of the two battling crews; a lot of sparks and flashes accompanied by a few black-outs with a commentary off screen from the official BBC launch. The only amusing part was the desperate effort made by the two cardboard boats in between the flashes and sparks to match up with what the voice was saying. I tried to suggest it was too early yet. 'Let the boys continue experimenting and then have a go,' I suggested. I argued with him but he was so keen to be a pioneer that reluctantly I had to release him. He very soon proved himself right and became one of the prime movers in putting television on the map, finishing up as Director of Light Entertainment at Alexandra Palace. A great loss to me but a great gain for the BBC.

Hide and Seek did us proud, providing us with four delightful friends: Lee and Betty, Pat and his sweet wife Babs. In addition, it had a good long run giving me plenty of time to work on plans for the future.

23

Being a dancer all my life necessitated a large amount of sleep, which made early rising a luxury I had to forego. Consequently I was considerably surprised to find myself early one morning having breakfast in a house in St John's Wood with a man I had never met before. My host was the autocratic Alex Korda, the mid-European talking-picture tycoon. An arresting personality, talking with a slight accent, and overworked to the extent that 8.15 to 9.15 was his only free time. I was expecting the usual Continental breakfast but, to my amazement, we started with porridge and cream, which my host seemed to relish as much as I did. I could only assume he was entirely obsessed with the production of his current film, *Bonnie Prince Charlie*.

Brilliant conversation followed—an eloquent eulogy on my success as a film actor. I made no attempt to argue or interrupt this interesting train of thought. Deploring the fact we had never met before, he assured me that this present venture would more than make amends. Stimulated by the early morning air, the porridge and cream, the savoury smell of eggs and bacon, including of course the brilliant conversation, I had no difficulty in feeling myself to be truly great. By the time we got to the toast and marmalade I was one of the best film comedians on either side of the Atlantic. He knew I could not ask for more money as I had already signed the contract—I could be praised to the skies with impunity. Then suddenly the convivial confrontation came to an abrupt end after we had knocked back our second cup of delicious French coffee. Rising to his feet, my host said with an imperious gesture, 'We will do something very big. We will work together all the time. We do something very important.'

And I never saw him again from that day to this. I didn't even know
if he was still in the country. I was left entirely in the hands of Marcel
Hellman, one of his producers and T. Freland was given the job of
directing. Marcel Hellman was a nervous little man and begged me
not to rewrite the dialogue of the script which was nearly completed.
I told him I wouldn't alter a word if it was good. He assured me he had
an excellent man. For the first time during the whole of my picture-
making, I never altered a thing and spoke the author's lines verbatim.
The dialogue was far better than anything I could invent. Here was a
young man after my own heart. His easy style was enchanting and his
humour irresistible. We thought alike and laughed at the same things.
I was so impressed that I asked him to collaborate with me on a new
musical I was preparing for production at the Palace Theatre.

With his typical modesty he replied, 'I would love to, but I don't
understand anything about musical shows.'

'That's exactly why I'm asking you. I don't want to proceed on the
old familiar lines, I'm searching for an entirely new approach.'

This eased his mind. The collaboration started and a new author
was introduced to the West End. For many years we worked together
in the very happiest of associations which enabled Cis and me to
remain at the Palace Theatre for many years producing three shows,
one after the other, and a fourth at the Phoenix Theatre. This rather
shy and self-effacing young man was Arthur Macrae. He had the same
light touch as Ronnie Jeans and the same subtle humour. Working
with Arthur was a joy. His dialogue was sparkling and original. He
wrote as he talked—it was just Arthur.

Opening a big musical is always a daunting task. A straight play is
difficult enough in all conscience but with a dancing chorus, a singing
chorus, trick lighting, setting up new complicated sets for the first
time, making necessary adjustments, band calls with chorus and principals, it is no picnic. It is a frantic race against time to get it all done for
a Monday night opening. Monday night and get on with it! That's
how it was in those days. At the mere suggestion of a mid-week
opening local managements would have been scandalised.

Our new show was called *Under Your Hat* and our starting date was
the Court Theatre, Liverpool. I sent my stage manager, Laurie Green,

in advance to supervise the 'get in' of the scenery, dresses, props, special lighting equipment, etc. I arrived on the Sunday just after midday with the intention of having a full dress rehearsal at seven o'clock, to find the theatre in a state of complete chaos. All the stuff that should have been there days before had arrived at the last minute in spite of all the meticulous planning in London. There had been no time to sort it out, so everything had been dumped on the stage, and there it stood defiantly in one enormous mass. This alarming contingency was further aggravated by the fact that not only were we opening a brand new, large scale musical with a big cast and chorus but a brand new theatre to boot, and a hefty gang of workmen were striving frantically to get it finished for the grand opening the next night. Quite an amusing little situation! It was impossible to move without bumping into carpenters, painters, plasterers, electricians and craftsmen of every trade. Any thought of a dress rehearsal that night was utter madness.

Stewart Cruikshank, the head of the Howard and Wyndham organisation, had arrived from London for the opening ceremony. I found a very worried man standing in the stalls. Without beating about the bush I told him straight away, 'We can't possibly open tomorrow night.'

He reeled under the blow and clutched the back of the richly upholstered seat, number 17 row E, to steady himself.

'But we must. We can't possibly postpone, we've got a host of V.I.P.s from Liverpool and a lot more coming up from London especially for the opening.' I pointed to the battle raging in the auditorium.

'But the theatre isn't even finished,' I protested. 'And look at that nightmare on the stage. We were delayed getting in. We couldn't get near. The carpenters were working at pressure trying to finish the job. Opening tomorrow night is out of the question.'

'We can't postpone. There's too much at stake. It would be disastrous. We must open,' he insisted.

I was equally emphatic. 'Quite impossible,' I repeated.

The richly upholstered seat, number 17 row E, received the full weight of a broken man, slumping helplessly into its accommodating softness. A pathetic sight. An elderly man and a nice one too. There were tears in his eyes. He looked like the manager of a cup final team that had just been defeated. He tried to continue talking but became incoherent, choking with emotion. Had it been anyone else it would have sickened me, but I repeat he was a nice chap, elderly and deserving respect. A critical situation, a dilemma. I saw his point. He knew in his heart it was hopeless, just as I did, but somehow I was moved to compassion. A crazy attempt to achieve the impossible would be at least exciting. I promptly decided to have a go.

'All right, I'll do it.' Once again the tears welled up. 'But I must have complete control in front as well as back stage.'

Unable to speak, he seized my hand and shook it warmly. Every feature of his face showing the deepest gratitude. He just managed to utter, 'Anything you say.'

In this mad attempt to beat the clock, without wasting another second I issued my orders. After that famous breakfast with Korda I still felt in pretty good shape.

'Instruct your house manager to remove half that scenery on the stage to a warehouse. He will be instructed what to take and what to leave. Drastic cuts will have to be made for the opening performance. I shall want a stage staff standing by, in relays if necessary. No arguments. It's got to be done. All work in the auditorium must cease the moment I start the dress rehearsal.'

Armed with this despotic power I felt no compunction in throwing my weight about even more, and got things done in double-quick time. Orders had to be obeyed. Ruthless cuts in the script enabled me to reduce the size of the piled-up chaos on the stage by two lorryloads, giving us room to manoeuvre. We started hanging the cloths and electrical equipment. The dresses I sent away to the wardrobe.

With the iron curtain down, a band call was in full swing with the principals and chorus in the stalls. This meant the workmen in the auditorium had to knock off for three vital hours. No arguments. Poor Stewart Cruickshank had to take it on the chin. He was ageing rapidly, but a man of integrity keeps his word. He suffered in silence.

The front of the house was chaotic—carpets still had to be laid— electric fittings to be wired up. The precious minutes were ticking away. At 7.30 on that Sunday evening we had twenty-four hours left to 'curtain up'. It was now a question of how to make the best of those precious twenty-four hours. I made a short list of the bare essentials before the full dress rehearsal could start. Rough lighting, entrances and exits of chorus, dialogue with cuts, skeleton run-through in the bar and musical numbers with the M.D. in the stalls. With hard slogging the process took three and a half hours.

At midnight we started the dress rehearsal and that was when the real fun began. I called the whole company on to the stage and delivered a fighting speech apologising for driving them so hard and promising I was going to drive them harder still. I explained we were about to attempt the impossible and open tomorrow night. In spite of their loyalty and goodwill, progress was slow and at 2.30 a.m. we had only got through half the first act.

As the architect of the theatre seemed to have decided that a pass door from stage to auditorium was unnecessary I had to get the carpenters to knock up a temporary bridge over the orchestra pit to enable me to dive into the stalls when I had the chance and look at the show. I could see all the bits I was not in, and sometimes I got my understudy to play one of my scenes so that I could go out front and watch that particular part of the show. I seem to have spent most of the vital dress rehearsal time going backwards and forwards over that beastly little bridge.

Another point completely overlooked was a means of communication between the prompt corner and the man working the front arcs, situated at the back of the gallery just under the roof; telephonic communication had not been installed. The only way to reach him was to shout, several times, and even then he didn't always hear. When I was trying to get him to iris out on Cis instead of blacking out, I shouted myself hoarse. No result. I tried making signs. No result. I was going mad. Arthur Macrae, who was watching the rehearsal from the stalls, couldn't resist the opportunity and said, 'Why not try carrier pigeons?'

Twenty-one and a half hours left to opening time. After a short break for coffee and sandwiches we resumed the battle and by 4.30 a.m. we had staggered through to the end of Act I whereupon I blew the whistle for half time. Sleep had become number one priority.

We continued the fight the next morning at 11.00 a.m. to finish the rest of Act I and then attack the most difficult part—the whole of the second act—with only five hours left. Could we do it? Everyone was in a terrible state of nerves. It called for another speech—and keep it short, I told myself, mustn't lose a minute. Again I addressed the company.

'Once more, dear friends, once more. Exhausted and overworked as you are, one last supreme effort. Five hours to go then over the top. The game's afoot and upon this charge cry God for Harry Cruickshank and St George.'

Then followed such a commendable display of loyalty that the entire company were on their toes which enabled me to work that much faster . . . but not fast enough. It was now afternoon.

By four o'clock we still had a hell of a long way to go. No time for a tea break. Must drive on. Cis to the rescue as always. Has tea sent in and hands it out to the company in the wings whenever any of them had a few minutes off stage—one of the many little things they loved her for. She knew that a cup of tea in a crisis works wonders and it happened at the right moment. Suddenly, everything blew up. Scene changes went wrong and had to be done again. Lighting cues were missed and had to be corrected. Two hours left and the most intricate part still to come. Madness to continue. The clock was winning. I struggled with the last scene. Three-quarters of an hour left. The queues outside the theatre were already forming for the opening night. I waded in, working with frenzied haste to sort it out. The queues outside were getting larger. Twenty minutes left. We were very nearly there, one final effort. . . .

And so, on a Monday evening in October, 1938, at 7.30, the curtain went up on *Under Your Hat*. Marvellous what a cup of tea will do at a crucial moment. The impossible had been achieved. The fact that the theatre was not quite finished, far from upsetting the distinguished audience, seemed to put them in a happy and receptive mood. Cis and I entered together to a gale of applause and from then on the audience sat back to enjoy themselves. The story amused them and, as I hoped, Arthur's dialogue produced an abundance of laugher. Fired by their enthusiasm, the spirited performance the cast gave belied their exhaustion and the numbers and dances exceeded my wildest hopes. The show went at a cracking speed without a hitch. I was excited. Too excited probably—I was the only one who boobed.

I had to do all my changes on the side of the stage, watching from the wings to keep in touch, and, of course, my mistake would have to include my dear friend Peter Hadden, who was nervously singing his number before a front cloth. Hoping he would go well I watched anxiously from the wings and automatically started to change. Off came the coat, tie and shirt, then the trousers. Just as Peter was about to make his exit I realised I was wrong. I had to play the next scene, which followed immediately, in the clothes I had just thrown on the floor. I shouted to Peter to sing the chorus again. Rather bewildered he started another refrain. I had thirty-two bars of music to get back into the clothes I had just discarded. Where the hell were the trousers? I searched madly and just as Peter made his exit the black-out came. The front cloth was flown and the lights came full up on the next scene. I found the trousers at once, pulled them on and entered holding them up, to meet Leonora Corbett and play an intimate scene. The audience got it at once, and every time I tried to hold her in my arms and grabbed the trousers as they fell, I got huge laughs. I was embarrassed at first, but it made the scene go so well that I was almost glad it had happened. By this time the audience were in such a happy state of mind that on the final curtain we received a heart-warming reception.

Arthur Macrae was delighted with his initial success in musical comedy and Stewart Cruickshank gave a vivid impersonation of a schoolboy just home for the jolly hols. Shaking me warmly by the hand he said, 'You've worked wonders. Lee Ephraim said you'd do it and you have. Congratulations, my boy.'

'I told you it was impossible,' I replied, 'but we seem to have pulled it off. I realised your predicament and decided to do my damnedest.'

Dropping his voice, the old boy spoke with controlled feeling, 'I can't thank you enough.'

'You don't have to, I've gained a salutary lesson. The word "impossible" should never exist in a producer's vocabulary and the simultaneous opening of a new musical and a new theatre over a short weekend should be sedulously avoided.'

The opening week at Liverpool repaid us handsomely for the ordeal we had endured. We were packed out. All the cuts and discarded scenery were restored in a few days and it was all working as originally planned.

Lee knew I wanted plenty of time to work on the show before coming to London, so he booked a six weeks' tour. We were sitting pretty in the provinces but London was another matter. Polish the dialogue, tighten, speed up, drill the chorus, were the order of the day. Was there anything else? Definitely. A vital point. Precision. The poor unfortunate company had to suffer yet another of my exhortations.

'Thank you for your co-operation, all your hard work during the tour. Next week when we go home, if London acclaims our united efforts as the provinces have done, well and good. If not, you will probably want to tear me limb from limb and march down Whitehall carrying banners with slogans "Hulbert Out"—"He's a slave driver" —"Don't work for him."

'But let me tell you we have a great potential. Think only of success and the cardinal factor, audibility. Let us be sure the audience can sit back and hear everything we say. Let us concentrate in these last few performances on immaculate articulation. In a word, precision. Think about it. Practise it. All the great artistes of today possess this essential technique. Oddly enough, an audience love to hear what you're saying. Precision applies not only to speech but to movement. You in the chorus, think of the perfection of the Covent Garden ballet—the touchstone of precision of movement.'

The year 1938 probably saw London at its gayest. The metropolis was in merry mood and received our efforts at the Palace with open arms. The boring speech on 'precision' seemed to have paid off. We received no letters of complaint about inaudibility. The gaiety of the show harmonised perfectly with the happy mood of the audience. Joy all round—even the press went to town, and to cap it all we created a television record.

My friend Pat Hillyard, who had now become the big noise in T.V. Light Entertainment at Alexandra Palace, asked me to collaborate in televising our first night. Nothing against that. A swell idea. Pat had a genius for invention and organisation. He had a camera in the foyer of the theatre, a camera in Cis's dressing room and a camera facing the stage.

He started with shots of the audience entering the theatre, shots of Cis and me being interviewed backstage just before we took the plunge and made our first entrance. Those agonising moments one always dreads—Cis was in a frenzy. I made a superhuman effort to appear calm and failed miserably. The realism of this display of first night nerves, I was told afterwards, was most convincing on the screen. It should have been—we weren't acting, it was for real. Pat's organisation was perfect. One scene led into another. His split second timing was uncanny. From the camera in Cis's dressing room he cut to the foyer, showing it now empty as the first nighters were in their seats, and then to the stage where the chorus finished dancing.

Cis and I making our first entrance together was to be the big climax to an exciting sequence. Being impossible to explain this to the audience —they knew nothing of the important part they were playing—Pat had to gamble on our getting a good reception. Quite unconscious of the moment of drama the audience played their part superbly. Pat's gamble came off. The whole thing was a great success, a definite step forward in those early days of television. All credit to Pat for blazing the trail.

He did some excellent work in those early pioneering days. He brought over the famous Parisienne floor show—the Lido—from Paris and in later years he put on a complete West End revue running at the Savile Theatre, *Here Come the Boys*, starring Bobby Howes and Jack Hulbert, the latter having succumbed to the persuasive power and charm of his old friend. The situation was reversed—he was no longer working for *me*, I was working for *him*. And it was then that I became a pioneer fanatic myself.

Lee was delighted with the first night reception and the notices. Betty Ephraim's dress designs added considerably to the colour and effectiveness of the production—such an important item in a gay musical—and that brilliant young composer Vivian Ellis once again excelled himself. His music bore that rare distinction of originality.

In fact, he was an exceptional young man with a breadth of mind expanding his field of composition. But it was probably his pungent sense of humour that helped to make his popular music so catchy and distinctive. Not only was he one of our best composers but an excellent writer of most entertaining and amusing prose.

24

When one has been away on tour for many weeks it is an immense joy to return to one's own home. Number 28 Curzon Street proved to be ideal. It gave us everything we wanted. It was light, airy and comfortable with plenty of room to move around. Pammie had her own quarters, Nanny had her own bedroom, and with *Under Your Hat* a big success at the Palace we settled down gaily to our daily round of home life. Cis organised the running of the house, catering, doing the accounts with our secretary, running the social side and looking after our friends; in fact, no actress could have been busier off the stage. This left me clear to deal with authors, composers, theatre business and everything to do with the stage. We never suffered boredom from a planned, rational life. The excitement of uncertainty is infinitely preferable. But when two people have been living together in perfect harmony for a considerable number of years, certain incidents recur so frequently that they become established routines. One we use a tremendous lot is the 'where-are-my-keys?' routine. It usually occurs when we are both pressed for time, which is always.

'*Now* what are you looking for?' enquires Cis.

'My keys,' I reply testily, searching everywhere. Then comes the irritating question.

'When did you last have them?'

'I can't remember.'

'Well, think,' says Cis imperiously. 'Did you have them this morning?'

'Definitely.'

'Well then, where did you put them?'

'Oh, for heaven's sake, isn't that what I'm trying to find out?'

Throwing everything about all over the room I was getting frantic. In these moments of stress, *one* always tries to calm the *other*. When I get het-up Cis always becomes cool and collected and when Cis gets panicky I become ice cold and composed. It was my turn to be calmed down.

'Now don't go mad. If only you would listen to me. You have no method. You should always keep them in the same pocket.'

'I always do,' I protested. 'But they're not there.'

'Look again.'

'What's the good? It's a waste of time.'

'Have you looked in your hip pocket?'

'I never put them there.'

'Here, let me look. What's this?'

'Well, I'm damned. Thank you, darling.'

'You see what I mean,' Cis says in triumph, 'no method. You must always keep them in the same place.'

Suddenly, Cis makes a dash for her handbag. In a flash the entire contents are emptied on the bed.

'Would you believe it,' she says. 'Now I've lost *mine*.' And the routine starts all over again.

Another short scene which is still enjoying a very long run is the 'Leaving-the-house-together'.

I am in the bath, the door suddenly bursts open and a voice says urgently, 'It's me. Oh, you're still in the bath. Now I don't want to keep on, but I am not going to be late for rehearsal. You know what the traffic's like. Now for heaven's sake get out of that bath and stop dreaming of a White Christmas.'

'I'm not. I'm shaving,' I reply, with complete justification. Cis becomes even more emphatic.

'You've got exactly half an hour. You know how long it takes to get down the Strand to the Savoy. I'm leaving at ten past ten.'

'O.K. I'll be there.'

'You won't be unless you're mighty quick and I tell you *I am not waiting*.'

Ten minutes later the door bursts open again.

'Oh really, Jack, you're *still* in the bath.' This undeniable fact I have to accept.

'Just getting out, darling,' I say.

'Now I mean it. *I am not waiting.*' The voice now has an ominous ring.

'Not to worry, darling, I'll be there.'

The time had come for action. Out of the bath in a split second—a quick rub down—into the bedroom—on with the clothes. From the hall below loud and clear comes the final call before the countdown.

'*Jack, are you coming?*'

'Two minutes,' I shout back. All this irrespective of the tolerant gentleman who occupies the flat above. Then finally from the hall below, 'I'm getting a taxi'. The tone is inexorable.

'On my way,' I shout back. Socks on—shoes on, but not fastened—tie on, but not tied—shirt on unbuttoned. End of countdown.

'*J-a-c-k, taxi's here. I'm going.*'

'On my way,' I shout as I dash for the stairs. The front door closes with a bang. Then comes the voice from the tolerant gentleman upstairs: 'Too late, She's gone.'

I stop the first taxi that passes, jump in, tell the driver to take the shortest route to the Savoy Theatre, finish dressing and arrive there just in time to open the door of Cis's taxi.

'Good morning, madam. Savoy Theatre.'

Cis just smiles. Anyone else would slap my face. How important it is to marry the right woman.

And so we were back in the London we had grown to love over the years. We felt at peace with the world and so apparently did the Prime Minister. He had just made the front page of most of the dailies. A photograph of a happy P.M. with a benign smile waving a piece of paper to the assembled photographers on his return from Munich. This master stroke of diplomacy was epitomised in the word 'appeasement' which accounted for the big smile. But the national press omitted to produce a corresponding picture of the man who had been appeased. He was wearing an even bigger smile, for a very good reason as was proved by subsequent events. Those halcyon days were short lived.

Soon after his triumphant return Mr Chamberlain went on the air and made an announcement which shook the world like an earthquake. Reading Mr Lyndoe the astrologer each Sunday in *The Referee*, I noticed with great satisfaction he persistently prophesied that Hitler would not go to war. I was stunned by Mr Chamberlain's announcement. Hitler was already on the march. What was Lyndoe going to say about it the following Sunday? His statement is worth recording: 'A madman against the stars.'

The Government acted quickly and closed all the London theatres. This was the second time in our lives that we were stopped in our tracks by the German menace. In 1914 we had had a big success with *The Cinema Star* but were closed down after a few nights and in 1939 we suffered a similar fate. Lee acted without hesitation and transported the show in its entirety to Blackpool, where we played for three weeks. By that time the Government had decided that the threat of an air attack on London had declined for the time being and, realizing the importance of stage entertainment in boosting the morale of the people, they gave the authority for re-opening. We returned to the Palace immediately and continued playing to capacity business as if we had never been away. We were right back to where we came in and all set for a long run.

The suffering and severity of hostilities had not yet affected London. We were in the year of the 'phoney war', a misnomer as it turned out because the enemy were marshalling their forces and preparing for the *Blitzkreig* which was yet to come, but as far as London was concerned all was quiet and peaceful. Theatres were flourishing. There was a feeling of 'make the best of it while you can'. Anything might happen. There was no such thing as a foreseeable future. We had challenged the might of the German war machine and that was all we knew for certain. No one could tell from day to day what was in store.

In the happy and carefree days of peace, when Cis and I bought 28 Curzon Street, it had cost us every penny we possessed. But we were happy. We had bought a beautiful home for ourselves and it was ours for keeps. Congratulations came from all our friends for acquiring such a valuable property, an asset for the rest of our lives. But now suddenly we are at war. This resulted in two proud property owners becoming more and more worried. Had we chosen the wrong time to buy a small portion of London? Had we done the right thing in putting all our savings into something that might be blown sky-high overnight, leaving us with nothing? What could we live on if the theatres closed again? The prospect was alarming. Everyone advised a quick sale. Holding on to property was dangerous. With the whole country carrying gas masks and the youth of Britain in battle dress, it was hardly a propitious moment for selling a West End residence. There was no incentive to buy.

We had practically given up all hope of getting it off our hands, when right out of the blue an offer came along and we sold 28 Curzon Street, complete with a mews house at the back, for just a little less than we gave for it. We were greatly relieved and moved all our furniture and belongings into the different repositories and rented a furnished house at number 6 Chesterfield Hill.

How were we to know that our lovely home in Curzon Street would come right through the war untouched, entirely unscathed and the two repositories would be hit in the Blitz and all our belongings and furniture would go up in flames? That was the *unforseeable* future. How were we to know we could have lived in our Curzon Street home with all our furniture and belongings right through the entire bombing and finish up the proud owners of property which today would be worth a fortune? In this year of grace, 1974, as I was thinking back on these incidents of some thirty odd years ago, I read in my newspaper that a similar property in Curzon Street, a few doors away, was sold for two million pounds. Fate had decreed we were never to be millionaires. But we have no regrets, only eternal gratitude for still being here and able to go on enjoying the fun and excitement of working on the stage.

After a year of the so-called 'phoney war', Hitler was ready to strike London and the provinces which he did, good and hard. It was an ill-conceived strategy, producing the exact opposite effect to what he had anticipated. Total war calls for retaliation. What we needed as a nation was a great leader who could be trusted implicitly and inspire the nation with confidence and the will to see it through. Only a superman would do, and that is exactly what we got. Cis and I never had the honour of meeting Winston Churchill but we were both so deeply affected by his fighting speech on the air of 'Tears, blood, toil and sweat' that we sent him a telegram of congratulations and received a wire by return of acknowledgment and thanks—a most treasured possession from one of the greatest personalities this country has ever produced. What a man! Keep him in mind, dear children, when you read in your history books about Alfred the Great, Hannibal, Julius Caesar and all those superstars of the past and your interest will increase a hundredfold as you realise how great these chaps really were.

In those dark days of the Blitz who would have thought that the public would flock to the theatre as an antidote against the violence and brutality of total war. Yet, over a period of six years, Cis and I did three big musicals at the Palace. Who could have foretold that Cis, in an E.N.S.A. uniform, would be taking out her own unit to North Africa and Italy to entertain the troops or that I should find myself in a dark blue uniform doing every kind of job a war-time policeman was called on to perform. It seemed impossible that the West End theatres could survive the fury of the enemy attacks on London, yet only one was wiped out—the Shaftesbury—where we had met and played together for the first time.

In those days of the Second World War we were all one, united against a common foe. A cordial camaraderie existed—a mateyness— a chumminess. The resilience of the British temperament showed itself to perfection. Where is it today? Can it be revived? This is the moment, but where is the man with the Churchillian touch?

The Victory Parade marched through the streets of London. The jubilant crowds shouted in exultation. Mighty few that day would fail to recall the tenacity and determination of that incomparable architect of victory. It was a great thrill for Cis. The crowds lining Charing Cross Road shouted for her song, *There's Something About a Soldier* as she stood on the balcony of the Phoenix Theatre where she was playing in *Under the Counter* at the time, and it happened again when we went to the Victory Supper at the Savoy in the evening. They hoisted her on to a chair and she sang it with such feeling that the cheers came just before the end. Proud moments in one's life, unforgettable.

A successful show on the stage or screen—in the same way as the moment I have described—never fades from the memory. Failure is fleeting, quickly rejected, but it has infinite value in promoting a full appreciation of success. It is essential to have a bunch of flops and we've had plenty. Our biggest disaster was *Under the Counter* on Broadway. The big success in London attracted the attention of the Schuberts, and Lee fixed a deal for us to appear at the Schubert Theatre. We opened and New York said definitely 'No'. Schubert wanted to take it off the next night and though dear old Lee managed to stay his hand we were off in ten days.

There was also *A Yank on my Tail* which lasted just over a week at the Vaudeville. A big musical called *Star Maker* took me a year to build. It was the last musical Cis and I played in together, but it never came to London. We couldn't get a theatre. There were two beautiful flops at the Duke of York's—one with that glorious artist Yvonne Arnaud, who next to Cis is my favourite comedienne, and the other a revival of *Dear Charles*—both absolute disasters.

So when Cis had her biggest success of all in *Gay's the Word* at the Savile I thought, as an artiste she was in a class of her own and she thought, as a producer I was the cat's whiskers. I can only plead a mad devotion to the job in extenuation of this flagrant lack of modesty and of course that slight inference that we rather like each other. We rejoiced like two kids at the prospect of a big success with *Gay's the Word* which was vindicated by a very long run, and that, try as hard as you may, cannot be guaranteed every time.

One is constantly asked when interviewed by the press or on television, what is the secret of a happy marriage. In my case the answer is unequivocal: find a woman like Cicely Courtneidge. Apart from her dedication to the theatre, her two great loves are running the home and loving her friends, which she does with the same vitality and enthusiasm which characterises her work on the stage. She never lets up. An amazing personality, blessed with a genius for organisation— the home, holidays, travelling, parties, even me. The latter has proved the most difficult, but I am gradually falling into line. She's got quite a bit to clear up yet but that indomitable Scottish blood will brook no defeat. It's merely a matter of time.

She specialises in throwing parties. Christmas, New Year, birthdays and anniversaries—she is infallible. One of her best efforts was on St Valentine's Day in 1966, our Golden Wedding.

The party was a smash hit. You could tell that by the noise. . . .

Index